Mysterious America

MYSTERIOUS AMERICA

LOREN COLEMAN

faber and faber
London and Boston

ISBN 0-571-12524-7
Printed in the United States of America

Library of Congress Cataloging in Publication Data

Coleman, Loren.
    Mysterious America.

Bibliography: p.
1. United States – Miscellanea. 2. Curiosities and wonders – United States. I. Title. .
E179.C64 1983   001.9'4'0973   83-16502
ISBN 0-571-12524-7 (pbk.)

For Mark A. Hall and Jerome Clark,
friends and Forteans extraordinaire

Acknowledgements

I deeply appreciated permission given by *Fate, Flying Saucer Review, Boston Magazine, People's Almanac,* and *Occult* for the revised use of material previously published. Thanks also to *Fortean Times* for serving as a forum for many ideas expressed in *Mysterious America,* through my column, "On the Trail . . .", published in that journal.

For the years of correspondence, information exchange, and intellectual stimulation, I would like to take a special moment to thank Mark A. Hall of Minnesota. Working away, unbeknownst to most of the rest of the world, Mark has painstakingly sorted through reams of material, checked into numerous Fortean mysteries, and thoughtfully ventured a few answers to these anomalies. Mark and I have carried on a dynamic interchange which many times propelled me into new Fortean directions. My long distance friend, therefore, has been with me on many of my excursions across America, in spirit, and I appreciate his assistance in the essence of this book.

And likewise, a sincere and long thank you to Jerome Clark, now the Associate Editor of *Fate.* Jerry and I worked closely, ten years ago, sorting through material collected for over a decade before that. Jerry Clark must be credited with assisting my words to flow from the ideas in my head, and the data in my hands. Jerry saw that river begin to flow, and it still courses its way through *Mysterious America,* thanks in part to Jerry's encouragement. Some material in this book reflects work done with Jerry Clark, and I appreciate his permission to use it.

A leader in the field of cryptozoology, Dr. Bernard Heuvelmans has influenced my life since I read his book on unknown animals. He has become a person I now call "friend" and truly feel very close to him in words, deeds, and some ideas. Bernard may not share my total view of what's up with our monsters, but we do agree in post-fieldwork methodology and hard work to attempt to understand the facts. With sympathy, Bernard, part of this is for you.

Some departed individuals who have had a great impact on my investigative life, and whom I would like to thank, are Charles Fort, Ivan T. Sanderson, George F. Haas, and Carleton Coon. I was happy to have personally known the last three. Charles Fort, whom we have to thank for the examination of unexplained things, or Forteana, helped me from afar, and by his works.

The body of a book is filled with information, especially a Fortean one like this. Dedicated correspondents and fellow researchers who have consistently shared their Fortean data with me over the last two decades include Robert Rickard, Tom Adams, Lou Farish, John Green, X, Steve Hicks, Joseph Zarzynski, Warren Thompson, Larry Arnold, David Fideler, Bill Grimstad, Gary Mangicopra, John A. Keel, Robert Neeley, Dwight Whalen, Walt Webb, Jim McClarin, Paul Willis, and of course, my deeply involved brother, Jerry Coleman of Illinois.

As the miles and days rolled by while I traveled about looking into the shadowy corners of this country, leads, clues and hints which made my investigative work more complete have been forwarded to me by an evergrowing body of Forteans. Although I am certain I shall leave someone out, I have found the following people helpful with these "bits and pieces": Michael Anthony Hoffman, Ted Bloecher, William Zeiser, Ron Westrum, Roy Mackal, Don Worley, Janet and Colin Bord, David Webb, Pat Bontempo, Doug Tarrant, Tom Bearden, Gray Barker, Jay Garon, Bob Betts,

Vincent Gaddis, Peter Costello, Robert Downing, Terry Colvin, Dennis Pilichis, Mary Margaret and Curtis Fuller, George Earley, Randall Eaton, Roberta Payne, Peter Rodman, Berthold Schwarz, Roy Robinson, Peter Jordan, Joseph Nyman, Rene Dahinden, Betty Hill, Richard Crowe, Tim Church, James Moseley, Carol Michels, William Corliss, Ray Boeche, Bob Tarte, Curt Sutherly, Paul Bartholomew, Constance Cameron, Rod Dyke, Bob Jones, David Downs, Wayne Laporte, Joan Jeffers, Joel Hurd, Allen Greenfield, Ron Schaffner, Gene Duplantier, Ramona Hibner, Tom Miller, Joan Thompson, Graham Conway, Jim Auburn, Jacob Davidson, Len Aiken, Thomas Archer, Stan Gordon, Ted Phillips, Michael Bershad, Hank Davis, Ron Dobbins, George Eberhart, Jerome Eden and Bjorn Kurten. Organizations need to be mentioned also, and I am especially happy with NEARA, MUFON, INFO, VESTIGA, the International Society of Cryptozoology, and Expanded Video of Portland, Maine.

I gained an immense amount of personal and professional support from my wife, Libbet Cone, and have appreciated her positive comments and helpful critiques. Likewise, my editor, Dennis Campbell, has been there when I needed him, and has assisted me in the birth of this project. Margaret Fitzpatrick's extra hours were filled with typing the manuscript, and I thank her. And a special thanks to Joel Eichler, for his support through the process.

I am grateful to all of those mentioned and unmentioned who have assisted my efforts in exploring those secret places in time and space which fill this book. I could not have made my treks without them.

LOREN COLEMAN
June 1983

Contents

On the Road Again . . .

"One measures a circle beginning anywhere."
—Charles Fort

INTRODUCTION: MYSTERIOUS AMERICA

Charles Hoy Fort was a unique sort of man. Born in Albany, New York in 1874, he was raised by a rather strict gentleman whose children addressed him as "They." Whatever molding this up-bringing did to the young Charles is truly unknown, but it certainly gave the man healthy doses of skepticism and humor as his mainstays in life. After modestly delving into zoology and journalism, and coming into a small but adequate inheritance, Charles Fort gave over his life to a strange existence—silent reading and research at the New York Public Library and at the British Museum in London. What Fort extracted from the eons of journals and newspapers slowly developed into a framework of thought unmatched before his time. Fort chronicled his information and dissections of his data in his four books—*The Book of the Damned, New Lands, Lo!,* and *Wild Talents.* (These have been reissued as the collective volume, *The Books of Charles Fort,* most recently by Dover in 1974.) Quite simply, in Charles Fort's words, he looked at "A procession of the damned. By the damned, I mean the excluded. We shall have a procession of data that Science has excluded."

The damned data Fort gathered covered so many marvels, mysteries, and monsters, that the list would go on for pages – including unidentified aerial objects, frog falls, disappearances of ships, red rains, earthquake lights, lake monsters, animal mutilations, psychic explosions, and much much more. Indeed, Charles Fort is credited with inventing the word "teleportation." Today, the people who study the wonders examined by Fort are called "Forteans." The strange and unusual phenomena we Forteans research and write about is often referred to as "Forteana." Such associations as the International Fortean Organization just outside of Washington, D.C., and the journal *Fortean Times* of London have sprung up in the wake of Charles Fort to carry on his work.

Charles Fort died in 1932, and probably would be embarrassed that such a subculture of followers has grown in recent years. He even refused to join the original Fortean Society of the 1920's which was begun by the likes of Ben Hecht, Booth Tarkington, Tiffany Thayer, Theodore Dreiser, Alexander Woollcott, Buckminister Fuller, Oliver Wendell Holmes, Clarence Darrow, Burton Rascoe, John Cowper Powys, and other intellectuals. Charles Fort would have laughed not a little that annual conferences are now held entitled "Fortfests" and that seminars on cryptozoology (the study of hidden animals, i.e. monsters) are commonplace.

I discovered Charles Fort in the late 1950's and soon joined the leagues of Forteans. In the 1960's, I began a ten year correspondence with the late zoologist Ivan T. Sanderson who once wrote: "I am an 'Fortean' and very proud to be labelled as such." Like Sanderson and scores of others I have worked with in this field, I am quite happy Charles Fort has influenced my life as he has. Fort was one of the first truly intellectual investigative reporters – long before Watergate was a household word. Through the 1960's and 1970's, as I jumped into the thick of the pursuit of the unknown, Fort's humor and skepticism served me well. We Forteans of the 1980's and beyond are carrying on his tradition in an intensive fashion – and have added fieldwork to the laborious bibliographical tasks he started in the British Museum and the New York Library.

In *Mysterious America*, I have set down my personal insights and experiences as a Fortean traveling around North America during the last twenty-five years. I have chased monsters and mad gassers; tracked down teleported animals; interviewed scores of people who have seen creatures from mysterious kangaroos to black panthers, or viewed entities from phantom clowns to shadowy nephites, and more. I have lived in Illinois, California, Massachusetts and Maine. To pursue Fortean phenomena, my travels have taken me to the four corners of the country, from the Pacific Northwest to the US Virgin Islands, from New England to the Southwest. My investigative mobile unit (i.e. my pickup truck) has crisscrossed the Midwest so many times that sometimes I think I could turn it loose and it would steer itself to the latest Bigfoot or UFO sighting. Presently from my bases in Massachusetts and Maine, I find myself going to places like Fort Mountain, Georgia, and Mystery Hill, New Hampshire, to examine strange structures built by ancient unknown peoples, or to various wooded areas in the Northeast to run down the latest phantom feline account. Everyday I open my mail and hear about a new Fortean event happening someplace in this nation that deserves my attention. The material rolls in in an ever increasing wave, and this searcher into the unexplained can barely keep up with the demand on his investigative time. It is a strange world out there, and some people may be too busy oftentimes to stop and notice. Since I have made so many treks on the trail of the inexplicable, I present this book to you, to share with you some of my excursions and adventures in Mysterious America. I hope it helps you to look beyond the horizon. If it does, and you would like to exchange information and ideas on the subjects explored, please write to me at Post Office Box 109/Rangeley, Maine 04970.

1
Reflections of a Traveling American Fortean

Often are the times when our thoughts turn to moving, weekend treks, taking vacations, going on holiday, and visiting family and friends in other parts of the country. If your thoughts also have a Fortean bent to them, if you mix your pleasure with furthering your own personal inquiries into the unexplained wonders around you, then some helpful hints toward making your next trip a worthwhile phenomenological investigative adventure might interest you.

You can do many things at home before you travel to your destination. A hefty amount of initial background research, before your journey, can save you hours of wasted time in the field. First, I always discovered it was important to find out what the specific locales I was going to and through have to offer. All researchers must ask themselves specific questions which apply to their own interests, but in general, I like to know if there are runes, mounds, monster-inhabited lakes, spook lights, Bigfoot country, haunted places, ice caves, panther-frequented valleys, and a whole host of more or less permanent Fortean wonders in the vicinity of my route or its predetermined end.

Finding these fixed unexplained locations by way of the Fortean literature is becoming easier – if you can get your hands on the right sources. George Eberhart's *A Geo-Bibliography of Anomalies* and Jim Brandon's *Weird America* are two of the best books with individual locale listings. Eberhart's expensive sixty dollar book might be available in a few libraries, and Brandon's quality paperback should be almost as difficult to run across in some bookstores. Both are worth the effort of the search, however. Brandon's *Weird America* is especially good since it is compact and offers a rather complete rundown on the individual Fortean sites. Since he used his own files as well as the items in the *INFO Journal* and *FATE*, Brandon was able to give a rather nice cross-section of what each state has or has had to offer. *Weird America* is a true Fortean guidebook. Brandon's 1983 book, *The Rebirth of Pan*, adds another chapter in his unique analysis of the cryptograms written on the face of America.

Amazing America is less helpful in terms of weirdness and Fortean activity. This is an exaggerated collection of the biggest, shortest, oldest, usually manmade attractions along the way. In fact, it serves as a good negative guidebook for it lets you know what things to avoid, at any cost. *Space-Time Transients* is a book to which you might wish to refer, but it is a teaser. *STT* lists some spots from the authors' computer printouts, but it leaves a lot out. And be on your guard, too. The data base is slanted towards Fortean phenomena, as seen through the pages of *FATE*. Because a couple of active writers (myself and Jerry Clark) did many pieces on Illinois mysteries, *STT* has a map demonstrating the especially active nature of Illinois Forteana – which is probably not quite the case.

Trento's *In Search of Lost America*, Fell's *America B.C.*, and others are good beginning places for individuals looking for ancient anomalous sites. Trento's checklist is not specific enough to be helpful, but it is a start. The National Geographic's *Guide to Ancient Treasures*, however, is excellent for it gives detailed highway, route and byway travel tips. Also, as I mention elsewhere (see

On the road, this time in Willow Creek, California, I stop for the obligatory Bigfoot researcher photo. This figure was carved by Jim McClarin, and closely matches the descriptions of the area's giant humanoids.

Appendix IV and Chapter Three), ancient sites labelled "devil" should be examined.

On certain other topics, such as where Bigfoot has been seen, John Green's *The Apes Amoung Us* gives an easy state-by-state breakdown to follow. Peter Costello's *In Search of Lake Monsters* does a fairly complete job of indicating where to find the watery beasts, and the novice will find it of assistance. *Mysterious America's* Chapter Nine and Appendix V give specific data on monster-inhabited lakes. Articles with seed catalogue-type presentations can be treasure troves of information on specific locations of particular phenomena. Mark A. Hall's spook light listing (see Appendix I) still ranks as my favorite; it is very detailed concerning what to expect to see and where.

Falls of strange items from ice to frogs, for example, appear to be one-shot affairs, but it is always good to understand a locale in terms of its total Fortean history. Falls, strange appearances, and permanent phenomena are natural candidates for lists, and *Fortean Times* and *INFO Journal* articles on these topics pinpoint the sites of the occurrences. The reader is referred to the Appendices of this book for a good collection of Fortean lists. For example, my list (see Appendix II) on the appearance of crocs and 'gators is an illustration of a seed catalogue worth having. David Fideler's *Anomaly Research Bulletin's* enjoyable listing of kangaroo sightings is another. Tom Adam's *Stigmata* has had many articles and maps on the mystery of the cattle mutilations, for those interested in that pursuit. For the American Fortean, lists are good guides.

Overall, these books and articles should give you a fairly good idea about where to target some of your efforts on your trip—as should *Mysterious America*. After going through the literature, you may wish to write some researchers who have been known to do extensive fieldwork in the locale of your interest. The best way to locate such individuals is by taking a deeper dip into the vast underground Fortean pool of organizations, newsletters, and journals. Contact could be made with *Fortean Times, Fate,* INFO, VESTIGA, NEARA, and others.

Personally, I enjoy finding out what is the most recent activity in an area I am heading for. Fellow researchers can often give me a lead, but another way I discover if anything unusual is hopping is by contacting the local area's newspapers before I take my journey. On the road, I also often stop at the regional weeklies to inquire about any folklore or if I know about some local, well-known wonder (e.g. The Devil's Tramping Ground, Lake Champlain Monster, etc.) then about that specifically. This is lots of fun, and I frequently feel like I am on a Fortean fishing trip. Sometimes I am casting out a line for a Bigfoot account, and I come up with a close encounter with a UFO. It is amazing—and keeps me on my toes.

While getting to and going through an area, I try to pick up local books written by local people on the regional folklore. (See *Mysterious America's* bibliography for the names of some of these local books.) Also, sometimes I come across some intriguing maps which have captured local legends in little pictures with quaint names, like the Cape Anywhere Sea Serpent, The Buried Treasure of Someplace Canyon, or the Headless Horseman of This Valley or That. These local legends are repeatedly new to me because they are part of the local people's traditions which have not appeared in a national tabloid or on an incredible television program. Undiscovered wonders still do exist. Finding such a Fortean gem can make a trip very worth the time and toil.

Another resource for finding out what unexplained happenings and places abound in any given province is simply talking to the local folks. Gas station attendants are a gold mine of information if you take the time to get out of your automobile and chat with them. The people at country stores, craft shops, and yard sales know a good deal about the countryside, and often are willing to share with you some unique incident or story if you are friendly and unjudgmental.

The worst possible source of Fortean knowledge, I have discovered, is located at the so-called "Information Bureaus." These sandtraps of the American vacationer give out little more than some insights into the nearest or newest tourist attraction. If you go to them with much more than a specific question about a specific location, do not expect much satisfaction. They have been able to tell me where, for example, a well known haunted house was, but frequently an information bureau has not been able to direct me to an interesting creek close at hand; I had to get that information from a service station operator. Another warning in your travels should be given about "Mystery Spots." In 80–90% of the cases, these tourist traps are optical illusions. Unfortunately, some completely worthwhile and topnotch Fortean sites have been labelled a "mystery" something or other. The most famous example of this is the 4000 B.P. megalithic structures at North Salem, New Hampshire, entitled collectively "Mystery Hill," a spot well worth a detour. A word to the wise will save you some time, either way.

Well, with all these hints and warnings in mind, it is time to take your trip. Get your tape recorder, camera, paper, pen, and money and take a Fortean adventure. With careful planning, a little research, and some friendly questions along the way, your journey anywhere in Mysterious America can be rewarded with some interesting Fortean discoveries. Enjoy yourself. And help enlighten others, after your return.

2
A Couple of Side Trips Into the Unknown

For almost a decade I have lived in the Boston area, and thus I sometimes forget how driving from the urbanized East Coast of the United States into the Midwest is a culturally shocking event. The megapolis of the Washington-New York-Boston complex often stymies life and the natural world, as well as the imagination of man. Despite some articles of recent years about the encroachment of wildlife into North American cities, these fingers of urban nature are generally nothing more or less than the occasional raccoon, opossum or deer. Only when you get away from the overcrowded, concrete jungle do you find the kind of space, the corridors of vegetation which allow the creatures of the netherland to roam freely. New England is beautiful and wild, but the temperate climate and open territory of the Heartland has reserved a special place in its soul for the kind of unknown animals I love to pursue. Be they ape-like, feline-formed, or thunderbird-shaped, the beasts of the Midwest make a Fortean's drive through Ohio,

Indiana and Illinois an exciting trek. From just such a journey, here are some stops along the way.

Phantom Panthers

Westerville, Ohio, is a town a mere mile from Interstate 270, the vast ring of highway which keeps the sprawl of Columbus so neatly contained. 270, like the others of its kind in America that separate wildlife from man, suburbs from the city, does serve as a barrier. But Westerville is not a suburban community of square little houses and clipped lawns; rather, Westerville is a gathering of cornfields, of country roads where speed limits are difficult to enforce, of homes and farmhouses here and there, *and* of course, trailer courts.

Most cities in the US move their corporate limits into an area, and among the new sidewalks, stop signs, and sewage systems they bring with them, they also introduce zoning laws which quickly eliminate trailer courts. Mobile home parks are forced, therefore, to move beyond the new city limits. In a way, the residents of trailers are becoming the new pioneers of our civilization. They relocate on the edges of the country, with often only a thin sheet of metal between them and the unknown. Very often, as quite a few researchers have discovered, many occupants of trailer courts find their confrontations with the unexplained more frequent than they desire. My travels led me, once again, to quite a number of trailers and their owners.

Following up on a lead supplied by David Fideler, I stopped by the Lake Estates Home Park in Westerville, Ohio, to check on the recent accounts of a panther seen thereabouts in June 1979.

Elusive, phantom panthers are nothing new to central Ohio. Back in 1947, Stanley Belt saw one near Kirkwood. The reports have come in periodical waves since then. Black panthers have been seen in virtual flaps in 1955, 1962, and 1973, in the Urbana–Springfield region of the state, and the Bluffton area was the site of the 1977 activity. Ron Schaffner's investigations of 1978 revealed sightings near Minerva. Not too surprisingly, the phenomena continue still.

Starting in late May, 1979, Delaware County Sheriff Bill Lavery began getting calls from residents who claimed to have spotted a large cat-like animal, a "cougar." In the village of Delaware, a big feline had killed some sheep, and in the nearby Sunbury, some people had actually spied the cat. As with the Bluffton, Ohio, panther reports I investigated in 1977, [See *Creatures of the Outer Edge* (Warner 1978) pp 209-217; or "Phantom Panther on the Prowl," *Fate* November 1977 pp 62-67.] the pattern of livestock kills, sightings, and foot-print finds was repeated in Delaware County, Ohio, in 1979.

In the midst of all of this "cougar" activity, the animal made a visit to the Lake Estates trailer court. Charles and Helen Marks, co-managers of the court for three years after having moved from Toledo did not think they were going to get involved in "cougar tracking," when suddenly on June 10, 1979, they found huge footprints at their doorstep.

This is the way Charles Marks described the course of events to me: "Someone had called the police, and said that the night before, they were fishin' out here (at the little lake next to the trailer court). See we got a lot of good fish in this lake here. It's stocked. He was out fishin' and he'd seen these prints. Then he called the Delaware Sheriff, and they came down Sunday morning. The guy showed them the prints; he'd staked them all out. Then we hightailed it out here to see what was going on." Helen Marks added: "We didn't know if it was a dead body or something. But it was these prints, some with claws, some without."

Charles Marks had some plaster of paris from the time he had repaired a broken leg of a pet, and Marks tried his hand at making some casts. His wife, in the role of "operations director," told Charles to make a cast of the more exciting clawed tracks, and thus these were the ones shown to the police. The authorities quickly labelled them as "dog prints" – an event familiar to anyone interested in mysterious feline accounts.

The Marks found over 200 prints in the small muddy and grassy fields across from their trailer, and next to the little lake. They are convinced they had discovered "cougar" prints, for they also came upon a patch of vegetation with clear signs of where the animal had lain. Helen Marks recalled: "And you could even see the tufts of grass sticking up between the place the head had rested, and the five foot long depression where the body was."

Later on that eventful Sunday, the discovery of the prints unbeknownst to them, three boys were out playing in their "fort" behind the trailer court. Quite suddenly, they encountered a large, tan panther in a tree. Donnie Grady, 12, said the cat jumped from the tree, landed on all fours, and fled. Ricky Smith, 10, obviously taking the encounter very personally, told of how the thing "looked at me and jumped from the tree." Travis, Ricky's eight year old brother, said "when it growled, I saw those BIG front teeth." The boys, residents of the trailer court, later saw the "cougar" on a near-by roadway, and then learned of the Marks' discovery of the prints.

More reported encounters with the panther took place during the next week in June. A woman on nearby Fancher Road was taking out some trash when she met the big cat – and promptly fainted. Other sightings filled the newspapers for a few days, but like many elusive creatures of the borderland Midwest, this one too faded from the view and the minds of the residents of central Ohio.

The percipients of such incidents, however, do not so quickly forget the events which touched their lives. This came clearly into focus in Illinois.

Big Birds

In 1977, Lawndale, Illinois, was visited by two big birds, one of which carried a ten year old boy a few feet before his fright-ened mother's screams seemed to make the bird drop the boy. [See *Creatures of the Outer Edge* pp 225-227; and FT 24 pp10-12.] My brother, Jerry Coleman of Decatur, Illinois, had been able to interview Marlon, Ruth and Jake Lowe on two occasions in 1977, within hours of the incident. During my 1979 trip I planned to reinterview the Lowes and inquire into the occurrences since the time of their encounter two years previous.

Their trailer (!) had not changed any since the photographs Jerry had taken in 1977, and the prophetic black birds on the shutters were still there to greet us.

Ruth Lowe was cautious, to say the least. This was a woman

Helen and Charles Marks display the plaster casts of the mystery phantom panther tracks found near their mobile home in Westerville, Ohio, on June 10, 1979.

Marlon (left) and Ruth Lowe (right) stand at the beginning and end of the distance the big bird carried Marlon, in 1977, in front of his Logan County, Illinois, trailer home.

who had obviously been hurt, but I was soon to hear the surprising depths of this sorrow. And harassment.

After Marlon Lowe was lifted into the air, and the media carried the story, individuals started leaving dead birds on the Lowe's front porch. Right after the first press mention, Ruth Lowe found a "big, beautiful eagle" spread out at the foot of their door. The next day, a circle of six birds was placed there. The authorities seemed unable or unwilling to help the Lowes.

The dimension of the human tragedy was great for this family. Turning to my brother, Ruth Lowe asked: "You know how red Marlon's hair was? He had the reddest hair you'd ever want to see on a kid."

Lowering her tone, she continued, "Well, he wears a hat all the time now. For a year the kid won't go out after dark. I started coming home early before he got off the bus to clean off the front porch. I had hawks, owls, you name it, I had 'em on the front porch here. And I started coming home early from work *just* to clean off that front porch. Now that's when I started getting hysterical when I found all the birds, the little notes, and got all the telephone calls. But about a month after it happened, I was washing his head, and I mean to tell you, the only red hair he had on his head was just the top layer. It was just as gray as could be."

After the initial shock, and her mistake of telling Marlon sent him into hysterics, Ruth Lowe cut his hair short and debated whether to put a color rinse on it. Slowly the locks of gray seemed to disappear. She reflected: "It grew out. It's not a red. It's not a blonde. It's a gray."

And the reason for the change was not shadowy to Marlon's mother: "It was the shock of it. And we are still putting up with a lot. The poor kid gets in one or two scraps a week."

Subdued, Ruth Lowe observed: "They called him 'Bird Boy'. He's quite a fighter now."

In juxtaposition to the human consequences of the 1977 encounter, there are the numerous confirmations of those scary days. "I'll always remember how that huge thing was bending its white ringed neck, and seemed to be trying to peck at Marlon, as it was flying away," Ruth Lowe commented, in a new detail which did not come out two years before. Although she said the massive size of the bird reminded her of an ostrich, the bird itself looked like a condor. She had spent some long hours in the local library to come up with a clue to what she had seen. She was certain that it was not a turkey vulture, as an area constable would have her believe.

"I was standing at the door, and all I saw was Marlon's feet dangling in the air. There just aren't any birds around here that could lift him up like that," Ruth Lowe told us.

And there were the other sightings which have continued quietly up to the present in the Lawndale area. In nearby Lincoln, one of the big birds was flying down the middle of the main street, when the cab company's dispatcher yelled over the radio: "There goes that son-of-a-bitch now." But his report was silenced.

A December 1977 account of the killing of one of the birds was similarly kept under wraps for fear of ridicule. Apparently a woman was on her way to work in Beason when she saw something like a "man standing in the road with something over its arms." (A description which conjures up the images of Mothman.) The woman collapsed, was hospitalized, and recovered some time later. A group of men, hearing of this report from the local grapevine, went out to the spot, killed a large bird and burnt it. Whether it was one of the big birds will never be known, but this kind of story demonstrates the level of emotion these creatures can activate in such generally calm Midwestern towns as Lawndale.

Ruth Lowe's sister-in-law was even involved in a frightening big bird run-in at Belleville, Illinois. A large bird landed on top of one of the mobile homes (!) in the trailer park where she lives. The thing flapped its wings once, took off over the trailers, and left many residents gasping in disbelief at its 18 foot wingspan. Needless to say, this creature was the talk of the trailer court for some weeks.

The local reports and the memories have given the Lowe family many haunted moments, for as Ruth Lowe knows and quietly told me . . . "They're still around here!"

3
Devil Names and Fortean Places

When Western Europeans landed in the New World and began spreading across what was later to become America, they discovered what the Amerindians already knew – there were some strange places in this new land. Certain locations were "strange" because the early explorers and settlers would see, hear, smell or feel strange things – weird globes of light, eerie screechings, sickening sweet odors, cold drafts of air as well as UFO's, mystery animals and other "inexplicables." The interface between these newcomers and the decidedly unexplainable phenomena produced place-names which attempted to reflect the notion that the locales were special, different and, indeed, strange. The names can take many forms, but I have long noticed an American historical acknowledgement of Forteana-ridden places by the use of the work "devil" in the naming of these locations. A few examples will illustrate this point.

Some of the more frequent sightings of California's phantom black panthers occur in the Diablo (Spanish for "devil") Valley, east of San Francisco. The Las Trampas Regional Park booklet notes the black cat is referred to as "The Black Mountain Lion of Devil's Hole" because it is frequently seen on the slopes of Mt. Diablo, and in the Devil's Hole area of the park. Mystery lights also turn up in the Mt. Diablo–Diablo Valley area frequently.

In 1873, a live frog was found in a slab of limestone in a mine on Mt. Diablo, and in 1806, Spanish General Vallejo encountered a man-like apparition (which had exotic plumage and made "diving movements") while battling the Bolgones Indians. Monte del Diablo is a very strange place.

The territory known as Devil's Kitchen in southern Illinois was avoided by the region's Amerindians because of their awareness of its sinister nature. Southern Illinois, in general, is a frequent host to mystery animals and UFO's as well as the site of pre-Columbian stone walls which form a rough alignment between the Ohio and Mississippi rivers.

Near Grand Tower, also in southern Illinois, is a small rocky hill known as the Devil's Bake Oven. South of that prominence is a longer hill known as the Devil's Backbone. Speaking of the Devil's Bake Oven, folklorist John W. Allen observes: "On those nights when the hill was flooded with gentle moonlight, visitors would report that they had seen a weird and mistlike creature . . . floating silently across their pathway to disappear among the rocks or in the dense bushes on the hillside. This disappearance was often followed by moans, wails and shrieks such as only a ghost can make."

Devil's Lake of Wisconsin has its share of geological oddities such as glacier scratches on unusual rock formations and petrified sand waves of an ancient sea, but it is the Amerindian mounds which are especially interesting. Three major effigy mounds are located in Devil's Lake State Park. One in the shape of a bear and another which resembles a lynx are at the north end of the lake. A bird-shaped mound is at the south end. Did the mound-builders wish to acknowledge real animals or phantom creature forms which haunted the shores of Devil's Lake?

From nearby Baraboo (a mere three miles north of Devil's Lake on Wisconsin 123), at least a decade ago, stories were circulating of giant ghost elephants. Or were they mastodons? August Derleth, author and follower of H. P. Lovecraft, likes this area of south-central Wisconsin because he felt it contains "Cthulhu power zones".

During the summer of 1970, campers at Devil's Lake complained of shadowy "somethings" prowling around their tents. Department of Natural Resources personnel stated no bears are found in the area. However, Bigfeet accounts are well known from Wisconsin. Devil's Lake is also the location of an 1889 lake monster report. Additionally, the surface of the lake is broken with the ghostly wake of a phantom canoe seen in the mists of cold, still nights.

The place does have an aura about it. Folklore tells of an Indian maiden and her lover leaping to their deaths. In general, the site is said to be a "place of many dead."

Devil's Lake, Wisconsin, is a spooky spot.

One of my favorite examples of the reflection of Fortean phenomena via a "devil name" comes from one corner of the inland town of Chester, New Hampshire, on Rattlesnake Hill. A cavern there of "great notoriety in all the country round" bears the name Devil's Den. According to local legends, the path leading to the cave "was always kept open, in summer and winter, by the passing to and fro of the evil spirits who frequented the place, though themselves invisible to the eyes of mortal men."

The poet J. G. Whittier put the Devil's Den traditions into verse, and the following two stanzas from his poem "Devil's Den" give deep insight into bedeviled places in general:

> 'Tis said that this cave is an evil place —
> The chosen haunt of a fallen race —
> That the midnight traveller oft hath seen
> A red flame tremble its jaws between,
> And lighten and quiver the boughs among,
> Like the fiery play of a serpent's tongue;

(courtesy of Bill Sanderson)

Locations with "devil names" often have a history of Fortean
wonders.

That sounds of fear from its chambers swell –
The ghostly gibber, – the fiendish yell;
That bodiless hands at its entrance wave, –
And hence they have named it The Demon's Cave.

• • •

Yet is there something to fancy dear
In this silent cave and its lingering fear, –
Something which tells of another age,
Of the wizard's wand, and the Sybil's page,
Of the fairy ring and the haunted glen,
And the restless phantoms of murdered men:
The grandame's tale, and the nurse's song –
The dreams of childhood remembered long;
And I love even now to list the tale
Of the Demon's Cave, and its haunted vale.

Simply stated, the strange events of the past are often remembered in the geographical names of the area. Place-names can be a Fortean's clue to the "haunted vale." I know of over one hundred and twenty-five places with "devil names" in the United States, and I am finding more correlations with this list and Forteana every day. (See Appendix IV.) I suspect many more etymological connections exist. My list of "devil names" is just the tip of the pitchfork.

Indeed, the United Kingdom abounds with fertile devil sites for the curious researcher. Evan Hadingham in *Circles and Standing Stones* writes: "There are countless names and stories connecting ancient sites with giants and devils, such as the Devil's Arrows alignments at Boroughbridge, Yorkshire, or the name Devil's Quoits associated with Stanton Drew."

Geographical "devil names" worldwide may indicate, as they seem to in America, locales high in Fortean energy and strangeness. These places deserve some extra attention, for from the stray sod to the fairy ring, from the haunted glen to the Devil's Den, there lies many a riddle to unfold.

4
Things that Go Bump in the Bay State

The Bay State's heritage of hauntings – both real and imagined – goes back nearly three centuries to the Salem witch hunt of 1692. That brief hysteria of accusations, trials and twenty executions has been documented and analyzed so often that the phrase "Salem witch trials" has passed into household usage. The same cannot be said of Massachusetts' myriad other recorded incidents of hauntings, cursed, apparitions, and unusual phenomena. Yet one need not look too far to find a rich harvest of the mysterious.

The Hoosac railroad tunnel that runs through the Berkshire Mountains has been associated with spooky incidents for more that 100 years. Its construction cost more than $15 million and 200 lives, and legend has it that the tunnel's dead do not rest easy.

On March 20, 1865, two explosive experts, Ned Brinkman and Billy Nash, were buried under tons of rock when their foreman, Ringo Kelly, accidently set off a blast of dynamite. Kelly disappeared immediately after the accident. Exactly one year later he was found strangled to death deep inside the tunnel at precisely the spot where Brinkman and Nash had died. Since then, many people have reported ghostly encounters with all three of the dead men.

In 1872, executives of the Boston and Maine Railroad were frightened by a moaning figure carrying a lantern through the darkened corridors of the Hoosac. In 1936, Joseph Impocco, a railroad worker, reported that he was saved from being run over by an express train when a spooky voice called out, "Hey Joe, Joe. Jump quick!" He leaped from the track just seconds before the train roared by.

Many people have mysteriously disappeared in the Hoosac Tunnel. In 1973, Barnard Hastaba set out to walk through the tunnel from North Adams to Williamstown. He was never heard from again.

Retribution is the motive attributed to Goody Hallet, the Witch of Wellfleet. Seduced at fifteen by pirate Sam Bellamy, she was later charged with murdering the child born of the union.

While awaiting sentence, so the legend goes, she signed a pact with the devil and escaped from jail. From then on, she haunted the dunes, summoned hurricanes, stirred up thick fogs, and set out false lights to lure ships onto the shoals.

In 1717, Bellamy's ship the *Widdah* was wrecked and his body cast ashore near Goody Hallet's ruined cottage. Not yet satisfied, her ghost continued to plague the waters of Cape Cod for the next eighty years, and on occasion she was sighted late at night dressed in red, dancing demonically on the Wellfleet village green.

Mad Meg Wesson, the Witch of Cape Ann, did not fare as well as the Witch of Wellfleet. Mad Meg wore a necklace of eels and kept as her familiar a raven with a peculiar jagged white marking under one wing. She heaved a multitude of curses in her time prompting hens to stop laying, fish nets to break, and pigs to devour their piglets.

In 1745, Sir William Pepperell led a military expedition against the French fortress of Louisburg on Cape Brenton. On the night before setting out from Cape Ann, Pepperell's troops gathered for a celebration at a local tavern. Mad Meg appeared at the door and cursed the campaign. Thereafter all military pursuits failed miserably.

One day the troops spotted a raven, its underwing zigzagged with white. One of the soldiers fired twice at the bird. His first shot broke the raven's leg, his second shot killed it. Two days later, the army triumphed at Louisburg, and when the soldiers returned to Cape Ann, they later learned that Meg had fallen down and broken her leg. Two days later – the day of the Louisburg victory – she had died.

Two hundred years after the fact such ghostly goings on can be dismissed as local legend or embellished half-truths. But dozens of additional phenomena simply cannot be explained away so easily. Many inexplicable incidents have occurred in two so-called window areas, the Quabbin Reservoir near Amherst and the Hockomock Swamp in southeastern Massachusetts, near Brockton.

On August 13, 1819, there was a huge blast and a flash of light in the sky above Quabbin. Afterward a bowl-shaped object, dubbed a whatsis, was found in the front yard of an Amherst professor. The object was about eight inches across, covered by a velvety nap of buff color and full of a stinking pulp that turned blood red and liquified on exposure to the air.

College authorities judged the whatsis to be an unknown form of fresh-water nostoc algae. Several more of the saucers were found soon afterward and similarly dismissed as nostoc, which forms blue-green colonies embedded in jelly. Nostoc, however, has never been known to arrive with a blast and a flash of light. Nor has it been known to stink and to dissolve redly on exposure to air.

Other Quabbin oddities include mysterious beehive-shaped caves in Pelham, Leverett, and Shutesbury, and the sightings of crocodilian creatures in the Dismal Swamp near Ware. Crocodiles between six and eight feet long were spotted in 1922. Since then, three crocs ranging in size from one to three feet have been captured in the swamp. Crocodilians are generally found only in tropical or semitropical climates.

On June 14, 1972, several fat, four-foot long eels were pulled from the water pipes in a house in Medford after residents complained of low water pressure. The eels are believed to have swum more than 100 miles through the pipes from the Quabbin Reservoir.

The Hockomock Swamp area claims its own share of strange occurrences. Because of its long history of evil, bedeviled and ominous occurrences, residents have recognized this area of the state for its strange and often sinister character and have, over the years, dubbed it "The Bridgewater Triangle." The Bridgewater Triangle or Hockomock Swamp region covers an area of approximately 200 square miles and includes the towns of Abington, Freetown, and Rehoboth at the angles of the triangle, and Brockton, Taunton, the Bridgewaters, Raynham, Mansfield, Norton and Easton within the triangle. Historically, residents of areas such as this one have acknowledged the haunted or bedeviled nature of these places by giving them names such as Devil's Kitchen in Illinois, Devil's Den in New Hampshire and Diablo Valley in California. In recent times, areas of strange unexplained activity—UFO sightings, mysterious disappearances, creature sightings and a high incidence of accidents, violence and crime—have been labeled "Triangles." The most famous of these is the "Bermuda Triangle." The term "Triangle" is now a commonly accepted way of describing what researchers of strange phenomena call a "gateway" or "window" area, that is, a location of focused unexplained activity. The Bridgewater Triangle seems to be one of these focal areas.

For thousands of years, the local Indians have recognized the extraordinary character of the Hockomock area. Indian history figures prominently in the lore of Hockomock. For the Indians, it has been a site that is especially sacred and sometimes especially evil. Several years ago, an expedition of Massachusetts archaeologists discovered an eight thousand year old Indian burial site on Grassy Island in the Hockomock Swamp. When the graves were opened, the red ochre within the tombs bubbled and dissolved mysteriously and every photograph taken of the site failed to develop. Recently, while clearing a path for Interstate 495,

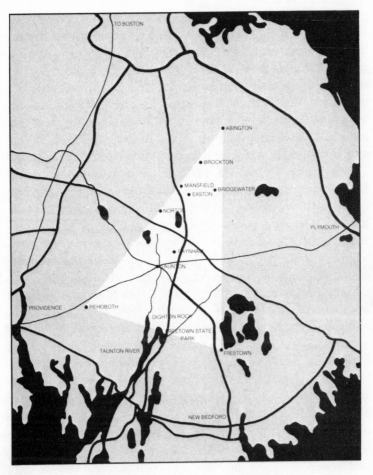

Massachusetts' Bridgewater Triangle.

workers in Norton discovered arrowheads, stone tools, pottery and other remains of prehistoric paleo-Indians who may have moved into this area after the glaciers receded more than ten thousand years ago. Archaeologists were not surprised by this significant discovery because this area of Massachusetts has one of the highest densities of pre-historic sites in New England.

The question of exactly who were the first new inhabitants of this area, is a matter of local controversy. On a site thirty miles up the Taunton River at the edge of the Hockomock Swamp, there is a mysterious forty-ton sandstone boulder which has been used by various nationalities as proof that they were the first "pilgrims." Dighton Rock, as it is called, sits on the river bank directly across from the Grassy Island Indian burial grounds. This rock is covered by a tangled pattern of carvings and hieroglyphics. Various national groups have interpreted these carvings in a manner that supports each group's contention that pilgrims or explorers of their nationality were the first to settle the area. Today, Dighton Rock in the main attraction of Delabarre State Park. It sits in a temperature controlled house, the walls of which are covered with exhibits that support first pilgrim theories of various nationalities – including Egyptians, Phoenicians, Vikings and Portugese.

Many Portugese-Americans live in the area, and lately the inscriptions on Dighton Rock have been most cited by adherents of the theory that the first settlers were Portugese. In Lisbon, there are royal charters indicating that in 1501, Gasper Corte Real embarked for the New World and was followed in 1512 by his brother, Miguel. Neither ever returned. However, among the spidery scrawls on Dighton Rock, there appears to be the date 1511, with the abbreviated name "M – COR" near it. To adherents of the Portugese pilgrim theory, these signs indicate that Miguel Corte Real arrived in mid-1502 and stayed for nine years. During that time, it is further theorized, the Portugese and Indians interbred and this intermingling is supposedly the reason why the Indians of this region were remarkably light-skinned. European explorers such as Verranzano and Roger Williams later remarked upon the light skin of these Indians, the Wampanoags or "People of the Dawn Light." The present day Portugese-American residents of the area believe this characteristic was passed on by the crews of Miguel Corte Real, and that he and his crew were the first pilgrims. There is, however, no certainty to this theory. The solid carved and cross-hatched forty tons of Dighton Rock remain as only another one of the many mysteries on the landscape of Hockomock and the Bridgewater Triangle.

Not only the swampy landscape of the Bridgewater Triangle, full of quicksand, rivers and murky reed-infested pools, is mysterious. The skies of this area also abound with strange appearances and disappearances. From colonial times comes the report of "Yellow Day" when the skies above the area shone with an eerie sulfureous yellow light all day long. In more recent times, many reports of strange lights and noises in the sky above the massive power lines that run through the swamp have been recorded. Regularly every January, "spook lights" – unexplained elusive balls of light – have been seen over the railroad tracks that run beside the Raynham Dog Track and through the swamp. In 1973, in Rehoboth, patrons of Joseph's Restaurant on Park Street believed they were visited by a UFO. The restaurant experienced a short power failure; when the lights came on, two large perfect circles were found imprinted in the dirt behind the restaurant. During the summer of 1978, a flap of many UFO sightings occurred throughout the months of July and August. The latest major flap occurred during the Spring of 1979. One of the most spectacular unidentified flying objects was seen by Jerry Lopes, a radio newsman at WHDH in Boston. Lopes encountered his UFO on the 23rd of March. He described it as shaped like home plate on a baseball diamond, with a bright red light on its top, a powerful white "headlight" on the bottom at the point and rows of white and red lights around the edges. Jerry Lopes saw this strange aerial apparition at the junction of Routes 24 and 106 – near the center of the Bridgewater Triangle.

Finally, in the skies of the triangle, there have been sightings of tremendous unknown birds. The most recent and dramatic sighting of one of these huge birds took place at 2 a.m. on a late summer's night in 1971. Norton police sergeant Thomas Downy was driving along Winter Street in Mansfield toward his home in Easton. As he approached a place known as "Bird Hill" in Easton at the edge of the swamp, he was suddenly confronted by a tremendous winged creature over six feet tall with a wing span of between eight and twelve feet. As Sergeant Downy drew to a stop at the intersection, the bird flew straight up and, flapping its massive wings, disappeared over the dark trees into the swamp. Downy reported the sighting to the Easton police as soon as he reached home. A patrol car searched the area, but the huge bird was not sighted again. For weeks after, this policeman with the feathery name was teased by his fellow officers who called him "The Birdman." Downy stuck to his story. Of course, he is not alone in ancient or recent history for the sighting of tremendous birds or bird-like creatures.

Again and again, these enormous birds appear in human history and folklore. They figure in the Indian legends of Hockomock and of many other areas throughout the Americas. Known as Thunderbirds in Indian mythology, these creatures were large enough and powerful enough to carry off a man. In recent times, these huge birds have been sighted by many people in Texas and throughout the Southwest. They have been reliably reported from the Midwest since 1948. In Lawndale, Illinois, I investigated the 1977 report that one of these huge birds carried a ten year-old boy for a distance of thirty feet through the air (See Chapter Two). Thunderbirds have also been seen in Northern Pennsylvania, in an area known as the "Coudersport Triangle." These Thunderbirds are not the only creatures of the Netherland to have appeared in the Hockomock Swamp region. Several other creatures that occur repeatedly in human folklore and legend have manifested themselves in the Bridgewater Triangle.

The most famous phantom creature to appear in the Bridgewater Triangle is the notorious Bigfoot. In the past ten years, all kinds of sightings of Bigfoot, ranging from almost certain hoaxes to incidents involving eminently responsible witnesses and organized police hunts have been reported. In Bridgewater, in 1970, heavily armed state and local police, along with a pack of hunting dogs, tracked what was reported to be a huge "bear." Since the creature was not found, police were never certain what it really was. They are certain, although bears have not been seen in the Bridgewater area for many years, that whatever the creature was it was not a hoax. Several very reputable citizens had had a good look at the huge creature before it lumbered off into the woods, and large definite tracks were discovered. In other parts of the country, people trying to make sense of the unexplained have often labeled these large hairy creatures "bears."

Around the same time as these "bear" sightings, there were several other reports of a large hairy creature walking upright in other places in the Bridgewater vicinity. Farmers reported killed and mutilated pigs and sheep. Another Bridgewater resident complained to the police that a large hairy creature walking upright was thrashing about in the backyards and woods of the neighborhood. Police investigated several times. One officer, lying in wait in his patrol car, reported that, entirely without warning, something picked up the rear of his car. The policeman spun the car around and when he flashed his searchlight, he saw something that looked like a huge bipedal "bear" running away between the houses. Nothing was found in further searches. However, there were several other sightings in the area. In Raynham, a night security guard at the Raynham Dog Track reported a series of horrible screams and screeches that frightened him and upset the dogs. Huge eighteen inch footprints were discovered in the snow south of Raynham. On separate occasions several residents reported seeing a tall furry man-like creature in the Elm Street – Bridge Street area of Raynham, I discoverd in my interviews with local authorities.

In 1977, outside of the triangle area in Agawam, Massachusetts, near Springfield, footprints were discovered in the snow, and again tales of Bigfoot circulated. This time, police determined that the incident was almost certainly a hoax. Previous sightings within the Triangle, however, could not be explained as hoaxes. Many area observers and even the police have, by now, become firm believers in the weird creatures of the Bridgewater Triangle. As one police officer said in 1970, "Nothing surprises us much anymore. Last week, a motorist ran over an eight foot Boa Constrictor. We still haven't learned where that came from."

Huge snakes have been sighted before in the Hockomock region. In 1939, Roosevelt era CCC workers, completing a project on King Phillip's Street at the edge of the swamp, reported seeing a huge snake "as large around and black as a stove-pipe." The snake coiled for a moment, raised its spade-like head and disappeared into the swamp. Local legends claim that a huge snake like this one appears every seven years. In addition to legendary serpents, great cats – "lions" or "phantom panthers" – have been sighted regularly in places throughout the Bridgewater Triangle. In 1972, in Rehoboth, Mass., a "lion hunt" was organized by local police. Residents of the area had been terrorized by what they reported as a large cat or mountain lion. Cattle and sheep in the area had been mysteriously killed, and carcasses were discovered raked with claw-marks. Police took casts of the animal's tracks and used dogs and a helicopter in an attempt to track it down. Nothing was caught. Similar incidents, however, involving phantom cats have occurred in other places throughout the Bridgewater Triangle – and across the nation. None of these mysterious felines has yet been captured.

Huge black dogs, as well as black panthers, have been reported within the Bridgewater Triangle. Both of these "creature-forms" have a long history in human mythology and folklore. Sir Arthur Conan Doyle's "Hound of the Baskervilles" has its ancestors in the many legends of the Hounds of Hell and of the Irish Pooka, huge black ghost-like dogs with eyes of fire. In 1976, a huge black "killer dog" was reported in Abington within the Bridgewater Triangle. The "dog" ripped out the throats of two ponies. Local firefighter Phillip Kane, the owner of the ponies, saw the "dog" standing over the bloody carcasses gnawing at their necks. He said that the "dog" eluded extensive police searches and, for a period of several weeks, terrorized the community. During the three days following the killing of the ponies police received 1000 telephone calls. School children were kept in at recess, and many home-owners and store-keepers armed themselves with rifles. The last time this "dog" was seen was when police officer Frank Curran sighted it

along some railroad tracks. The officer fired a shot but "missed."
The "black dog" merely turned away and walked off slowly in the
other direction. And into another dimension?

The coastal areas of Massachusetts are also fecund territory for
weird phenomena. The sands of Singing Beach in Manchester
keen strangely when they are walked upon; all attempts to recre-
ate these sounds under laboratory conditions have failed.

Twice during the last century, in 1819 in Nahant and 1871 at
Cape Ann, hundreds of North Shore residents reported sighting
a forty-foot-long chocolate-brown sea serpent. More recently, in
1964, a sleek unidentifiable creature about the size of a seal was
reported to be haunting St. Mary's Cemetery in Quincy. The
creature, described as being black with short legs and dragging
tail, uttered shrill cries and always appeared near running water.

There have been a host of other random oddities in many other
towns around the state. On September 7, 1954, in Leicester, frogs
and toads fell from the sky and landed on rooftops and gutters
throughout Leicester center and on Paxton Avenue. In Pittsfield,
during February of 1958, patrons of the Bridge Lunch Restaurant
were surprised to see an old-time steam engine with half a dozen
coaches go clattering by on the railroad tracks outside. Railroad
officials said that steam engines have not operated on that line
for many years. On October 22, 1973, a Sudbury woman noticed
sparkling fibers gathering on wires and tree branches. When she
looked upward, she saw a shiny globular object disappearing in
the clear sky to the west. She collected many of the strange fibers
which have been found in other places and are known to ufologists
as "Angel Hair." She then quickly sealed them in a jar before they
evaporated. Scientists at the University of Massachusetts confirmed that the fibers were not spiderweb, but could not determine further what this Halloween substance was.

One can devise all sorts of explanations for unusual events. They
might be the result of hoax, coincidence, or natural forces that
have yet to be understood. Psychic energy, the power of suggestion and the fertility of imagination may be contributing factors.

(courtesy Naval Historical Foundation)

On many occasions during the 19th century, Massachusetts' North Shore was visited by this sea serpent. This print specifically shows the Gloucester monster.

One might concede that supernatural or extraterrestrial forces are at work.

The public still treats such phenomenon with a healthy skepticism. But there are indications that people are beginning to believe there may be more to our haunted heritage than meets the eye. In 1974, for example, the director of the Barnstable Housing Authority allowed a family to move from one public housing unit to another. The reason: the tenants had complained that the rooms were haunted.

Creatures Aplenty. . .

5
A Case Study:
The Dover Demon

Often, people ask me what happens when I investigate a sighting, how do I hear about it, what steps do I take to verify the status of the witness in the community, and several other related questions. All accounts are different and various methods are used at any one time, but in essence, Fortean fieldwork is a form of investigative reporting and scientific inquiry. To get an insider's look at one such examination of an outbreak of sightings, I have asked Walter Webb, Assistant Director of the Hayden Planetarium at Boston's Science Museum, for his kind permission, to publish his sterling report on the systematic investigation of the Dover Demon.

Walter Webb, the first researcher to hear about and examine the details of the Barney and Betty Hill UFO abduction case, completed the Dover Demon report in September of 1977.

Introduction and Background

In April of 1977 the town of Dover, Massachusetts, provided the setting for one of the most baffling creature episodes ever

41

reported. Generally recorded as the wealthiest town in Massachusetts, Dover (pop. 5000) is a heavily wooded community situated just 15 miles southwest of Boston. During a 25½-hour period on April 21-22, four teenagers claimed to have made three independent sightings of a small gnome-like entity with an enormous head, large round glowing eyes, and long spindly limbs. In all three circumstances the bizarre creature – tagged the "Dover Demon" by investigator Loren Coleman – was allegedly spotted within a two-mile-long zone along narrow paved roads. The vegetation in this rural-suburban area alternates between wooded land and pasture, and houses generally are spaced several hundred feet apart. No UFO was reported by the witnesses.

On April 28, one week after the sightings, Loren Coleman happened to be at the Dover Country Store when a store employee, Melody Fryer, told him about William Bartlett's sighting and his sketch of the creature. Mrs. Fryer promised to get Coleman the sketch. Two days later the investigator obtained two of Bartlett's drawings. The following day, May 1, Loren interviewed Bartlett, and on the 3rd he questioned John Baxter and Abby Brabham (Will Taintor was quizzed about two days after that). Also on the 1st Coleman gave the Dover Police Department a copy of one of Bartlett's sketches in case other witnesses should come forth. On the 4th Loren contacted *The Real Paper* in Cambridge. The newspaper interviewed Coleman as well as Bartlett, Baxter, and Dover Police Chief Carl Sheridan on the 7th.

It was on May 12 that the Framingham radio station WKOX, searching for local news stories, happened to call the Dover police station and thereupon was informed about the creature sightings. WKOX/WCVF-FM aired the story the next day. On the 14th the Associated Press and the *South Middlesex News* (Framingham), having heard the WKOX report, also called Coleman for more information. Finally, the first newspaper accounts appeared – *South Middlesex News* and *The Real Paper* on the 15th and the Boston *Globe*, Boston *Herald American, Patriot Ledger* (Quincy), and other New England newspapers on the 16th. Local and national television picked up the story.

I actually was aware of the Dover affair on May 14. My informant, a Needham resident, only made brief mention of it, and I passed it off as a probable hoax. Three days later, however, my administrative assistant (at Boston's Charles Hayden Planetarium) and a visitor (a witness in another UFO case) almost simultaneously brought my attention to the newspaper stories.

Since there appeared to be several observers of the creature and the sightings occurred as close as four (air) miles from my home in neighboring Westwood, I could hardly pass this one up. I visited the Dover police station on the evening of the 17th and obtained the addresses and telephone numbers of Bill Bartlett and Loren Coleman. When I called Loren, he suggested I join him and two other local UFO investigators in sort of a "pool coverage" operation.

The four of us represented five UFO/Fortean organizations, and we happened to be from four different towns surrounding Dover. The team consisted of Coleman, who is consulting editor of INFO (International Fortean Society), an honorary member of SITU (Society for the Investigation of the Unexplained), and co-author of *The Unidentified* (Warner Books, 1975); Joseph Nyman of Medfield (MUFON/APRO); Ed Fogg of Foxboro (New England UFO Study Group); and myself (APRO). Loren proved especially valuable to our joint effort not only because of his initial investigation into the Dover sightings but also because of his knowledge of and rapport with young people. He is a social worker at a school for emotionally disturbed boys.

Together, on May 21, we interrogated witnesses Baxter, Brabham, and Taintor as well as Baxter's mother and Taintor's parents (Bartlett was confined in a hospital with mononucleosis). Afterward Loren led us to the three sites where the "demon" was alleged to have been seen. At these places we took photographs and measurements. On June 11 we finally questioned Bartlett and his parents.

Additional information concerning the youths' reliability was obtained from the police, teachers, and the principal of the school. I concluded my own investigation on August 7, with interviews of Bartlett's two companions (nonwitnesses in his car at the time of his sightings) and with a telephone call to one of the teachers.

The Bartlett Sighting

On the evening of April 21, William Bartlett, 17, of Dover, was driving around in his VW with two friends, Mike Mazzocca, 17, and Andy Brodie, 17, of Sherborn. Bill recalled that the sky was clear and stars were visible (confirmed by the National Weather Service at Boston's Logan Airport; temperature was 55°F at the time of the sighting, according to Blue Hill Observatory located ten miles from Dover). Although Bartlett hadn't been drinking, he said he had smoked a little marijuana in Norwood about an hour before his sighting. He emphasized, however, he had only a few puffs and was positive his head was clear during the crucial moments of the encounter.

About 10:30 p.m. (EST) the trio was driving northward at about 40 or 45 miles per hour on Farm Street, approaching Smith Street, when Bill said he spotted what he at first thought was a dog or cat creeping along a low wall of loose stones (the wall was about two feet high) on the left side of the road. (The site is almost opposite the L. B. Taylor mailbox on Farm Street. Immediately next to the wall is a single row of trees, and beyond is an open field.) The figure appeared to place its hands and feet carefully on the stones as if it weren't sure of its path over the wall.

Bathed in the car's high-beams, according to Bartlett, the creature grabbed onto a rock with long fingers, slowly turned its head toward the approaching car, and stared into the light. In the next instant, the witness said he realized it wasn't a dog or cat. The entity possessed an unusually large head shaped like a watermelon and about the same size as its trunk. In the center of the head glowed two large, round, glassy, lidless eyes, shining brightly "like two orange marbles" in the glare of the headlights. No other features were detected on the head; there was no discernable nose, mouth, or ears. The head seemed supported on a thin neck.

The creature's body, according to Bartlett, was thin with long spindly arms and legs and large hands and feet. The shape reminded the witness of a "baby's body with long arms and legs." Its skin was hairless, with something like dirt smudged on it, appeared to be the rough texture of a shark ("like wet sandpaper"), and was a peach color – "an exaggerated skin color, like Fred Flintstone in the Sunday comics" (quote from *The Real Paper* interview). The tint was lighter, almost whitish, near the hands. The entity's size appeared to be about that of a monkey, three and a half to four feet tall. Although no tail was visible, Bartlett admitted one could have been present but hidden behind the figure.

The following two paragraphs quoting Bartlett were taken verbatim from *The Real Paper* interview and best describe what happened next (parenthetical remarks are mine):

"I really flew after I saw it. I took that corner at 45, which is pretty fast. (In several timed re-enactments, the sighting lasted a maximum of five or six seconds. By our actual tape measurement, his vehicle would have passed within about 20 feet of the creature.) I said to my friends, 'Did you see that?' And they said, 'Nah, describe it.' I did and they said, 'Go back. Go back.' And I said, 'No way. No way.' When you see something like that, you don't want to stand around and see what it's going to do.

(Continuing nearly a mile beyond the site, Bill turned left on Glen Street and then turned around.)

"They finally got me to go back, and Mike was leaning out of the window yelling, 'Come on, creature!' And I was saying 'Will you cut that out?' (He said he was still shaking at this point.) Andy was yelling, 'I want to see you!' I was trying to get them to shut the windows." (The entity was gone.)

I questioned both Mike and Andy separately. I asked them why neither saw the alleged creature. Mike, who was sitting in the front seat beside Bill, said he was looking at his own side of the road. Andy, on the other hand, was in back and said he wasn't sure but thought he was talking to Mike at the time. Mike said Bill was "pretty scared" after seeing the creature and didn't want to go back. Andy agreed that Bill "sounded genuinely frightened." At first the two youths didn't believe their friend's description of a big-headed creature with large glowing eyes, long fingers grabbing the rocks, etc. But Bartlett's fright was convincing, and both Mazzocca and Brodie soon accepted the witness's story. They urged Bill to make a drawing of the creature when he got home so they could see what it looked like.

As soon as he returned home, Bill said he took out his sketchpad and drew the figure as he recalled it. (Quote from *The Real Paper*: "I draw a lot. I train myself to remember what I see as soon as I see it.") He is an excellent amateur artist and showed us some of his work; he is a member of Boston's Copley Art Society. Mr. Bartlett told us his son was upset when he came home and described to his father what he had seen. Both Mr. and Mrs. Bartlett are convinced Bill saw "something," that he is "very honest and open," and not the kind to play pranks or make up stories. He is not a drama student nor is he a science-fiction buff.

The Baxter Sighting

The second encounter reportedly occurred about two hours later (April 22) 1.2 (air) miles northeast of the Bartlett location. Around midnight John Baxter, 15, of Dover, left his girlfriend's house (Cathy Cronin) at the south end of Millers Hill Road and proceeded to walk north toward the end of the street where he hoped to hitch a ride home.

After a half hour, he had walked nearly a mile (.95 mile by our speedometer) up the left side of Millers Hill Road when he said about 50 yards away (100 feet by our measurement) he glimpsed the silhouette of someone approaching him on his side of the road (paved).

As he got closer, John said he could see that the figure was very small and thought it might be a kid he knew who lived on the street, M. G. Bouchard. He called out, "M.G., is that you?" There was no response. Both the witness and the shadowy figure continued to walk toward each other.

When they were about 15 feet apart (about 25 feet by our measurement), the figure stopped. Baxter also halted. The witness said he again called out, "Who is that?" It was very dark, and he could barely see the figure. (Logan Airport reported scattered clouds at 25,000 feet at midnight becoming overcast by 1 a.m. The temperature remained at 55°F at Blue Hill.)

As John took another step toward the figure, suddenly it scur-

(Above) Bill Bartlett's drawing of the Dover Demon.
(Below) Bartlett at the Farm Street stone wall, the location
of his sighting.

ried very rapidly to the left down a shallow wooded gully, across a low wet spot, and up the opposite bank. The witness said he could hear the creature's footfalls on the dry leaves as it ran.

Baxter scrambled down the slope after the creature for about six to eight feet and then stopped. Across the gully he could see the being (about 30 feet away by our tape) standing with both feet "molded" around the top of a rock a few feet from a tree. It was leaning toward the tree, the long fingers of both hands gripping the trunk for support (the tree's diameter was about eight inches). The digits of the feet, according to Baxter, could be seen in the dark curled around the rock because of the rock's lighter color. He was unsure of the exact number of digits on each hand and foot.

The figure was now clearly outlined against an open field providing the witness with his best view. The dark silhouette resembled that of a monkey except for a large "figure-eight" head. The creature's eyes showed up as two lighter spots in the middle of the head and peered straight ahead at the observer.

After staring at the entity for what seemed like a few minutes, Baxter said he began to feel uneasy about the situation he was in. He said he didn't quite know what sort of creature or animal confronted him, and it looked as if it might be ready to spring. At this point the witness said he backed up the slope, his heart pounding, and "walked very fast" down the road (another .15 mile or 800 feet) to the intersection at Farm Street. There he was picked up by a Dedham couple who dropped him off at his home (about 1 a.m.). He estimated observing the figure less than ten minutes (probably considerably less).

John said as soon as he got home, he drew a sketch of the creature (as Bill had done) allegedly before he knew of Bartlett's own sighting. Although *The Real Paper* implied that John's mother doubted the creature existed, she told us her son "never made up stories" and she believed "he saw something." We were unable to talk to Mr. Baxter, who was recovering from a brain-clot operation. *The Real Paper* stated that Mr. Baxter didn't believe his son made up the story. However, he was also quoted as saying: "The only thing that bothers me a bit is that he's an avid science-fiction fan." John readily admitted his scifi interest which includes writing his own stories. But he denied this had anything to do with his sighting report.

When we visited Baxter's claimed encounter site, we spoke to the owner of the nearest property, Alice W. Stewart. She was aware of the Dover Demon stories. We asked her if she had noticed or heard anything at all peculiar near her house that night. She replied she hadn't. Her dogs were inside the house at the time.

The Brabham-Taintor Sighting

Bartlett said he was unaware of Baxter's confrontation with the demon until five days later (April 26). At that time John, who had heard about Bill's sighting, showed Bill his own sketch of the entity. Bartlett said he was "amazed" because it was the same creature he had seen. Although Bill didn't see John until the 26th, on the 22nd he did tell his close friend, Will Taintor, 18, of Dover, about his strange experience.

That night, about midnight on the 22nd (almost 24 hours after the Baxter sighting), Will was driving Abby Brabham, 15, to her home in Sherborn. They were about a quarter mile out of Dover center on Springdale Avenue when Abby said she saw something in the headlights in the left lane of the road. (The site is atop a culvert crossing the east branch of Trout Brook 1.2 miles east-northeast of Baxter's location and 2.3 miles northeast of Bartlett's.) A creature of some kind was crouched on all fours facing the car and looked like a monkey or small ape, with several important exceptions: its head was very large and oblong; the body appeared hairless and tan or beige in color; and there was no nose, mouth, ears, or tail. The facial area appeared somewhat lighter around the eyes which were round and glowed bright *green* in the headlights. (Abby was questioned closely about the eye color, and she felt positive about the green hue.)

Taintor's car was traveling about 40 miles per hour, and by the time he said he noticed the creature in the road, he managed to catch only a fleeting glimpse (for perhaps a few seconds). He recalled having the impression of something with a large head and tan body crouched in the road, with its front legs raised in the air. He was certain it wasn't a dog. Will thought it might have been as large as a goat, and Abby guessed it was the size of a German shepherd. Apparently neither witness noticed hands or feet.

As the vehicle drove past the creature (perhaps as close as eight feet away by our measurement), Abby asked Will to speed up and get out of there. Although she thought she had viewed the creature for as long as 30 to 45 seconds, a timed re-enactment placed the length of Abby's observation at only about five seconds.

As they drove on, Will said he suddenly remembered the Bartlett sighting and only then did he begin to question Abby more closely about specific details, features he was aware of from his conversation with Bill (Will's own sighting proved brief and unspectactular). Taintor said he deliberately asked Abby leading questions about the creature's appearance – about details he knew were *not* true – in order to check her story and description against Bartlett's. According to Will, he divulged nothing to Abby about Bartlett's sighting until after theirs had occurred. Abby agreed she hadn't known about the other sighting reports.

Cloud conditions during the third sighting, according the Logan Airport, were overcast at 20,000 feet, with broken clouds at 7000 feet. The temperature at Blue Hill Observatory was 65°F.

When we interviewed Will and Abby, Will's parents were present. Like the parents of the previous boys, Will's parents believed their son and Abby were telling the truth and they saw something real. Mr. Taintor tended to think a conventional animal of some kind was mistaken for the demon, while Mrs. Taintor speculated an unknown creature might be involved.

Evaluation

After hearing the four teenagers tell their stories, the four of us who conducted the investigation agreed unanimously about the witnesses: we were impressed by them, especially Bill Bartlett and Abby Brabham.

Bartlett, who claimed the first sighting and who became the central figure in the case due chiefly to his widely publicized sketch, was overwhelmingly endorsed by townspeople. The following represent typical responses:

Dover Police Chief Carl Sheridan described Bartlett as an "outstanding artist and a reliable witness."

Science teacher Robert Linton, one of the first adults to talk to Bartlett outside Bill's parents, said the youth "seemed extremely sincere and I had to believe him."

Mike Mazzocca and Andy Brodie, Bill's two companions during the sighting, agreed their friend was "pretty scared" (Mike) and "sounded genuinely frightened" (Andy) after seeing the creature. Although they themselves didn't glimpse the demon, they became convinced Bill's account was true.

Mr. Bartlett testified his son was upset when he arrived home. After hearing Bill's story, he said he believed Bill saw "something," an animal of some kind. Bill's parents assured us their son was "very honest and open" and not the type to make up stories. As also pointed out before, he was not a scifi fan nor a drama student.

Loren and I questioned Bill's science teacher on separate occasions. Robert Linton, 35, has taught at Dover-Sherborn for seven years and is greatly liked and respected by the students. On April 25 – four days after Bartlett's encounter and also the first day back to school following spring vacation – the teacher said he overheard Bill discussing his sighting with students as they entered the classroom. He asked Bill about it, whereupon the youth described his experience and drew a picture of the creature. Linton told us Bartlett was convinced he saw the creature, that it "scared the hell out of him," and that the others later saw the same thing, too. The instructor asked his student if he had anything to smoke or drink beforehand. Bill replied, as he had to us, that he puffed a little marijuana that evening but felt he was "straight" during the sighting. Linton accepted Bartlett's story.

In the midst of all of the endorsements for Bill Bartlett's reliability, we came across only one curiously negative opinion. It was expressed by one of Bill's teachers who desired that his name not be divulged. Joe Nyman received the name through another teacher. When Joe telephoned the anonymous instructor (his name is on file), this individual implied that Bartlett was a troubled frustrated kid with very low credibility, that he cut classes, hung around the student's smoking lounge with John Baxter, and belonged to a clique that included Baxter. The teacher summed up his low opinion of the witness by stating: "If I had to pick someone to pull something like this, it would be Bartlett."

Loren confronted Bill with these charges, saying they came from a "source" at school. The youth denied the accusations. He said the smoking lounge happens to be a central meeting place for students whether they smoke or not (both Bartlett and his parents said Bill doesn't smoke cigarettes although he does puff pot out of school occasionally). He said Baxter is only one of his friends, and he was detained only once this year for cutting a class.

Loren went back to the teacher with Bartlett's denials, but he refused to change his opinion and stuck to his remarks. Because this individual is the only person we uncovered who held an unfavorable view of this witness, and since it was such a total contrast to the opinions of others, we believe the teacher's motives may be suspect. Our reasons for thinking this have to do with things that can't be revealed without giving away the instructor's identity. In addition, he was the only person who refused to allow his name to be published. Of all the witnesses, we were *most* impressed by Bill Bartlett — as a healthy well-adjusted teenager, as a careful observer, and as an excellent artist.

Regarding John Baxter, Loren Coleman felt some uneasiness about his testimony during Loren's May 3 interview. The investigator thought John might have been a bit defensive owing to some initial resistance he may have received to his story. However, we all agreed he appeared much more relaxed during our interview on May 21. Baxter's mother told us John "never made up stories," and she believed "he saw something." Although Mr. Baxter apparently agreed, it will be recalled he told *The Real Paper*: "The only thing that bothers me a bit is that he's an avid science-fiction fan." John admitted writing scifi stories for fun but rejected the notion that this played a role in his sighting claim. While we all agreed Baxter's account of his experience had the ring of truth as we listened, to what extent his scifi interest might have influenced his sighting, or his account of it, is a troublesome feature that can't be completely ignored.

In the case of Abby Brabham and Will Taintor's assertions that they also witnessed the Dover Demon, Abby's story proved quite convincing to us, especially when she declared adamantly: "I know I saw the creature and don't care what happens!". It will be recalled that Will was already aware of the Bartlett sighting and yet failed to "capitalize" on it by embellishing his own observation. In fact, his own description was meager compared to Abby's because he caught only a fleeting glimpse of the creature. This lends credibility to Will's account. At the time Abby claimed she didn't know about the earlier sightings until Will mentioned Bartlett's *after* their own encounter.

Other comments from Dover residents concerning the witnesses in general:

High school principal Richard Wakely told Loren: "I don't think these kids got together and invented it." Were they troublemakers? "No. They're average students."

Michael Dowd of the Dover Country Store: "I'm a sucker for anything. But the kids trust me and they're really upstanding kids. I don't think they're making this up" (Dover-Sherborn *Suburban Press*).

An unidentified officer at the Dover Police Department: "At first I was going to ask one of the witnesses to give me whatever it was he was smoking, but I know all four, and I know that, to all of us, they're very reputable people" (*South Middlesex News*).

What arguments, if any, support the hoax hypothesis? A skeptic might draw up the following scenario: all four youths were either close friends, acquaintances, or knew of one another at school. The teenagers seemed to agree there is little for kids to do in Dover, especially during spring vacation when the alleged sightings occurred. Perhaps inspired by a science-fiction film or by Tolkien's little goggle-eyed creature known as Gollum (suggested in a letter to the Boston *Globe*) or even by a creature in one of Baxter's own fictional yarns, Bartlett might have got the others to go along with a little prank, aided by sketches from

Bartlett and Baxter, to "liven things up" around town. Alternatively, perhaps they themselves were the *victims* of a hoax perpetrated by other equally bored youths. In any case, there can be no denying the youths received a lot of attention, both locally and nationally in the press, as a result of this incident. Loren Coleman reported Bill and John became quite popular at school, and Bill enjoyed recognition as an artist by having his sketch published in the newspapers. Abby and Will were invited to appear on Television Channel 44's "Club 44," where they described their encounter.

However, equally logical counter arguments balance or even outweigh the hoax scenario. Perhaps first and foremost, Bill Bartlett's emotional upset during and immediately following his sighting was attested to by both the two companions and his father. His fright appeared geniune, not staged. While John Baxter's scifi interest tends to complicate his sighting claim, both Bill and Abby appeared quite convincing in our presence. Loren was the first investigator to interview all four witnesses when their stories were still rather fresh and before the media coverage. He was especially impressed at that time by Bill and his testimony (Loren's insight as a social worker proved extremely helpful in this regard).

None of the four was on drugs or drinking at the time of his or her sighting so far as we were able to determine. As students at the same high school, it would be surprising if the witnesses were not at least aware of each other. None of the principals in this affair made any attempt to go to the newspapers or police to publicize their claims. Instead, the sightings gradually leaked out. Finally the teenagers' own parents, the high-school principal, the science instructor, and other adults in Dover whose comments were solicited didn't believe the Dover Demon was a fabrication, implying the youths did indeed see "something." (The sole doubter we encountered was the teacher whose damning remarks were somewhat suspect.)

As for the idea the witnesses were victims of somebody else's stunt, this seems most unlikely, chiefly due to the virtual impossibility of creating an animated, life-like "demon" of the sort described.

If these young people saw "something," what sort of creature did they see? Theories have ranged all the way from an escaped monkey to an unknown animal or extraterrestrial visitor. Mr. Bartlett's belief was that although the creature could have represented something supernatural or extraterrestrial, he was certain it had a "more plausible explanation," such as an escaped laboratory animal of some sort. Mrs. Bartlett told us her neighbor suggested a sick fox because there is a disease that makes a fox swell up grotesquely and lose all of its hair. Joe Nyman asked a veterinarian about this and discovered in such cases where the hair falls out and the body swells, the skin of the fox becomes *dark* (the Dover creature possessed a light color). However, the greatest objection to the sick fox-escaped monkey/lab animal hypothesis is the simple fact the demon bore absolutely no resemblance to any of these animals (sick or healthy). All of the witnesses agreed their creature was hairless *and* lacked a nose, mouth, ears, and tail. Besides, if the animal were someone's escaped monkey or lab animal, it seems strange that no one came forth to identify it.

Interestingly, all four witnesses thought the most likely explanation for what they saw was that the creature must have been an unknown terrestrial animal that, until now, managed to escape detection in Dover's dense woods. Bill and Abby believed it must be a water creature of some kind since it was seen not far from water in all three instances. John said it wasn't like any creature he'd ever seen. He thought an unknown earth creature "seems a little more realistic" than the notion it might have come from space. He considered, then rejected, the idea that a "very mishapen monkey" could have been the source of the sightings. It seems very unlikely to this investigator that any unidentified earthly creature the size of the Dover Demon could dwell so near large population areas and remain hidden from the eyes of science until now — and then be glimpsed three times in one 25½-hour period, only to disappear back into oblivion. However, the fact that all the observers preferred an earthly explanation to an extraterrestrial one provides futher credibility for their reports.

Loren was the first to note some resemblance between the Dover entity and the famous Kelly, Kentucky, "little men" incident of 1955 (the subject of Chapter 17). Yet major differences about, not the least of which were the Kentucky creatures' large floppy ears. Like the Dover Demon, the Kelly being has never been reported before or since. I asked Ted Bloecher, co-chairman of MUFON's Humanoid Study Group, if he recalled anything in his humanoid file that matched the description of the Dover Demon. He replied in the negative. The Dover occurrence is a Type E event in the Bloecher classification system, that is, "no known association between entity and UFO." Using Ted's witness credibility scale (0-9), I assign a 4-5 rating to the Dover Demon case.

In some respects, the Dover entity resembles some of the gnome-like critters of fairy folklore. For example, the Cree Indians of eastern Canada have a legend about the Mannegishi, who are supposed to be "little people with round heads and no noses who live with only one purpose: to play jokes on travelers. The little creatures have long spidery legs, arms with six-fingered hands, and live between rocks in the rapids . . ." (Sigurd Olson, *Listening Point,* Knopf, 1958)

The Dover Demon is a disturbing, bizarre affair. There are many frustrating, troublesome aspects about it. Like the Kelly encounter, it is without apparent precedent. But despite the doubts and questions this episode raises, I believe a hoax is unlikely and the report should be classified as a *low-weight unknown.*

6
The Teleporting Animals

The look to me is that, throughout what is loosely called Nature, teleportation exists, as a means of distribution of things and materials . . .

Charles Fort in *LO!*

The Summer of Synchronistic Species

Giant out-of-place lizards, all of the same species, were the plague of Florida during the summer of 1981. Florida is well known for its semitropical climate and frequent reports of exotic introduced animals, from walking catfish and piranha, to jaguars and jaguarundis. However, the 1981 rash of monitor lizard encounters is noteworthy because of the underlying synchronization and the nagging notions of teleportation.

Meandering Monitors

The LaMancha Golf Course in Royal Palm Beach was the sight of the first man–lizard meeting. Course Superintendent James

Kilgore was crossing the fairway on Saturday June the 20th, when he saw what he at first thought was one of the alligators he often had to chase off of the course.

"It was feeding on something. I never did see what," Kilgore said.

He soon discovered the thing was a six foot, five inch long Nile Monitor lizard. Kilgore pursued the lizard in his pick-up truck, and lassoed its head and body. "I threw the other end of the rope over a tree and lifted the lizard off the ground, then I just backed the truck up under him," the Superintendent told reporters.

The folks at Lion Country Safari were given the Nile Monitor by game commission officials, and happily added it to their display of two other Nile Monitors. No one knew the origin of the golf course monitor but theories flew. One Lion Country zoologist was quoted as saying: "It must have been imported (from Africa) and then escaped into the canal system."

Perhaps. Anyway, another Nile Monitor popped into official consciousness on Tuesday July 14th. A North Miami man had driven home Monday evening July 13th, and parked his automobile in his driveway. The next morning he opened his hood and found a five foot Nile Monitor lying across his engine. He quickly called game officials. "It's a bit startling to open your hood to change the oil and find a creature like that," noted game commission spokesperson Lt. B. F. Lampton.

It must have been a busy week for the Florida Game Commission, because right before the North Miami incident, a drama had begun to unfold in Hypoluxo, north of Boynton Beach, Florida. On Sunday, July 12th, Donald Wilton, a 79-year old retired carpenter and "primitive painter" was sitting in his living room reading. Then, he repeated later, "around dusk . . . I heard a noise. I opened the door to the garage and the thing scooted by me. It looked like an alligator."

It was no alligator; it was a five foot, thirty pound Nile Monitor.

Wilton called the game officials on Monday, but got brushed aside. They assumed he was talking about a small garden variety lizard, or an iguana. The advice they gave was to get a broom and "shoo" it out; or if that did not work, just to leave the garage door open, and it would leave, they said, when it got hungry. It took

Lindsey Hord gets a good grip on the Nile Monitor he captured at Hypoluxo, Florida. Its origin remains unknown.

until Wednesday – and after the North Miami encounter – for Wilton to convince them that a biologist and not a broom was needed. On Wednesday evening, Alligator Coordinator Lindsey Hord stopped by Wilton's house and was surprised to find a young, five foot long, monitor lizard, and not a foot long gecko. Hord corralled, tied up and taped the lizard's mouth shut. "You always take care of the mouth first." Hord said.

Lt. Lampton of the Florida Game Commission casually noted that two years ago a Nile Monitor had turned up near South Bay, Florida. Behind all the press jokes about the "Dragonslayer" Lampton seemed worried: "We have to be concerned since there have been two caught in the past two days." The Commission was not even talking about the golf course monitor; I discovered this information through contacting newspapers in Florida's east coast. Three Nile Monitors in a little over three weeks. Four in two years.

After the Hypoluxo lizard was taken to Commission offices, its adventures continued. It soon escaped from its enclosure (or did it teleport?), and hid behind some filing cabinets. It took three officers several minutes to recapture the Nile Monitor. "I'd rather deal with an alligator any day." Lampton said.

Crazy Crocodilians

For some people in America, alligators were exactly what they were dealing with during the summer of 1981.

Alligators have fascinated me for years. Charles Fort was delighted by the croc reports also, and some of his most interesting words on teleportation can be found in his passages on the crocodiles in England. From 1836 through the 1860's, Chipping Norton and Over-Norton in Oxfordshire were visited by young, usually foot long crocs. Along with Fort's work, and my list of some eighty-odd accounts, the concept of the "crazy crocs" (as Bill Grimstad labelled them) has been firmly planted in the sphere of Fortean study. So it was not surprising that during the crazy summer of 1981, the 'gators would pop up.

Two media exploited stories of escaped alligators kept the press busy. Even though these 'gators' origins were known, they are of interest to explorers of the unknown. Mainly for two reasons; first, the closeness in time of the alligators' escapes and captures suggests some synchronization; and second, the fact the 'gators' owners stepped forward bodes well for the teleportation of the large number of supposedly ownerless crocs that keep turning up everywhere.

Briefly then, on June 17th, Albert the Alligator escaped from the Denver Zoo and took up residence in the City Park's Duck Lake. The five foot five inch alligator was recaptured on July 16th. In Indianapolis, Oscar, Charlie Mudd's four foot pet alligator escaped on July 4th-Independence Day. Oscar decided to live in a neighbor's pond in the front yard of Gerald and Joyce Cannon. Oscar was recaptured on July 20th, ending Indianapolis' most recent croc caper. (Back in September of 1959, the city's Fall Creek was the host for a foot and a half long alligator.)

A short four days after the capture of Oscar, another crocodilian hunting expedition was formed. Officials who probably did not venture close enough to truly identify the animal, began looking for what they said was a four foot long "caiman" in the Kings River, near Laton, south of Fresno, California. Fish and game wardens were especially concerned because this area is a popluar swimming spot. This caiman appears to fit more clearly into the Fortean croc catalog than either Oscar or Albert.

California's central valley has a long history of strange animals and cryptozoological wonders. The Trinity Alps Monster (apparently a giant salamander?) and Folsom Lake's "alligators" intrique me. In the Tulare Lake Basin, Corcoran, California, a six footer was sighted during the summer of 1930. And in nearby Folsom Lake, a series of sightings of 'gators occurred between September 1957 and June 1958. In recent years, the reported finding of a dead alligator on the shores of Folsom Lake has reached me.

Pattering of the Penguins

Folsom Lake's elusive alligators once had to share their watery retreat with another enigmatic beast we Forteans have had to deal with now and then. In April of 1972, a penguin was stolen (by

Police officials were baffled by the penguin which mysteriously appeared on the shore of Monmouth Beach, New Jersey, so they confined it to jail before humane society workers relocated it to a zoo.

"pranksters," the reports say) from the Sacramento Zoo. After its alleged theft by these alleged pranksters, the penguin was found swimming and feeding in that Fortean hot-spot, Folsom Lake. It took six months for officials to end its freedom, and then the animal died three weeks after its return.

Not so strangely, another gateway of Fortean creatures, Loveland, Ohio, had a recent penguin incident. During a late summer's hot spell in September of 1978, two penguins supposedly escaped from a safari exhibit on Kings Island, ten miles from Loveland. One penguin was struck by a car and killed in Foster, but the other black and white creature caused havoc in Loveland for several hours. Darrell Merritt, a service station attendant, said: "I walked in here about 7 o'clock in the morning. Then this guy came to the door and said there was a penguin behind my station. I thought he must have been drunk. I went out and looked. I had to see for myself, you know." What Merritt saw was a penguin. After waddling around town a bit, the penguin was finally captured by two volunteer firemen.

Loveland, Ohio, is perhaps best known for the frog-mouthed "trolls under the bridge" sighted in March 1955, and investigated by Leonard H. Stringfield. Ron Schaffner and Richard Mackay interviewed the police officers involved in the March 1972, Loveland incident in which a four foot tall creature described as a frog, or lizard was seen. Loveland does seem to be one of those focal points we need to watch. Whether for frogs or penguins, who knows?

But back to penguins of late. As 1981's summer came to an end, a strange visitor appeared on the shore of Monmouth Beach, New Jersey—a South American rockhopper penguin. On Saturday, August 29th, the skinny creature was spotted on the beach, and spent the next several days, first in jail, then with the humane society, next at the Bronx Zoo, and finally now at San Diego's Sea World. The bird's origin remains unknown, and a deep mystery to officials who have been unsuccessful in theorizing an explanation to answer all the questions the rockhopper raised.

7
Alligators
In The Sewers

The story of alligators haunting the sewers of major American cities is a modern urban mystery.

Most people have heard the rumors about alligators-in-the-sewers, in large part, because of Thomas Pynchon's 1963 novel, *V.* Pynchon wrote of the cute little pet alligators purchased as Florida souvenirs but eventually discarded, growing and reproducing in the sewers of New York City. Moving through the underground system, they, Pynchon told us, were big, blind, albino and fed off rats and sewage. Pynchon envisioned an Alligator Patrol going into the depths of the sewers, working in teams of two, with one man holding a flashlight while the other carried a twelve-gauge repeating shotgun. As no one before him had, Thomas Pynchon wove the rumor of alligators-in-the-sewers through the fabric of his fascinating work of fiction. But where did Pynchon's fiction end and fact begin?

The reworking of the alligators-in-the-sewer legend in the 60's only served to further confuse its origins. Folklorist Richard M. Dorson repeated the oft-told tale that marijuana harvesters in pur-

(courtesy *Olathe Daily News*)

Boys and out-of-place alligators still tangle. In March, 1979, these two young men found this alligator in a small creek near Stilwell, Kansas.

suit of the elusive strain "New York White" (what did you think happened to all those seeds flushed down toilets by nervous pot users?) were experiencing difficulties because of the alligators swimming around in the sewer system.

Finally, the last word (supposedly) was heard from the realm of Science. The herpetologists Sherman and Madge Rutherford Minton, in their book *Giant Reptiles,* inform their readers that "One of the sillier folktales of the late 1960's was that the New York sewers were becoming infested with alligators . . . We . . . would assure New Yorkers that alligators are not among their urban problems."

But alligators and other crocodilians are one of the most frequent creatures to be involved in Fortean events (see Appendix II), and to find actual records of alligators-in-the-sewers is an easy task.

Accounts of alligators falling from the sky would seem to be a rarer and less defensible form of crocodilian mystery, but no less an authority than the U.S. Weather Bureau related such a fall for July 2, 1843, on Anson Street, Charleston, South Carolina. Also, the *New York Times* carried an item on a December 1877, fall of alligators. They fell on a turpentine farm in Aiken County, South Carolina.

Alligators, caimans and crocodilians have materialized in cottonbins in Texas, express trains in France, hot water ditches in Illinois, and basements in Kansas. It is no wonder the reports of alligators slithering and slinking through the New York City sewer system are more than baseless rumors.

But surprisingly, the origins of the New York stories go back beyond the 1960's, back to the 1930's. On June 28, 1932, "swarms" of alligators were seen in the Bronx River, and a three footer was found dead.

On March 7, 1935 a three foot alligator was caught alive, in northern Yonkers while at Grass Sprain, a six foot 'gator was found dead. A barge captain at Pier 9, East River, on June 1, 1937, captured an alligator four feet long. Five days later at the Brooklyn Museum subway station, a New Yorker caught a two footer.

Perhaps the most exciting story of alligators in the sewers in the 1930's, however, is the one told in the *New York Times* of 1935. Some teenagers living in the East 123rd street neighborhood encountered, and killed a seven and a half foot long, 125 pound alligator. That chilling account gives one pause about current urban problems.

Some of these alleged discoveries are unusual, as, for example, the "alligator five and a half feet long . . . found near the bank of the Rock river, at Janesville, Wis., frozen to death," in 1892.

I have compiled a list (see Appendix II) of eighty-plus encounters with erratic alligators for the years 1948-1983, but the actual, supposedly true recording of an alligator in a sewer proved to be a rare occurrence. I was able to discover just such an event, nevertheless, recorded as fact from, not surprisingly, New York City.

The incident may or may not have taken place, but its publication in a no nonsense fashion in a highly regarded and respected newspaper must have lent much credibility to the story. In contrast to the common notion that the alligators-in-the-sewers motif is a product of the sixties, the following article is from the *New York Times* of February 10th, 1935, and is given here in its entirety:

ALLIGATOR FOUND IN UPTOWN SEWER
Youths Shoveling Snow Into Manhole
See The Animal Churning In Icy Water.
SNARE IT AND DRAG IT OUT
Reptile Slain by Rescuers When It Gets Vicious —
Whence It Came is Mystery.

The youthful residents of East 123rd Street, near the murky Harlem River, were having a rather grand time at dusk yesterday shoveling the last of the recent snow into a gaping manhole.

Salvatore Condulucci, 16 years old, of 419 East 123rd Street, was assigned to the rim. His comrades would heap blackened slush near him, and he, carefully observing the sewer's capacity, would give the last fine flick to each mound.

Suddenly there were signs of clogging ten feet below, where the manhole drop merged with the dark conduit leading to the river. Salvatore yelled: "Hey, you guys, wait a minute," and got down on his knees to see what was the trouble.

What he saw, in the thickening dusk, almost caused him to topple into the icy cavern. For the jagged surface of the ice blockade below was moving; and something black was breaking through. Salvatore's eyes widened; then he managed to leap to his feet and call his friends.

"Honest, it's an alligator!" he exploded.

Others Look and Are Convinced.

There was a murmur of skepticism. Jimmy Mireno, 19, of 440 East 123rd Street, shouldered his way to the rim and stared.

"He's right," he said.

Frank Lonzo, 18, of 1743 Park Avenue, looked next. He also confirmed the spectre. Then there was a great crush about the opening in the middle of the street and heads were bent low around the aperture.

The animal apparently was threshing about in the ice, trying to get clear. When the first wave of awe had passed, the boys decided to help it out. A delegation was dispatched to the Lehigh Stove and Repair Shop at 441 East 123rd Street.

"We want some clothes-line," demanded the delegation, and got it.

Young Condolucci, an expert on Western movies, fashioned a slip knot. With the others watching breathlessly, he dangled the noose into the sewer, and after several tantalizing near-catches, looped it about the 'gator's neck. Then he pulled hard. There was a grating of rough leathery skin against jumbled ice. But the job was too much for one youth. The others grabbed the rope and all pulled.

Slowly, with its curving tail twisting weakly, the animal was dragged from the snow, ten feet through the dark cavern, and to the street, where it lay, non-committal; it was not in Florida, that was clear.

And therefore, when one of the boys sought to loosen the rope, the creature opened its jaws and snapped, not with the robust vigor of a healthy, well-sunned alligator, but with the fury of a sick, very badly treated one. The boys jumped back. Curiosity and sympathy turned to enmity.

"Let'im have it!" the cry went up.

Rescuers Then Kill It.

So the shovels that had been used to pile snow on the alligator's head were now to rain upon it. The 'gator's tail swished about a few last times. Its jaws clashed weakly. But it was in no mood for a real struggle after its icy incarceration. It died on the spot.

Triumphantly, but not without the inevitable reaction of sorrow, the boys took their victim to the Lehigh Stove and Repair Shop. There it was found to weigh 125 pounds; they said it measured seven and a half or eight feet. It became at once the greatest attraction the store ever had had. The whole neighborhood milled about, and finally, a call for the police reached a nearby station.

But there was little for the hurrying policemen to do. The strange visitor was quite dead; and no charge could be preferred against it or against its slayers. The neighbors were calmed with little trouble and speculation as to where the 'gator had come from was rife.

There are no pet shops in the vicinity; that theory was ruled out almost at once. Finally, the theories simmered down to that of a passing boat. Plainly, a steamer from the mysterious Everglades, or thereabouts, had been passing 123rd Street, and the alligator had fallen overboard.

Shunning the hatefully cold water, it had swum toward shore and found only the entrance to the conduit. Then after another 150 yeards through a torrent of melting snow – and by that time it was half dead – it had arrived under the open manhole.

Half-dead, yes, the neighborhood conceded. But still alive enough for a last splendid opening and snapping of its jaws. The boys were ready to swear to that.

At about 9 p.m., when tired mothers had succeeded in getting most of their alligator-conscious youngsters to bed, a Department of Sanitation truck rumbled up to the store and made off with the prize. Its destination was Barren Island and an incinerator.

Teddy May, the Superintendent of the New York City sewers during the 1930's, began hearing reports from his inspectors of sighting alligators, but May did not believe them. May refused to approve these 1935 reports with the inspectors' notations on alligators. Indeed, Teddy May hired extra men to watch the inspectors and tell him how they were getting their liquor down in the sewers. The word came back to the "King of the Sewers" that his men weren't drinking, but the reports of narrow escapes from alligators persisted. Bound and determined to lay the claims to rest, Teddy May decided to go down and have a look for himself.

A few hours later, May returned, shaken. His own flashlight, Robert Daley wrote in *The World Beneath the City,* illuminated the truth behind the rumors. Teddy May had seen alligators two feet in length and longer. Avoiding the dangerously fast currents in the main sewer lines under the major avenues, the alligators had taken to the smaller pipes in the backwash of the city. The alligators had settled in, and Teddy May was now faced with the task of ridding his sewers of the 'gators. Within months Teddy May felt he had finished that task. The methods he used were unorthodox, but then his prey was rather unusual. Rat poison got rid of some as did forcing some onto the main trunk lines where they drowned or were swiftly washed out to sea. A few alligators were hunted down by sewer inspectors with 22's on their own free time. Teddy May rid New York City of its alligators in the sewers – or so he thought.

In 1938 five alligators were caught in New Rochelle, New York, and sightings of alligators-in-the-sewers in New York City were recorded for 1948 and 1966.

Alligators in the sewers are neither rumor, folktale or myth, but a real part of the underground world of some of our larger urban centers. For, although this discussion has focussed on New York City, recent accounts seem to indicate alligators are also prowling the sewers of other diverse locations. The widespread nature of this phenomenon remains to be seen

8
Giant Snakes

Mystery animals have long held the interest of humans, and specifically the tales of giant snakes have captivated audiences since prehistoric times. For example, from ancient Chinese literature are the stories mentioned by Shan Hai King of the giant Pa Snake, a fabulous monster capable of swallowing whole elephants and ejecting the bones three years later. Carvings of great serpents are often found on the monuments and temples of the Toltecs, Aztecs and Mayans of ancient Mesoamerica. One excellent carving from Mexico shows a large snake in the act of swallowing an elegantly costumed woman who appears lacerated and crushed in the snake's jaws.

Giant snakes, the Bigfoot of the reptile world, tend to have characteristics almost ghost-like in nature, on the one hand, yet frighteningly physical on the other. To complicate the picture even further like the reports of teleported alligators, penguins, flamingos, or even lemurs, some cases of *real* out-of-place giant snakes do turn up.

Looking at the winter of 1959-1960, for example, I find people discovering giant, flesh-and-blood snakes in three spots in North America, in places where they should not have been. Late in September, 1959, William Hayden of the Bronx, New York, found a five-foot black snake in his backyard and popped it in his bathtub for safekeeping. Not too surprising perhaps, but the next day, on September 29th, Hayden found a five-foot boa constrictor curled around an ash can outside his apartment. Meanwhile, Reid Trail decided to have the twelve-foot python he ran over and killed near Roanoke, Virginia in December of 1959, stuffed because people would not believe him. And from Montreal, during this snake-filled winter, apartment tenant Marc Rivard was shocked to come home one February evening and discover a seven-foot-long boa in his front living room.

Other similar cases of out-of-place giant snakes have occurred from the 16-footer killed in a field in Lock Springs, Missouri, in 1897, to the five-foot boa captured in Champaign, Illinois, in 1972. These incidents are far more common than one might suppose.

But on a totally different level of reality, something besides pythons in toilet bowls have crept from the fringes of the borderland separating mystery animals from actual zoological specimens.

Giant snakes, creatures of the outer edge like Bigfoot, phantom panthers, black dogs and thunderbirds, have been seen in this country and elsewhere for centuries. The giant serpents and snakes of the shadow world of cryptozoology have many of the same characteristics of their brethren – namely, they are generally described as monstrous in size and dark in color, are never caught, and exhibit behaviors much more aggressive and daring than one would expect of these normally timid and retiring reptiles.

The history of incidents with giant snakes is a long one, and can best be examined through a few highlights from the Western Hemisphere. Some of the most intriguing accounts have issued from Brazil, and some of these have been brought back from the Amazon hinterland by the extremely colorful character, Major Fawcett.

In 1906, twenty years before he vanished without a trace in the Amazon, Major Percy Fawcett was sent by the Royal Geographic Society to make a thorough survey of the Rio Abuna and Acre

Major Percy Fawcett meets his giant anaconda along the Rio Negro, Brazil, in 1907. Similar monstrous snakes have been reported throughout America.

Rivers. Thirty-nine at the time, Major Fawcett was known for two sometimes contradictory character traits: he was a dreamer whose dreams led him to envision lost jungle cities of fantastic wealth and splendor; he was also a scrupulously matter-of-fact military man who reported exactly what he saw in detailed and down-to-earth observations. His memoirs, striking for their contrast of visionary dreams and earthy rankness, relate many strange adventures—including an encounter with a giant anaconda of the Amazon.

Fawcett ran across the giant snake in 1907. With his Indian crew, he was drifting along the Rio Negro when he spotted the snake. Fawcett reported that a great triangular head appeared at the bow of the boat, and when he shot the creature in the spine the body of the snake thrashed the water all around the boat. With great difficulty Fawcett convinced his crew to approach closer to the bank where the great snake lay. The Indians feared that the injured reptile would attack the boat or that its mate, as often happened, would come to destroy the hunters.

Fawcett then stepped onto the shore and cautiously approached the snake. According to Fawcett, the snake measured 45 feet out of the water and 17 in it, a total of 62 feet. The snake's diameter for such a great length was surprisingly small, only about 1 foot. The beast was not dead and emitted an awful odor from its mouth. Fawcett was told of many others, including one super giant of over 80 feet long that was said to have been killed by the Zrajchan boundary commission. The common length of the anaconda does not usually exceed 25 feet. Yet, Fawcett's tale is only one of many made by South American jungle guides and explorers who report giant snakes from 75 feet to even 150 feet in length. These giant creatures are said to have eyes the size of plates and a weight of several tons.

Closer to home, far from the teeming jungles of the Amazon, in the summer of 1944, a huge snake known as the Peninsula Python caused excitement along the Cuyahoga River in the wooded valley between Akron and Cleveland, Ohio. The creature first appeared on June 8, 1944 when Clarence Mitchell saw it sliding across his corn field. The Peninsula Python left a track the width of an automobile tire, and Mitchell reported the creature to be about 18 feet in length.

Two days later, Paul and John Szalay reported a similar track in their fields, and two days after this second sighting, Mrs. Roy Vaughn called out the fire department when the giant reptile attacked her hen house. The snake climbed the fence to her chicken coop and devoured a chicken.

Now that the snake was accepted as fact, theories abounded as to where it had come from. Two years before, a carnival truck had supposedly smashed up in a cemetery in the valley, and it was speculated that the python might have escaped from this wreck. As I have discovered many times before in my investigations of "circus train wrecks" as the source of any given mystery animal report, the story could never fully be tracked down.

The Cleveland and Columbus Zoos offered rewards for the live capture of the Peninsula Python, and the news services began to carry the story which aroused overseas interest from servicemen whose families lived in the valley.

On Sunday, June 25th, the sirens blasted to report the creature had been sighted near Kelly Hill. The town emptied as countless residents headed off to the hill in search of the Python. The hunters trampled through tangled thorn bush and burrs only to learn later that it was a false alarm.

Two days later, on June 27th, the snake leaped down out of a dead willow and frightened Mrs. Pauline Hopko. It also frightened her milk cows who broke their halters and ran off across the fields, and her dogs who cowered under Mrs. Hopko's skirts. Mrs. Hopko was left holding the milk pail. The snake was sighted also by Bobbie Pollard and some other boys at this time, but it disappeared before the Mayor's posse arrived on the scene.

Again, two days afterwards, Mrs. Ralph Griffin saw the snake rear up man-high in the middle of her back yard. Again, the creature avoided the posse. Then Mrs. Katherine Boroutick saw it in her back yard where it came crashing down out of her butternut tree when she was out by the river throwing out some trash. The posse found broken tree limbs and another track to the river bed. Professional searchers now came into the area, and the snake was reported a few more times in the fall. However, hunters said they never got word fast enough to get a shot at the snake. By first frost, residents waited for the buzzards to find a huge carcass of a snake dead of cold, but the Peninsula Python was never sighted again, dead or alive.

Throughout the United States, from the period of the Peninsula Python and before, accounts of giant snakes have circulated. Reports from the area around Bridgewater, Massachusetts tell of CCC workers encountering huge coiled serpents along the pathways through the Hockomock Swamp as mentioned in Chapter Four. From Hastings, Michigan, come tales of the 20 foot long Carter's Snake, so named because it was always seen near Carter's Lake. Near another lake, Reynold's Lake in Kentucky, local people began to take their hogs inside because of the fear their giant snake would devour their livestock after it got its fill of frogs. The era of a snake as "large as a stovepipe" is gone only because nobody uses stovepipes any longer, but the reports of giant snakes continue.

Recent years have had their share of monster snake accounts. The Zodiac News Service reported in January 1975 that hikers in the northern Appalachian mountains had sighted a 40 foot long giant snake. The slithering monster had reportedly been seen by more than a dozen hiking parties since it was first viewed in 1919. Legend has it that the giant snake, which witnesses have seen on Broad Top Mountain, survives Pennsylvania's harsh winters by crawling into warm coal mine shafts. Researchers who checked out one sighting claim the monster left behind a long trough in the earth four to six inches deep.

Curtis Fuller brought the readers of *FATE* up to date on the latest giant snake report in the May 1979 issue. Fuller detailed Eileen Blackburn and her daughter's (October 1978) experience near Cascade, Montana. The giant 20 to 30 foot long snake reportedly had coils at least three feet across. Cascade Police Chief Earl Damon said he had other giant snake reports from area people.

Like so many other mystery animal encounters, the Blackburns' had their run-in while they were traveling in their automobile. Mrs. Blackburn was not sure if she hit the giant cobra-like creature, or if it struck her car.

In days past, the giant snakes attacked not cars, but horses. One of the classic accounts is given in John Keel's *Strange Creatures From Time and Space*. The Kenton, Ohio, individual out horseback riding was Orland Packer (not Parker, as given in Keel's book). On June 9, 1946, an 8 foot long snake with a diamond shape on its flat head bit at Packer's horse, taking off a patch of the horse's hair. Packer was thrown and broke his ankle. His wife reported in 1970 that her husband used crutches for two years and suffered from excessive sweating and fever long after that. As with the maladies and chronic illnesses which haunt UFO, Bigfoot, and other witnesses of strange phenomena, Packer's condition appears to be related to the giant snake he saw.

What are we to make of all of this? Snakes, and serpents were very prominent in the religions of the early civilizations of the Old and New World. The snake appears to have been widely worshipped as a source of supernatural power. In the ancient cultures of the Americas, hints of the extent of the influence of giant snakes in the religions of these peoples is seen in the cult of Quetzalcoatl, the feathered serpent of the Aztecs, to the monumental earthworks of the giant Serpent Mound of Ohio. The ancients were in touch with the importance of giant serpents in their lives.

During the era of Modern Man, we have all lost contact, in varying degrees, with the meandering supernatural powers slithering through the world. In recent years, the increase in reports and the realization of the importance of UFO's, Bigfoot, phantom panthers, and other denizens of the unknown, have merely reflected man's renewed sensitivity to the borderlands of reality.

The investigation of giant snake sightings is another step in this direction.

9
Lake Monsters

In the spring of 1969 a fool-proof electronic detector called "Simarad," used to provide a graphic profile of the sea bottom, drew the outline of a 200 foot long "dinosaur" at 55 fathoms in Raspberry Strait off Kodiak, Alaska. Electronics specialists had mounted the device in the pilot house of the *M/V Mylark,* a 65 foot shrimp boat, and cruised the strait on an assignment that had nothing to do with monsters or any other kind of unexplained phenomena. They were astonished and flabbergasted when the image appeared. "We know the object is there," one of the researchers said. "Now we need to find out what it is."

Two months before the Alaska discovery, in March 1969, fishermen on City Island Bridge in the Bronx, New York, nearly dropped their casting rods when they spotted an enormous creature much bigger than a whale swimming upriver, apparently not at all bothered by the fact that it was passing by one of the world's largest cities. Shortly afterwards the creature was seen by witnesses at Little Neck Bay, Queens, and from there, chased unsuccessfully by Harbor Police.

Since neither of these stories can be laid, one assumes, to hoax or wishful thinking, we must search elsewhere for answers if we can find them. But if answers are scarce, there is certainly no shortage of questions, and we do not have to cross the Atlantic to uncover "Loch Ness monsters." As we shall see, we have plenty of our own in North America.

Canada has several native monsters, the most famous of them Okanagan Lake's "Ogopogo" in British Columbia. The same province lays claim to "Caddy" in Cadboro Bay, as well as an unnamed creature lurking in the depths of Cowichan Lake north of Victoria. Ontario has "Hapyxelor" in Muskrat Lake and Manitoba "Manipogo" at the northern tip of Lake Manitoba. The monster of New Brunswick's Lake Utopia is still being seen regularly. During July of 1982, Sherman Hatt told of sighting the creature which he said was "like a submarine coming out of the water with spray on both sides. It was about ten feet long and put me in mind of the back of a whale."

The United States has a long tradition of lake monster legends stretching back into the folklore of its first residents, the Indians. One of these tales, related by David Cusick in a pamphlet, "History of the Six (Indian) Nations," published in 1828, was collected from the Oneida branch of the Tuscaroras. The legend tells how long ago a great reptile, the "Mosqueto," rose from Lake Onondaga (near

(courtesy New Brunswick Museum)

Charlotte County, New Brunswick's Lake Utopia Monster has a long history of involvement with local fishermen. Many sightings were reported during the last century, as this print illustrates. The most recent sighting was reported in 1982.

Syracuse in upstate New York) and slew a number of people. The Indians also said that "2200 years before the time of Columbus" a great horned serpent appeared on Lake Ontario and killed onlookers with its overpowering stench.

A strikingly similar beast figures in legends of the Indians of Nebraska, who told the first white settlers that a monster lived in Alkali Lake near Hay Springs. The legends seem to have some truth in them, if we are to credit the testimony of one J. A. Johnson, who is quoted in the July 24, 1923, *Omaha World-Herald:* "I saw the monster myself while with two friends last fall. I could name 40 other people who have also seen the brute.

"We had camped a short distance from the lake on the night before and all three of us arose early to be ready for duck flight. We started to walk around the lake close to the shore, in order to jump any birds, when suddenly, coming around a slight raise in the ground we came upon this animal, nearly three-fourths out of the shallow water near the shore. We were less than 20 yards from him.

"The animal was probably 40 feet long, including the tail and the head, when raised in alarm as when he saw us. In general appearance, the animal was not unlike an alligator, except that the head was stubbier, and there seemed to be a projection like a horn between the eyes and nostrils. The animal was built much more heavily throughout than an alligator. Its color seemed a dull gray or brown.

"There was a very distinctive and somewhat unpleasant odor noticeable for several moments after the beast had vanished into the water. We stood for several minutes after the animal had gone, hardly knowing what to do or say, when we noticed several hundred feet out from the shore a considerable commotion in the water.

"Sure enough the animal came to the surface, floated there for a moment and then lashed the water with its tail, suddenly dived, and we saw no more of him."

Another of America's long-lived monsters belongs to Lake Champlain in Vermont's Champlain Valley. The first white man to see it was the lake's namesake, explorer Samuel de Champlain, who in July 1609 observed a serpent-like creature about 20 feet long, as thick as a barrel and with a head shaped like a horse's. Its next recorded appearance was on July 24, 1819, when pioneers in the Port Henry area sighted a lake monster in Bulwagga Bay.

The Lake Champlain Monster was seen by 21 people in 1981, but the sightings dropped off to only ten incidents in 1982. Therefore, by the end of the summer of 1982, 170 reported sightings had been recorded by Joseph Zarzynski.

Perhaps the biggest news coming out of the summer of '82, regarding the Lake Champlain Monster, was the passage of resolutions by the Vermont House and the New York Senate protecting the lake monsters "from any willful act resulting in death, injury or harassment."

That something exists in Lake Champlain I at least am not prepared to dispute. But the oddest aspect of the whole affair is not the sightings themselves – though certainly they are odd enough – but the baffling query raised by Marjorie L. Porter in *Vermont Life* magazine: "If the unknown creature is a huge aquatic mammal or a reptile, the question remains: how could it survive when the lake is locked solid with ice?" – as it is every winter. (For more on Champ, see the next Chapter.)

Alaska's Illiamna Lake, 80 miles long, hosts a number of monsters of various sizes, all described as possessing broad blunt heads, long, tapered bodies and vertical tails. Witnesses usually state that the monsters' color is similar to that of "dull aluminum."

These things, whatever they are, have been around for quite a while. The Aleut Indians have been familiar with them for many years and display a healthy respect for the creatures. This "respect" sometimes has escalated into downright fear. Earlier in the century, according to Aleut testimony, a monster upended one of their boats and swallowed up a crewman. For some considerable time afterwards the Indians conscientiously skirted that section of the lake.

Since then several fishermen have hooked the beasts with extremely heavy tackle, and bush pilots flying over the lake have seen them at or just beneath the surface of the lake's clear waters. No one has yet been able to formulate a satisfactory explanation for these beasts, though some theorists have speculated that they may be beluga whales which have entered the lake from the sea via the deep Kvichak River. Long time residents of the Illiamna region scoff at this notion, however, pointing out that beluga whales, common enough sights in the area, have paper-white backs, tapered heads and horizontal tails.

At one period in the last century Lake Michigan claimed a mysterious watery inhabitant. In its August 7, 1867, issue the *Chicago Tribune* went so far as to assert, "That Lake Michigan is inhabited by a vast monster, part fish and part serpent, no longer admits of doubt."

The *Tribune* reported that not long before crews of the tug *George W. Wood* and the propeller *Sky Lark* had seen the creature lashing through the waves off Evanston. They said the thing was between 40 and 50 feet long, with a neck as thick as a human being's and a body as thick as a barrel. On the morning of August 6th, fisherman Joseph Muhike encountered the same or a similar animal on the lake a mile and a half from the Hyde Park section of Chicago.

During the summer of 1879 another monster appeared in Illinois, this time in Stump Pond in DuQuoin. One night a man named Paquette had been fishing on the lake when something rushed through the water creating enough disturbance to rock his boat. Unnerved, Paquette headed for shore, vowing not to venture out on the water again during the late hours. A year later, in July 1880, two miners reportedly saw a 12-foot "serpent," its body the thickness of a telegraph pole and dark green in color, heading their way from one-eighth of a mile out. They chose not to avail themselves of the opportunity for a closer look.

Reports of a monster in Stump Pond continued until 1968, when the body of water was partially drained and its fish cleared out with electric stunners. The largest fish weighed 30 pounds apiece; impressive as fish go, but certainly not big enough to be mistaken for anything else. Needless to say no monster showed up; but still witnesses stuck to their stories. One of them, 66 year old Allyn Dunmyer, had a frightening experience several years before. "I was in my boat fishing for bass when it happened," he said.

"Something came up from the bottom, struck the boat underneath so hard I nearly tipped over."

Dunmyer had seen the monster – or monsters – before. "I think there are more than one of the critters in the pond," he told a reporter. "I've seen them, so near the surface that their back fins were sticking out of the water."

One man, wading in the pond's shallows, stumbled onto something sleeping underneath the algae which covered part of the water. He thought it looked like a large alligator.

The monsters that supposedly inhabit Lake Waterton in Montana are called "Oogle-Boogles" by local people, though no one knows just how that name got started. Flathead Lake in the same state boasts similar beasts, which have been described variously as between 5 and 60 feet in length. This is not the only inconsistency in the reports – there are enough inconsistencies to give any conscientious researcher a severe headache. But then consistency is not a virtue found in most monster lore. That does not have to mean, however, that therefore monsters do not exist. The vast majority of witnesses are obviously sincere and stand to gain little, aside from ridicule, for coming forth with their stories.

While some monsters, as we have seen, are long-time residents of certain lakes and rivers, others appear only once or twice and disappear. The creature observed in Michigan's Paint River in 1922 was apparently one of the latter. In the words of a lady who saw it, "I was walking down the hill toward the river to visit a girlfriend who lived at the bottom of the hill. A Mrs. Johnson was walking up the hill and we met on the knoll about halfway, which was very near the river. We got a very good look at this animal – both saw it at the same time, and stood stunned, speechless, watching it till it went out of sight. Mrs. Johnson, as if to check on her sense, asked me in Swedish: 'Did you see what I saw?' I assured her that I did. She went on ejaculating in Swedish, very excited, saying: 'It had a head bigger than a pail.' She then made me walk up the hill to our house, and I had to verify everything she said to my mother.

"My report? Yes, it did have a head much bigger than any pail I knew of; the head stood straight above the water; the body was dark color; the body did not move like that of a snake, but in an undulating motion. We could see humps sticking out of the water, and I recall counting six of them. How long? This is difficult to recall. It was swimming north up the river between two bridges. This distance could be the length of a city block, and this monster must have been nearly half of that bridge, but we followed its wake on up the river."

The monster of Big Chapman's Lake, near Warsaw, Indiana, evidently was also a one-timer. On August 16, 1934, H. W. Scott was fishing from a boat when the head of something rose from the water not far away. The head was two feet across, Scott reported, and it had "large cow-like eyes." That unfortunately is the extent of the description given in an *Indianapolis News* account of the sighting. The same source lists two other witnesses who allegedly saw the creature about the same time: Scott's wife and a Mrs. George Barnwell.

Another one-timer, a black fish about six or eight feet long with no visible appendages, rammed into a fisherman's boat and dented its fiberglass body one day in the summer of 1970. Ronald J. Haller was floating down the Missouri River between Fort Benton and Lewistown, Montana, when the collision occurred. Haller swung his boat around and followed the fish upstream with a movie camera.

To the best of my knowledge Haller's film has never been released, but the witness and his lawyer are known to have shown it to wildlife authorities, who so far have not identified the creature.

The monsters of inland America cannot be disposed of easily. (See Appendix V to view the extent of the accounts.) Are we to simply consider seriously the notion, entertained by some theorists, that zeuglodons and plesiosaurs have survived hundreds of millions of years in our lakes and rivers, much less that these creatures have done so completely undetected by zoology? As in the case of black panthers, common sense and our knowledge of the workings of the natural order unequivocally dictate that these things cannot be – yet they are. In a sense they are the UFO's of the natural order.

They share with UFOs, panthers, Bigfoot and other related anomalistic phenomena a kind of nebulousness, appearing from time to time within our vision but forever beyond our reach.

10
Champ

"I still have nightmares about the monster. The thing is chasing me, and I'm running to get away. After I saw the monster and took his picture, I had the dreams all the time, but then I got in touch with Zarzynski and the nightmares went away for a while. Now, with all the public pressure and people saying I didn't really see it, the dreams have started again. It's frightening, and sometimes I wish I hadn't told anyone about the picture, or I hadn't seen the monster."

Sandra Mansi, soft-spoken and matter-of-fact, was telling me about her life since she had become an instant celebrity thanks to the *New York Times* and *Time* magazine. It was late August of 1981, following a stimulating day at the first scientific seminar devoted to a study of the monster that has been reported lurking in the waters of Lake Champlain the past 300-plus years.

"I have been very careful about the people I tell about my experiences," Mansi said. "Someone recently was amazed when I told them I was going to the seminar, and began asking me if I believed in ESP, UFOs, and the tooth fairy. I didn't even tell that person I had seen and photographed the monster."

I have interviewed hundreds of witnesses who have had encounters of the monstrous kind – Bigfoot, sea serpents, or lake monsters. However, in all the research and field work I have done in the last 25 years, the story unfolding at Lake Champlain is one of the most fascinating I have investigated. The Lake Champlain monster, or "Champ," as it is called, is not a new story, but recent developments at the lake, including the Mansi photograph, have made the area a hotbed of unexplained-phenomena activity and media attention.

The first white man to see the Lake Champlain monster was the lake's namesake, explorer Samuel de Champlain, who in his journal entry for July, 1609, tells of having observed a serpentine creature about 20 feet long, as thick as a barrel, and with a horselike head. Champlain wrote that the Indians called the animal a *chaousarou*.

Between the time of Champlain's sighting and the 1800's, there were no known reports of Champ's existence, perhaps because the area was sparsely settled until just before the War of 1812. Previously, the only Europeans in the Champlain Valley were mostly Jesuits and soldiers, and they left no stories of any missionary or military encounters with the creature. By 1810, however, the monster sightings resumed, as about 150,000 settlers looking for inexpensive land had found their way to the lake.

The early pioneers discovered they had quite a lake to conquer. Lake Champlain is the United States' largest body of water other than the Great Lakes, occupying portions of what is now Vermont, New York, and the Quebec province of Canada. It is almost 110 miles long and 13 miles wide, with a maximum depth of 400 feet. The surface area is 436 square miles. The action of ancient glaciers carved out the lake, and as the ice sheets retreated they left behind a finger of inland sea that at different times was connected to the ocean. Like Loch Ness in Scotland, Okanagan Lake in British Columbia, and scores of other deep, cold-water lakes in the northern temperate zone, Lake Champlain appears to be an ideal home for monsters.

The early inhabitants soon found that the lake was indeed the residence of a monster of its very own. Accounts of the time, published in the *Plattsburgh Republican*, tell of how, in 1819, pioneers were alarmed by the beast as it stuck its head above the

(Mansi/Gamma Liason)

Even a black and white reproduction of Sandy Masi's striking original color photograph of Champ still offers every hint
of why researchers feel it is the best evidence to date of a
monster in Lake Champlain.

surface of Bulwagga Bay, near what is now Port Henry, New York.

Between the arrival of the steamboat, around 1870, and 1900, according to one historian, the lake's creature was reported on at least twenty occasions. Noteworthy in reviewing this series of sightings is the fact that in all but two incidents, the monster was seen by a number of people at the same time, and that the witnesses included men and women of unimpeachable character. On August 30, 1878, for example, the yacht *Rob Roy* was becalmed off Button Bay Island; soon the yacht's party of six saw a large monster swimming rapidly by, its head occasionally projecting through the "smooth as glass" surface of the water. On November 5, 1879, three University of Burlington (now Vermont) students saw the monster – 15 feet of it visible above the water – travel gracefully from Appletree Point, near Burlington, around Rock Dunder, and head for Essex. On July 9, 1887, the creature made a spectacular appearance as a group of East Charlotte, Vermont, picnickers saw it come around a bend, its flat snakelike head visible above the water, and make straight toward them. As it grew closer at a terrific speed, several people screamed, and the monster whirled to the right and disappeared under the waves. On August 4, 1892, the American Canoe Association's annual outing, at Willsborough, New York, was abruptly ended when the monster surfaced near their gathering, and canoeists scattered in panic.

The ridicule experienced by today's witnesses was not found during the "monster scare" of 1870 to 1900. People came forth readily to tell of their encounters. P. T. Barnum was so struck by the idea of possibly corralling the monster and adding it to his traveling exhibits that he offered $50,000 for the "Champlain Sea Serpent" carcass. No one produced a body, although the sightings continued.

In 1915, according to a subsequent *New York Times* account, several observers saw the monster stranded in the shallows at the entrance of Bulwagga Bay near the Crown Point fortifications. The animal, said to be 40 feet long, lashed the waters in an attempt to escape its fate. Soon it released itself, swam for the Vermont side, and finally sank "submarine fashion, leaving a wake which was well defined on the glassy surface of the lake."

The next series of monster sightings occurred in the 1930's and 1940's. One especially close encounter was experienced by a Mr. and Mrs. Langlois, who were fishing in their motorboat off Rouses Point, New York in August, 1939, when the monster headed for them and the couple hastily veered to avoid being hit. As they fled for shore, the monster disappeared below the lake's surface. In 1943 Charles Weston watched through binoculars as a large animal churned up the water off Rouses Point. In 1945, one Winooski, Vermont, woman aboard the SS *Ticonderoga* described how she and other passengers witnessing a bridge dedication saw the beast raise its head from the water nearby.

Through the 1950's, '60's and early '70's, sightings of the Lake Champlain monster were infrequently reported. But that all changed with the arrival on the scene a decade ago of Joseph Zarzynski, a dynamic investigator, lecturer, and social science instructor at a junior high school in Saratoga Springs, New York, who has organized the Lake Champlain Phenomena Investigation and made the search for Champ his life's passion. Zarzynski's no-nonsense approach to monster hunting has meant that those who for years had been ridiculed because they saw something strange in the lake now had a sympathetic ear.

I have known "Zarr" for almost a decade now, and have found his research thorough and his method enthusiastic. The towering, six-foot-six Zarr's friendly manner and confident style make him one of the most trusted cryptozoologists in the country. His nature induces witnesses to confide in him because they quickly learn that Zarr believes because he knows—he has cruised the lake, sonared its depths, and dived its bays.

Zarzynski has also talked to the scores of witnesses who have seen Champ, becoming the lightning rod that monster sighters have been searching for. His rewards are new Champ reports and old accounts uncovered.

A case in point is Sandra Mansi, a 34-year-old tinsmith and amateur photographer with no previous exposure to the world of controversy. Largely because of Zarzynski's stewardship, Mansi has been able to navigate some choppy waters on her way to sharing with the public what Zarzynski calls "the single most impressive piece of evidence" for Champ. Indeed, without Zarr, Mansi's incredible photo might have never been made public.

Mansi's adventure began on July 5, 1977, as she, her husband-to-be, and two children from a previous marriage, were picnicking and sightseeing along the Vermont side of Lake Champlain, north of St. Albans. The group decided to get a closer look at the lake, and cut across a farm field. The day was bright and sunny, and the water shimmered royal blue, luring the family to the lake's shore.

As she sat there, watching her children play in the water, Mansi saw an object near the middle of the lake. At first, she thought it was a large fish, then the hand of a diver surfacing, but finally she realized it was the grayish brown head and long snakelike neck of a creature breaking the lake's surface. The thing's head seemed to be twisting around, scanning the countryside, Mansi later told me. Although scared to death, she rushed to get her Kodak Instamatic camera from her car, and snapped one shot of the beast. Once the photograph was taken, she grabbed the children and hightailed it out of there.

Mansi had observed that the monster had skin "like an eel" and was "slimy looking," but still had a hard time explaining it to herself in terms of any known animals. Therefore, Mansi and her family cautiously began to joke about the sighting, as a way of living with their strange experience. "We had trouble rationalizing it, so we decided to call it a 2,000-pound duck," she told participants at the August seminar. "It's easier to live with a 2,000-pound duck than something you don't know."

Fearful of the jokes and ridicule she might be subjected to outside her family, Mansi hid the picture for three years. Finally, encouraged by friends and the growing interest in Champ promoted by Zarzynski and his investigation, Mansi, by now living in Winchester, New Hampshire, produced the photograph for scrutiny by some academic types allegedly interested in the monster. The fact that Mansi had lost the negative, and had never known the *exact* location of the sighting, led to some difficult moments until Mansi was introduced to Zarzynski.

After interviewing Mansi, Zarzynski contacted other figures in the field of cryptozoology to help him evaluate her evidence. Dr. Roy Mackal, a University of Chicago zoologist famed for his Loch Ness work, and J. Richard Greenwell and Dr. B. Roy Frieden, both of the University of Arizona, examined Mansi's photograph and subjected it to computer tests. According to Frieden, a professor of optical sciences, no evidence of a montage or superposition could be found. Greenwell and Mackal were similarly convinced that Mansi had a picture of an unknown animate object in the lake.

Since the Mansi photograph's first publicity, Zarzynski has been deluged by witnesses bringing forth new and old sightings. Among them: spring, 1980, near Fort Ticonderoga, two dark humps were seen swimming by in the lake; in April, 1981, something 25 feet long and dark was sighted near Port Henry, New York; on July 6, 1981, a cake-decorating class in Panton Cove, Vermont, was disrupted when a 20-foot blackish hump was seen moving toward some children playing in the water. Said one class member: "It was exciting. I've never believed in the monster before."

As the interest in Champ increased over the summer of 1981, sparked in large part by the publication of Mansi's photograph in the *New York Times* and *Time* magazine, Zarzynski and others decided a serious conference was needed to examine all the evidence for the existence of Champlain's beast. The seminar, entitled "Does Champ Exist?," took place on August 29, 1981, in Shelburne, Vermont.

In the morning session, Zarzynski ran down the historical background of the Champ sightings and introduced the audience of 200 people to the Mansi photograph. Projected on a wall-size screen in an old barn on the shore of Lake Champlain, the vivid blues and browns of the photograph presented an image few conference members will soon forget. The showing was coupled with Zarzynski's impassioned plea for state governments and environmental groups to help protect the monster.

Next, Mansi, despite being visibly frightened, told the story of her experience. Conference goers knew the details, but it was the first time Mansi, who now lives in her native Vermont, had spoken publicly. She stirred the audience when she forcefully answered the question raised by the title of the conference: "You don't want to ask me if I think Champ exists. I've seen him, almost on a first-name basis. I've photographed Champ."

The afternoon's session presented analyses by cryptozoologists Mackal and Greenwell, as well as their theories about what the creature might be. Two major camps have developed to explain Champ. The leader of one, Greenwell, is convinced that Champ is a plesiosaur, an extinct marine reptile, not unlike the Loch Ness monster. He feels that both creatures, and others in Northern Hemisphere lakes, were trapped in the inland lakes formed at the end of the last ice age.

In frank disagreement with Greenwell's theory is Mackal, who is certain that these temperate-zone lake monsters are relics of an early era, related to zeuglodons, primitive whales thought to have died out 20 million years ago; he also believes they have access to the oceans, via waterways.

Despite debates over what exactly the Lake Champlain monster may be, the seminar did introduce a new period of credibility to Champ watching. Although Mansi is often afraid she has opened a Pandora's box for herself and other monster researchers by releasing her photograph, Zarzynski believes her picture has put a nice cap on the issue. Some 100-plus sightings have been investigated by Zarzynski, but the Mansi photograph, he feels, is the one piece of evidence that Champ researchers have needed to compel the broader public to open its eyes to some rather strange goings-on right in its midst.

As I left the first scientific seminar on the Lake Champlain Monster, and headed back to Boston, I turned on the radio to find the song "Puff the Magic Dragon" by Peter, Paul and Mary playing. In the past, such conferences would have left me feeling as if my time had been wasted on examining something as elusive as a puff of smoke, but after Zarzynski's pioneering work and Mansi's photograph, the Lake Champlain Monster appears to be an actual creature frolicking in the autumn mist. Champ, indeed, apparently is a four hundred year part of America's watery wildlife.

11
The Phantom Panthers

Phantom panthers have an unusually high attraction to automobiles – especially with people in them.

In 1958, near Rome, Georgia, a big black panther leaped against a motorist's car and left muddy pawprints on its side. In 1948, two wildlife officials told of a 350 pound varmint which lunged at their car, crashing into its side, and then fled into the woods near Quakertown, Indiana.

One of the first attacks on an automobile and its passengers happened early in this century near a city which has hosted many phantom panther accounts. Many pages could be spent recounting hundreds of cases found in my files of American mystery feline sightings. Let me, however, dwell on the phenomenon reflected through the "window" of Decatur, Illinois. Like UFO sightings, phantom panther sightings often occur in waves in specific locations.

The creature which terrified the Decatur, Illinois area in July 1917, was called "Nellie the Lion" by reporters. Nellie first angered and frightened the public by attacking Thomas Gullett, a butler at the Robert Allerton Estate, southwest of Monticello, while he was in the garden picking flowers.

After nearly a month of 300 men posses, close encounters of the panther kind, and finds of *two* sets of tracks, things began heating up.

Chester Osborn, Earl Hill, and their wives were driving near Decatur when the lion pounced on their car. The attack took place at 10:30 p.m., on July 29th. Hill and Osborn, sitting in the front, saw Nellie standing in the weeds next to the road. It leaped, struck the car's side and fell onto the highway.

Osborn and Hill rushed back to Decatur to summon the police. The lion was still there when they returned. It soon disappeared over an embankment. Further search parties could not find it.

Soon after that, "Nellie" disappeared mysteriously forever.

After Nellie was gone, several years passed before the reign of the panther would return to central Illinois. Panther stories began circulating again in the Decatur area after September 13, 1955, when a woman saw one slinking along a road. The next evening, two truck drivers spotted the "cat" in the vicinity of Rea's Lost Bridge. Other persons reported hearing its scream in the night. The animal was described as "long, low-slung and jet black with gleaming eyes."

Then, on the 25th of October, 1955, game warden, Paul G. Myers, surprised a black panther near Decatur and shot it. Despite the fact that he, like scores before and after him, thought he had wounded it, Myers never found a body.

1963 had barely opened when a giant cat began frightening residents of Fisher, Urbana, and Mahomet in Illinois' Champaign County. Sheriff Everett J. Hedrick of Urbana, said reports described something about five feet long "and very dark, possibly black," adding, "It's just about impossible for the animal to be a panther. It might be a mountain lion that somehow got loose in this area." This time, around 300 men joined the posse. Needless to say the animal eluded them but its tracks – between a large dog's and a mountain lion's – were baffling.

Sightings of the animal continued well into 1963. One of them, made by farmer, Bill Chambers of Mahomet, is sufficiently detailed to be worth quoting in full:

In regard to the Mahomet cougar, I have seen it twice. The last time was just a fleeting look at daylight before it was light enough to shoot. The first time was the day before, just before sunset on June 2, 1963.

The cat was hunting in clover and was unaware of me, apparently. I was about 300 yards from him when I first saw him, or it. I was on the road in my pickup and the cat paid no attention to the truck so I drove into a lane and coasted down a little grade to within what I estimated to be 190 yards.

I had a set of sandbags that I use on my shooting bench and I put them on top of the truck cab to give me a steady shooting position. . . . (through the scope) the head was visible but seldom still enough for a target and the head is a poor place to shoot a cat anyway.

The cat spent several minutes near a big weed clump with little showing until he jumped on something in the clover. When he did this I had laid my rifle down and was watching with my 8x binoculars and the tail was clearly visible.

A little later, he sat up facing straight at me and with the sun down and directly at my back, I was looking at the lighted side all the time and he appeared jet black except for two tawny streaks under the jaws extending two or three inches down his neck. Before I could get the rifle on him again, he settled back down in the clover.

I was within an ounce of getting the shot off three different times in 10 or 15 minutes but the cat kept moving and I never got my shot off.

The next day, I stepped the distance from the truck tracks to the weed clump and got 187 steps. The clover there, averaged 12" tall which would make him about 15" tall at the shoulder. The fact that I was looking down on him a little might bring his shoulder height to about 14." Tail and all, I would say he was between four-and-a-half and five feet and probably closer to the four-and-a-half feet. The only tracks I could find measured two-and-five eighths inches in soft wet ground and had no claw marks like a dog would make.

Strangely, in May and July of 1962, near Urbana, *Ohio* – which happens to be in Champaign County – a major "black panther" flap was occurring. Over a dozen people said they saw the "all black, big" cat "with a long tail and big eyes." In the midst of the sightings, one individual came forward to say he had seen a black panther in 1955 when he was driving west of Urbana. Of the 1962 accounts, one incident involved Mr. and Mrs. Darrell Goff's viewing the panther jumping eight feet from a tree, and leaving behind tracks with "distinct claw marks." What is incredible is the interesting fact that in separate Champaign Counties, near separate Urbana's – in Illinois and Ohio – two major mystery feline flaps could be so closely timed.

Returning to the survey of central Illinois' flap: during the early morning hours of June 30, 1963, George W. Davidson of Decatur, Illinois, aroused by the sound of dogs barking in the neighborhood, chased a "large cat" into a tree. As he approached, however, it leaped on him, scratched his face and dashed away over a five-foot fence. He said the animal was three feet long and dark in color.

A black panther reappeared in Decatur, Illinois, at 2:00 a.m., June 25, 1965. A Mrs. Rogers was pulling into her driveway when a "black, big cat-like animal" suddenly loomed in her headlights. Before the witness could move the thing had escaped into a field close to her home. According to the sheriff's report, "the animal stood higher than her car's headlights. She showed (an investigating officer) a paw print in the dust of her driveway which was made by the animal. . . . The print (was) about four inches across and apparently made by a member of the cat family as opposed to the dog family."

Three days later the cat startled three children on an outing in Lincoln Park on the south end of Decatur; as they took off running it gobbled up a sack lunch one of them had dropped.

A "mountain lion" loped rapidly across the road in front of Anthony Viccone's car at dawn of June 27, 1967. Viccone told me he knew it was a "mountain lion" because he had seen them on television. Driving south of Decatur, the witness said at a "conservative" estimate the creature was six-and-a-half feet long and its color was a shiny "metalic" bronze. "It wasn't a bobcat," Viccone insisted. About twenty sheep had been killed in the area in recent weeks.

Then, in 1970, throughout Illinois, an "invasion" of mystery animals began. It started and ended in Decatur.

In January, west of Decatur, an employee of the Macon Seed Company saw a large black animal he described as a "cougar." William F. Beatty, president of the firm, told me that he had found tracks left by the animal, which he said had twice torn down his electric fence. Two days later game warden, James Atkins, investigated, concluding that the animal was a beaver – a most unusual beaver to be sure, since the footprints Beatty discovered were "very large" and had claw marks.

Finishing out the year of 1970, a large black panther and its half-grown cub appeared in a field outside of Decatur on December 11th, and were observed twice during the day by members of the Clarence Runyon family. The Runyons thought the animals may have been the reason forty chickens disappeared from their farm during the summer. The Department of Conservation's investigation produced no results. The 1970's brought reports of mystery kangaroos to Decatur and Illinois, but those will not be discussed here.

All of these reports seem to bring into doubt the theory that these mystery cats are merely the eastern subspecies of the puma, *Felis concolor*, repopulating its old niches. The puma is extremely shy and does not attack automobiles or humans. But perhaps most importantly, the puma is tawny in color, not black.

A mystery cat seen in North America is, more often than not, described as a "black panther." Generally, one thinks of the melanistic leopard of Africa and Asia as the black panther, but it is the puma of the New World which is the usual flesh and blood answer to these accounts of large, black cats. The problem remains, however, that besides being behaviorally worlds apart from the phantom felines, the puma has allegedly only once displayed the black color phase.

In 1843, a melanistic puma supposedly was killed in the Carandehy River section of Brazil. There is no record of what became of the body. Perhaps it was a black jaguar, after all.

But then the whole subject of melanistic or black felines is shrouded in mysterious happenings.

All the zoology texts indicate melanism in the Felidae, the family of cats, apparently runs the highest in the moist tropics and sub-tropics. The most frequent numbers of black mutations appear to occur in the jaguar (*Panthera onca*) of Latin and South America, and the leopard (*Panthera pardus*) of Africa and Asia.

The black jaguar found in Central and South America is comparatively rare. Right now, throughout the nations of the world, not more than thirty populate zoological gardens. Of these, a large percentage are zoo-bred animals. Black jaguars, therefore, are not that common in the wild, and seem frequently to be concentrated in specific areas such as the jungle of Guyana Massif. As far as I have been able to determine, no black jaguars have ever been captured in the United States, although the spotted variety often ranges into some states of the Southwest. The black jaguar is a stocky beast, and quite different from the descriptions of our phantom felines, or "black panthers."

The black leopards of Africa and Asia are referred to as black panthers, and therein lies the good deal of confusion among people seeing the "panthers" of the plains and cities of the USA. Within any litter of spotted leopards, the chances are high that one of the kits will be black. Among leopards of Asia, especially, the frequency of births and survival of black offspring is common. Some laymen have wrongly viewed the black leopard as a separate species and labeled them black panthers. Since a majority of the mystery cats are reported to be black, the phantom felines are tagged "black panthers" by the press and the witnesses. Because of such semantic games, the Illinois Department of Conservation, for example, can make ridiculous statements like the following:

> Now and then, rural communities in Illinois have a panther scare that reduces normal, thinking individuals into children that are afraid to step out in the dark. Usually, the alleged animal is said to be a black panther, not a cougar (puma). Cougars are not black, and black panthers are not native to the Western Hemisphere. In Africa and Asia where panthers do roam, the black panther is a rare animal because it is a freak, a melanist.

(courtesy Audubon Park and Zoological Gardens)

New Orleans' beautiful melanistic phase of the leopard (*Panthera pardus fusca*) is also referred to as a black panther.

But it is not that easy to dismiss the "black panthers" of North America.

Take, for example, the "black panthers" of California.

California is a state where recent estimates claim about 2,500 mountain lions may roam. But some of the most concentrated and interesting "black panther" reports are found within the range of the California puma. The problem of "real" mountain lions and the "unreal" phantom cats is brought into clear focus in California.

For several years, large black cats have been sighted near Ventura, in the Conejo Valley. A full-fledged hunt for two of these full grown black panthers was conducted in 1964, but things did not come to a peak until 1967. During the afternoon of the 12th of December of that year, Henry Madrid of Montelvo was installing a fence around the Ventura County sewer plant. Henry spotted a black panther pacing restlessly back and forth on the steep mountainside near the treatment facility. He and fellow workers, Dick Simmons, Fred Salinas and Manuel Portillo, kept an eye on the panther while the county sheriff deputies were notified. Taking in the situation quickly soon after they arrived, the deputies pointed their squad car in the cat's direction, and bounced off in hot pursuit toward the hillside. The obligingly flat field stretched out before them, but it proved to be merely a thin, dry crust over a bed of sludge. The chase ended with the police car plunging hood-deep into a sea of sickening muck. By the time a tow truck arrived to rescue the deputies from their smelly predicament, the black panther had long disappeared.

This was the first in a series of incidents that led many to believe the Ventura County black panther was an omen of a sinister nature.

Soon after the deputies' disaster, Kenneth French and his wife saw the black cat on January 9, 1968, near a mountainside while they were out driving. The couple debated whether to report it. "Finally my husband stayed to keep an eye on it while I went to get a sheriff's deputy," Mrs. French later told reporters. "Apparently, the cat ran away just after I left. My husband and I aren't the type to report weird things, and it's pretty embarrassing to have people think you go around seeing black panthers! Whatever kind of black cat it was, it was bad luck."

The "bad luck" of this black panther was to even trap an airman on a sheer, six hundred foot cliff on the 23rd of December,
1967. It took rescuers four hours to get him down after he went
hunting for the panther. Ventura County's black panther was
never caught, despite the airman's and many others' efforts.

Not to be outdone in the annals of Californian claims to phantom pantherdom, the accounts from Northern California far
outweigh those from the southern portion of the state. All of the
sightings from the north are centered around the San Francisco
Bay area.

In Marin County, a survey of the San Rafael newspaper, *The
Independent Journal,* for the years 1957-1975, reveals a total of approximately thirty separate sightings of large, mountain lion-like
animals. More often than not (75% of the total), the color of the
creature is not given, but in fifteen percent of the reports, the cat
is said definitely to be black. A confused picture of what is being
seen, "black panther" or puma, exists. Further mystery is added
when such an incident as the one in June, 1963, when two women
collecting watercress at a creek were chased home by a "panther,"
calls to mind behavior unlike *Felis concolor.* In March of 1975, a
large powerful-looking "panther" sauntered through downtown
Fairfax, California, and jaywalked across the busy Sir Frances
Drake Boulevard, leaving townsfolk shuddering in its wake. The
Humane Society of Marin attempted to track it down and capture it, but gave up empty-handed. Roubert L. Dollarhite, Director of Operations of the organization called the Fairfax sighting
"extraordinary," saying it is unusual for mountain lions to approach
urban areas. Mystery feline or common mountain lion? These panther accounts merge into those from Mt. Tamalpais and Mill
Valley, also in Marin County, of a chattering five foot tall, "earless
mountain lion" and Bigfoot seen in 1963, 1975, and 1976. What
are we to make of this swirling phantasmagoria of mysteries? But
things get crazier way out west.

South of Marin and San Francisco, in December of 1973, a flurry
of reports of a five-foot-long, 150 pound, "dark black" (how dark
can black get?) panther made it into the papers. Navy Lt. Comdr.
Thomas Mantei's collie, Cleo, supposedly even treed the cat in
a eucalyptus in a gully behind Mantei's San Jose hillside home.

Meanwhile, east of San Francisco, in what is generally known as the East Bay area, a series of UFO reports and black panther sightings were coming to an end. It started in the East Bay in the Spring of 1972, when two men in the space of three days called Gary Bogue, Curator of the Alexander Lindsey, Jr. Museum in Walnut Creek to tell him of their sightings of black panthers. Neither knew the other, and no press coverage had stimulated the reports. One man watched the cat through binoculars when he was at home for lunch. The other witness was walking his Irish Setter when his dog started barking at a large black cat up in a tree. The five foot long beast jumped out of the tree and ran off.

About twelve miles from the first reports and three weeks later, a woman and her neighbor reported they were looking out the back window, watching a black panther chase cattle. The panther also strolled over to her pool and took a drink. (This daytime pool-drinking behavior was also reported from witnesses in Southern California in 1972, and Ohio in 1977.)

Still no publicity and East Bay's cat continued to be seen. A month after the swimming pool incident, the Concord Naval Weapons Depot Commander called authorities to report a black panther on the grounds of his facility. Animal Control officers and several military personnel observed the mystery feline through binoculars. All agreed it was black and puma-sized. They called out one of the officers with his .357 magnum rifle, and the cat vanished.

During the Fall of 1972, a rancher living at the base of Mt. Diablo noticed his ducks and geese had begun disappearing. The fowl were not being ripped apart like a dog would do, but were totally devoured. The rancher and his wife also heard what sounded like heavy guttural purring outside their bedroom window. Then one midnight, there was a loud thump on their roof, their horses made lots of fuss, and the family German Shephard scratched to be let in. Well, they sure as hell knew something was up! The rancher grabbed a flashlight, went outside and saw a large black panther turn, look at him, and walk calmly away. Tracks about five inches across were found.

The naturalist at the Las Trampas Regional Park was the next person to see "it," beginning about three months after the rancher's encounter. The naturalist and others frequently saw the black panther in the company of a tawny-colored cat-like animal chasing deer. This is not the first time two different colored mystery cats have kept company. We are reminded of the August 7, 1948, Turner boys sighting from Richmond, Indiana. The patterns of the mystery felines were and are being played out in California.

The Bay area's phantom panthers have also shown a preoccupation with automobiles. For example, on Wednesday morning, the 19th of December, 1973, Larry Rephahn told Fremont police he almost struck a black mountain lion as it dashed across Niles Canyon Road near Joyland Park.

Indeed, stepping back from the California accounts, what we see is part of that circle we can start measuring anywhere. The "black panthers" do not seem to be "black mountain lions." The Californian mystery cats reflect and repeat patterns found in the ufological sphere. Like UFO sightings, these cat sightings occur in waves ("flaps") and in specific locations ("windows"). 1973 appears to have been a big year around the San Francisco Bay area for sightings of large, black panther-like creatures, while at the same time, it was the "year of the humanoids," to use David Webb's phrase, elsewhere in America.

As for "windows," I have as already stated long noticed an American historical acknowledgment of weird phenomena by way of place names including the word "devil."

Interestingly, some of the more frequent flap-related sightings of the Californian black panthers have taken place in the Diablo (Spanish for "devil") Valley. One booklet on the Las Trampas Regional Park noted the black cat was referred to as "The Black Mountain Lion of Devil's Hole" because it was frequently seen on the slopes of Mt. Diablo and in the Devil's Hole area of the park.

So, in a smoke screen of actual *Felis concolor* in California, something else appears to be going on. Flaps and window areas exist where people are viewing creatures unlike mountain lions. Mountain lions are not black. Mountain lions do not usually chase people. Nor do they prowl during the day. These mystery cats do. The differences are many.

A good report of a phantom panther cannot be shrugged off easily. The conventionalists, unwilling to admit they are stumped, usually try to ignore the mystery cats or explain them away in terms of known animals. The fact that the pumas or mountain lions (*Felis concolor*) are still to be found in scattered parts of the New World makes it easy for the rationalizers to dismiss individual sightings as hoaxes, mistakes, or descriptions of normal pumas stepping briefly outside of their usual territory. In the Northeast, from New York State, and in the Great Smokies of the Southeast, *Felis concolor* is making a comeback. However, knowing the characteristics of our phantom felines, I am not easily distracted by such flimsy explanations.

From my studies of mystery felines, I have come to see they all run in specific behaviorally predictable patterns, be they seen in Australia, England or the United States. They all have an uncanny liking for automobiles. Most leave pointed toe, or clawed prints with otherwise cat-like features. They are extremely dangerous to human beings, in contrast to real pumas, which attack when driven by starvation to such an act. In all of North America, there are no more than ten recorded cases in which *Felis concolor* has attacked people; with phantom panthers, unprovoked assaults are the rule. There is a growing body of cases linking some of the mystery cat attacks on people and automobiles with the ability to interfere with the electromagnetic systems of the cars.

We have here the bare hints of an enigma so vast that its only immediate parallel in variety, quantity and distribution of reports is that other great mystery, with which it seems to have some oblique connection: the UFO problem. The major difference is that this question of phantom panthers has received practically no attention from Ufologists and Forteans, the vast majority of whom do not even appear to recognize its implications. When I began researching the accounts of phantom panthers over two decades ago, I was shocked to learn the subject had been so ignored by Forteans. Through my efforts and those of Mark A. Hall, Jerome Clark and Robert J. M. Rickard, only in recent years has the vast importance of these cases come to the fore. Even most of those who have granted its relevance to our area of interest have not been able to grasp its magnitude. But we are apparently dealing with thousands of sightings, spanning at the very minimum, two centuries and five continents, of unexplained, large and highly dangerous cat-like creatures.

The phantom felines are so oddly elusive that inevitably they remind one of Ivan Sanderson's dictum about Fortean phenomena: "We'll never catch them." Witnesses have shot at them without apparent effect, set traps, conducted "safaris," and done everything possible to bring a specimen in for examination. Like UFO's, the mystery cats possess that weird tangible intangibility that makes understanding so difficult and investigation so frustrating.

As a *Toronto Star* editorial writer once expressed it, black panthers are the "flying saucers of the animal world." When talking about the supposed reports of "pumas" in New York in the 1950s, a State Conservationist called them "feline flying saucers." It is in the United States, as opposed to England or Africa or Australia, where I have been able to examine the subject the closest, and have come away the most perplexed. For in America, there are large cats – the puma or mountain lion – but in spite of this, the reports of phantom panthers float above the normal, and give notice to the world that something strange is taking place.

12
Maned Mystery Cats

An "African" lion loose in California? The November, 1979 sightings of a fully maned cat are some of the more recent pages in an elusive chapter of the phantom feline mystery.

Fremont, California, the site of past reports of black panthers, is across the East Bay from San Francisco, but fringed by some of the wilder regions of northern California. At 5:27 p.m., on the night of November 10, 1979, Fremont residents near the Coyote Hills Regional Park relayed to police the disturbing fact that a large male lion was roaming loose. One caller told the authorities, after swearing he was not drunk, that he heard roaring at the corner of Alvarado and Lowry Boulevards.

Soon a massive search was organized. Based on the 6:28 p.m. reports of several residents who saw the lion near Alvarado Boulevard and Whitehead Lane, the "safari" began in the Alameda Creek area. More than forty policemen, firefighters, animal control workers and East Bay Regional Park District personnel were involved in the unusual chase. At one point, tracking dogs and a Bay Area Rapid Transit helicopter were included.

Shortly after 9:00 p.m., Fremont Police Officer William Fontes came face to face with the big cat under the Fremont Boulevard-Nimitz Freeway overpass, as the feline meandered down the Alameda County Flood Channel. When Fontes shined his flashlight in the face of the lion, it growled but did not attack. Days later, when a local owner of a forty pound chow-chow puppy came forth claiming his dog was the lion, Fontes said: "The puppy in no way resembled the 300 to 400 pound animal observed in the flood control channel."

On the 10th of November, after Fontes' sighting, the lion was last seen near Newark Boulevard and the Turk Island Dump at about 10 p.m. and then the search was called off due to darkness.

Charles Johnson, maintenance supervisor at Coyote Hills Regional Park commented after the search that he thought the lion still lurked in the park. He felt the hunters did not do an adequate job in their "safari" through the park. "They didn't check that underbush while I was here," Johnson observed. "They just flew the helicopter over it and turned on sirens to scare the lion."

During the following days no one saw the lion again. Fremont Police Identification Officer Karen Burhardt and an animal track expert from Marine World Africa USA labeled tracks found in the flood channel as those of "a large cat," but the lion seemed to have disappeared from the Fremont area.

Large, maned mystery cats – seemingly male African lions – are nothing new. Reports tick back over the years, from various parts of the United States and Canada. There appears to be a direct relationship between these "African lions" and the "black panthers" we have become so accustomed to hearing about, but more on that later. Let's look at a short history of the maned mystery felines.

Soon after the turn of the century, the famous "Nellie the Lion" incidents drew headlines in central Illinois. The furor started in July 1917 when Thomas Gullet, a butler at the Robert Allerton estate southwest of Monticello, was attacked while he was in the garden picking flowers. Gullet's injuries were only a few scratches, but despite the fact the animal had been seen near Camargo a few days earlier, this event served as the stimulus for massive lion hunts.

Thomas Gullet had described "Nellie" as an "African lioness," as did the Allerton Manison's chief housekeeper, Mrs. Shaw. On the 15th of July, Mrs. Shaw spied "Nellie" as a 300 man posse searched for the lion on another part of the estate. But "Nellie" was not alone. Apparently, her male companion was nearby. On the 29th of July, a lion pounced the automobile in which the families of Chester Osborn and Earl Hill were riding near Decatur.

James Rutherford was driving a hay wagon past a gravel pit on the 31st of July, when he spotted a "large yellow, long-haired beast." Throughout central Illinois during the Summer of 1917, many witnesses viewed "Nellie" or her maned counterpart. Like all the other mystery cats, "Nellie" was never caught or killed, and her origin remained elusive to the authorities.

A few years later, and in a neighboring state, another fully maned lion was reported scurrying about. In the midst of a mystery cat flap in which black panthers and tawny mountain lion types were being seen, a giant animal rushed a fishing party of four adults and two children in the Elkhorn Falls, Indiana region. The incident occurred in the early evening hours of the fifth of August, 1948.

According to Ivan Toney, who lived nearby, "About 7:30 p.m. a man came to the house and wanted to use the phone to call the sheriff. He said he and another man, along with their wives and two children, were fishing along the banks of the pool at the foot of the Elkhorn Falls. Their car was parked on the road near the gate leading to the falls. He said the animal came up the stream from the south. When they sighted it, they started running for the car. They reached it but the animal lunged at the car, then plowed through the fence into the sandy bar along the stream's edge."

The creature "looked like a lion with a long tail," the witnesses asserted, with bushy hair around the neck. This is a trait of the male of the African lion. Deputy Sheriff Jack Witherby examined the tracks and said they were like "nothing I have ever seen before." Witherby, after completing his investigations of the incident, issued a warning to persons in the area who fish along streams at night.

Two days after the Elkhorn Falls incident, two farm boys, Arthur and Howard Turner, saw a strange beast near a plum tree not far from the gate leading into their barnyard. On a rise of ground to their right, another animal stood 200 feet away. Arthur raised his rifle to his shoulder and blasted away. The animals wheeled around, jumped a gate and disappeared down a lane.

The Turner boys described one of the animals as "having the appearance of a lion." It was large-headed, shaggy and brown in color. The other looked like a black panther. Tracks were found, but their dog "Shep" refused to help the Turners and the authorities search for the mystery cats.

The following afternoon, farmers northwest of Abington, Indiana, watched two animals identical to those the Turner boys had seen. And the next morning, the two beasts were sighted by others in Wayne County. Although other varmint reports continued coming out of Indiana in the late forties and fifties, none specifically mentioned the maned lions again.

The *Omaha World Herald,* Monday, August 2, 1954, told of the latest sighting of what appeared to farmer Arnold Neujahr to be an African lion. "He reported he saw a lion as he topped a hill two miles west of Surprise," the newspaper informed. "The surprised lion, he said, dived into a ditch and disappeared into some trees. The lion had a mane, he said." (How else would one expect to find a lion seen near Surprise, Nebraska, but surprised?) One woman living in Surprise, the newspaper continued, said she saw a lion and mate running across her front yard. A similar incident took place in nearby Rising City. The Omaha paper ended by noting that these stories closely paralleled those which touched off a lengthy lion hunt near Ceresco, November 12, 1951. Ceresco is 32 miles east of Surprise.

In June of 1960, near Kapuskasing, Ontario, Leo Paul Dallaire had yet another experience. He reported seeing an animal resembling an African lion on his farm. Dallaire said it was light tan in color, had a mane, was at least three feet tall and five feet long. The animal also had a four foot long tail with a bushy end.

Meanwhile, back in the Midwest, ten years later, Tom Terry and about five other people called the Winnebago County Sheriff's office to report they had seen a lion near Roscoe, Illinois.

In late May of 1970, Terry and his friends were working at the Parthenon Sod Farm on Burr Oak Road along with the owner, George Kapotas. The seven of them were loading sod onto a semi-truck one Friday morning when George saw something run by with a bag of raw meat in its mouth. The meat had recently been used to feed two stray dogs wandering around the farm. The two dogs went in pursuit of the animal. "We thought it was a dog," Tom Terry said. "It seemed kind of funny that one stray dog would steal two others' meat."

Terry and his friends climbed on the truck and saw the thief was a lion. At about the same time, Kapotas noticed the same thing. Kapotas got pretty close to the lion, but had to give up the chase. Then on the other side of the field, Terry and his friends piled into a van to join the dogs who were still running after the beast. "We found the dogs sitting by a gate across the field," Terry noted. "They didn't move. They looked shell-shocked."

Driving slowly past the dogs, the search party found the animal on the top of a hill. "He turned and looked at us," Tom Terry later told a sheriff's deputy. "He must have been eight feet long. He had a mane and a long tail. It looked . . . well . . . like a regular lion." When they got about 80 feet from it, the "regular lion" jumped a fence and disappeared. "Nobody believes me. I wouldn't believe it, if I were in someone else's shoes," Terry said.

After the local authorities were called, this all prompted a small "safari" of law enforcement officers, complete with a state police airplane, in the area of the sightings near Interstate 90. After searching for one and a half hours, they failed to find the lion. The usual teletype inquiries requesting information on escapees from circuses and animal shows elicited negative results. But a week later something caused two ponies, one horse and four calves on the Lyle Imig farm near Rockford, Illinois, to bolt through two barbed wire fences. The prowling beast left tracks described as five inches long and four and three-fourths inches wide with a span of about 40 inches between each pawprint. Larry Black of the county's Animal Welfare League said they were like those of a "huge dog" but he was baffled. He said a similar but smaller set of tracks also was found at the scene. Of the larger tracks, Black noted: "It isn't a dog's; it's something else and we're going to find out what." Lyle Imig rounded up his livestock and returned them to his farm. He said once back the "very excited animals wouldn't leave the shed."

Late in August of the same year along the east bank of the Rock River near Rockford, it seems the same "lion" was still exciting local animals. Dogs began to bark vigorously in the area after a "roar" was heard. Dorsey Hailey swears he was not kidding when he said he heard a lion roar in the vicinity of his home. "It sounded just like a lion," he said. "Like the lions they have in the Milwaukee zoo." His wife who was out hunting dewworms at the time agreed. And of course so did the neighbors' dogs who were barking. Sheriff's deputies and neighbors with flashlights searched through the late August night, but found no trace of the beast.

In 1976, a farmer in Georgia, watched a weird animal in his pasture. J. H. Holyoak was driving a pickup truck down to check on his cows in Berrien County, Georgia, that day. Suddenly, he saw this "thing" and thought it was a dog chasing his cattle. When he got within 50 to 100 feet of the animal, he noticed the "thing" resembled a half-panther, half-lion. Specifically, Holyoak said it looked like a panther all over its body except for the mane it had on its neck, just like an African lion.

J. H. Holyoak's son, Ken, a farmer in his own right and a University of Georgia graduate, added these details in a 1979 interview: "He told me the animal was big and was trying to catch a calf. He shot the animal with birdshot and saw blood running out of it, but it didn't do much damage. The animal crossed the fence and ran off into the woods."

Ken Holyoak noted the "lion" was seen in the forest and swampy woods between Alapaha and Enigma – an interesting name for a town considering the circumstances. He felt sure his father knew what he had seen because "it was daylight, and there was no mistake about it." His father, J. H. Holyoak was raised in the mountains of Arizona, killed mountain lions there, and knew the difference between them and this "African lion" in Georgia.

In 1977, in Arkansas, where people at Dierks were reporting

panthers as "black as the ace of spades," a maned lion attacked two dogs at Dover. Beginning with sightings at the turn-of-the-century, the authorities have been faced with trying to account for all of these maned mystery cats.

More often than not, the police in the United States try to explain away the maned lion sightings as dogs; as we saw with the Fremont case of 1979.

Such dog explanations buried the Cincinnati, Ohio's suburban Croesbeck lion report of April 1971, and the Tacoma, Washington, July, 1976, story. Indeed, the Tacoma lion was described by "all sorts of people" as having "a shaggy black mane, light brown body, and a black tuft at the end of a long tail." Police fanned out, shot off their shotguns and revolvers, endangering mainly themselves, and did not catch or kill the lion anywhere near Washington and South 56th, where it was seen. Instead, they caught a part-collie, part-shepherd dog named Jake at the city dump and labeled poor Jake the "lion."

The answers to the maned mystery cats are beyond the sphere of dogs and escaped circus animals.

An Answer From the Pleistocene

Mystery felines closely resembling male African lions are not as familiar as the "black panthers" of Fortean literature, but they are just as elusive.

As the accounts demonstrate, these "African lions" have some unique traits. Indeed, the maned mystery cats seen in America have some particular characteristics which separate them from the so-called "black panthers" in whose company they are often found. Besides being social, the mysterious maned lions appear to be more forthrightly venturesome, retreating less quickly than the black panthers, but then again not attacking as frequently either. Comparing them overall, the maned lions seem more even tempered, less timid and yet not as aggressive as the hauntingly hyperactive black phantom cats. Why?

There are many levels of reality in the shadowy world of cryptozoology. I feel there may be a concrete, flesh and blood, if you will, answer to some accounts of mystery cats in America. I will

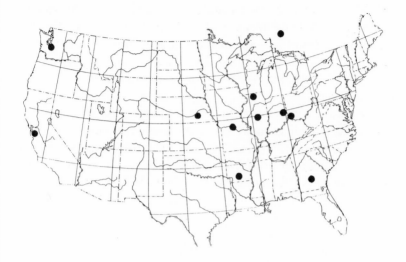

Each dot represents the locations of maned mystery cat
sightings in North America during the 20th Century.

Assurbanipal hunting lions – lions which may be closely
related to the cave lion (*Panthera leo spelaea*) and the American
lion (*Panthera leo atrox*).

here explore and develop a suggestion made by Mark A. Hall of Minnesota that the "black panthers" and "maned lions" may be only two slices of the same pie, and that the answer seems to lie in the survival of relict populations of *Panthera leo atrox* (*Panthera atrox* or *Felis atrox*, to some), the giant American lion of the Pleistocene.

When one begins to imagine the great felines of the American Ice Ages, thoughts usually run to the images of the sabertoothed cats. The classic Rancho la Brea painting rushes into our consciousness; *Smilodon* the lion-sized sabertooth on the back of some grazing mammal flashes to mind. The two prehistoric animals are stuck together in the tar pits, soon to be immortalized for thousands of years in the gooey mess. But a rarer (or maybe more intelligent?) visitor lurks in the background. There, larger by a third is another cat. This cat is *Panthera leo atrox.*

Fossils of *atrox* have been found in forty sites, from Alaska to Peru, from California through Nebraska to northern Florida. This giant lion was killed by Paleo-Indians, and Dr. Bjorn Kurten has written of the evidence suggesting they were around until as recently as 10,370 years, plus or minus 160 years, before present. Do they persist in isolated pockets today? Why should we even consider such a notion?

Panthera leo atrox was closely related to the Eurasian cave lion, *Panthera leo spelaea.* An unbroken range of lions fringed the top of the world during the Pleistocene, with a distinctive subspecies in each hemisphere. *Pantherea leo leo,* the so-called modern lion of Asia and Africa, is the reduced remainder of *P.l. spelaea.* But the cave lion seems to have actually persisted into historic Europe. Xerxes' expedition through Macedonia in 480 B.C. had to put up with such "annoyances" as the killing of some of his draft camels by lions. Some authors of ancient Greece – Hereodotus, Aristotle, Xenophon, and others – wrote of their contemporary lions. Investigators such as Dawkins and Sanford see no difference between the cave lion and the modern lion. And Dawkins, Kurten, and many others feel *spelaea* and *atrox* are identical. Because men lived for so long with the cave lion, we can learn much about these lions from the prehistoric artists of Europe, for theorists and fossils do not tell us much about what the animals looked like. One reindeer shoulder-blade from France clearly shows a cave lion with a tufted tail. F. Ed. Koby studied prehistoric drawings and sculptures of the large Ice Age cats and found two types. One was a heavily built feline with neither mane nor tufted tail; the other was a lion with mane and tufted tail. The art of palaeolithic man reinforces the idea that the prehistoric lions showed some quite clear differences between males and females. As C. A. W. Guggisberg wrote on the cave lion in art in his excellent overview: *Simba: Life of the Lion:* "Two lions in the *Grotte des Trois-Freres,* of which one is maned, turn their heads towards the viewer and stare at him with big eyes."

The giant American lion *P. leo atrox* reflected this sexual dimorphism, as would be expected, through the different limb sizes of the fossil finds. The sexually linked differences in the cats is the key to the lock which opens the mystery of the phantom feline question. Only lions are social. Only lions show wide physical differences between sexes.

The behaviours demonstrated by the mysterious maned cats of America are exactly what one would predict of a male *atrox.* And the more aggressive huntress *atrox* would resemble the "black panther." The latter are more frequently seen, and definitely more aggressive than their maned male counterparts – following closely the pattern of the African and Asian (modern?) lions, *P. leo leo.* The black panthers, our female *atrox,* are the mystery cats consistently reported with the cubs, or young. They are downright nasty but intelligent. The strutting, careful maned male *atrox* are no dummies, either.

And the fossil *atrox* was a bright cat. Thirty sabertoothed *Smilodons* ended up in the La Brea tar pits for every one *atrox.* Because of that amazing ratio, many an author has discussed the intellectual superiority of the lions of La Brea vs. the sabertooths. In Kurten and Anderson's *Pleistocene Mammals of North America,* for example, they also note that *atrox:* "had a larger brain, relative to body size, than any of the Pleistocene or living lions of the Old World."

Added to its intellectual abilities are various natural selective processes which would have helped *atrox* adapt as the New World changed. One of these is the tendency towards melanism on the fringes of the lions' range. One good example of this is the darkly colored (with black belly and head manes) Cape lions of South Africa. The reports of the "black panthers" may be evidence that the females have been able to effectively use this genetic adaptation. Then the stage would be set for what we find in mysterious America today . . . large maned lions doing what males do (sleeping, mating, regally walking about) . . . and aggressive black cats doing what females do (hunting, killing, raising young). Whether or not *P. leo atrox* is the answer remains to be seen, but for now, it seems to fit.

13
Mystery Kangaroos

The place is Chicago's Northwest Side. It is early in the morning, nearly 3:30 a.m. The date is October 18, 1974; a normal day for *most* people, but for patrolmen Leonard Ciagi and Michael Byrne of the Chicago Police Force, a very strange drama is unfolding. Earlier, the patrolmen had responded to the call of an incredulous homeowner who claimed a kangaroo, of all things, had been on his porch. It was easy for the police officers to laugh about the report a couple of hours before, but now that Byrne and Ciagi had cornered the five-foot-tall marsupial at the end of a darkened alley they had to come to grips with the situation.

And to make matters worse, the kangaroo was growling.

Byrne, understandably reluctant, attempted to handcuff the animal. It was at that point, as he later told reporters, that the kangaroo "started to scream and get vicious." The battle that followed was not soon to be forgotten in the casebook of Chicago's finest.

"My partner got kicked pretty bad in the legs. He (the kangaroo) smacks pretty good, but we got in a few good punches to the head and he must have felt it."

Byrne then added, "Too bad we didn't have our nightsticks there. Then we could have really hammered him."

The media had a field day. Newspapers from coast to coast blared with such headlines as **"KANGAROO STAYS A JUMP AHEAD OF POLICE"** and **"KEYSTONE KOPS GO ON KANGAROO KAPER"** in huge block letters the day following the encounter.

Short of using their guns, the men stood little chance of subduing the animal. Handcuffs were certainly of no use, so, nightstickless and battered, the pair backed off. As additional squad cars began to arrive, the animal leaped over a fence and took off down the street "going 20 miles per hour," leaving only a mystery and sore shins in its wake.

And it is a mystery. Little known to the public-at-large, mystery kangaroos have turned up all over the Midwest and continue to do so on a semi-regular basis. When these phantom creatures do make an appearance they are never claimed. I am not describing escaped pets, or for that matter, animals that "got away" from the local zoo. What I am discussing, instead, is a strange type of phantom indeed – "animals" that may not be animals in the conventional sense of the word. Animals, which for reasons unknown, see it fit to appear in areas that host the majority of "monsters" and UFO activity. Animals, that for technical and other considerations, cannot, *but do,* exist.

In this report I shall examine the stuff that fantasies, dreams, and – perhaps more frequently – nightmares are made of.

The legacy of mysterious marsupials of the Midwest has been an active one since the snarling kangaroo attacked the two Chicago policemen in 1974. But before I examine the bizarre events of more recent years, let me peer at some kangaroo sightings in America before them.

In a rather obscure book by Robert H. Gollmar, *My Father Owned a Circus,* I find the first record of an errant kangaroo. In his chapter on the tragedies affecting the Gollmar circus, he told of the day that a big cyclone struck New Richmond, Wisconsin. The storm occurred on June 12, 1899, and the circus happened

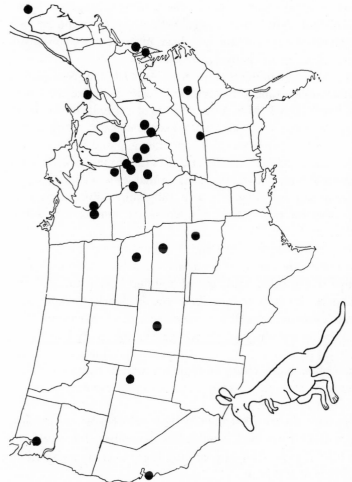

Mystery kangaroos have been seen throughout America, but a major portion of the sightings has been concentrated in the Midwest.

to be in town. According to a local historian, Ann P. Epley, writing in 1900, in the midst of the storm a Mrs. Glover saw a kangaroo run through the backyard of Mrs. Allen. Robert Gollmar takes issue with the claim the creature was an escaped circus animal. "I have no recollection of the circus owning a kangaroo; I particularly doubt it in 1899," Gollmar writes. Too often the escapee theory has been used without any basis in fact, and we run across it many times in the kangaroo stories.

Around the turn of the century, near Mays Landing, New Jersey, something like a kangaroo was to add weight to that region's tales of the "Jersey Devil." Mrs. Amanda Sutts of Yardville recalled seeing and hearing the "Devil" in 1900 when she was a girl of ten.

"We heard a scream near the barn one night and ran out of our house," said Mrs. Sutts. "We saw this thing that looked like a kangaroo. It wasn't such a great big animal – it was about the size of a small calf and weighed about 150 pounds. But the noise is what scared us. It sounded like a woman screaming in an awful lot of agony."

The sound of a woman screaming is nothing new to researchers of the unknown. The peculiar sound – also described like that of a baby crying – often spills out of haunted houses to bathe the locale in eerie vibration. Strangely, the awesome "Bigfeet" seem to emit this sound, as well as those elusive phantom panthers that prowl the landscape. And, of course, the legendary banshee is famous for its terrible scream. Often, a myriad of "unrelated" unexplained phenomena have the same element in common. When studying mysterious Fortean occurrences, the sensation is encountered quite frequently.

Mrs. Sutts reported that she saw the Devil's tracks many times, always around the family barn. She remembers the footprints were from eight to ten feet apart and led to a large cedar swamp at the rear of the farm.

The lore of the New Jersey Devil is a mixed bag of Bigfoot, panther, and thunderbird reports – as well as some obvious hoaxes. Over the years, many eyewitnesses have reported seeing the thing. In general, the reports indicate that the Jersey Devil had the face of a horse, the body of a kangaroo, sometimes the wings of a bat, and often seemed half human and half animal. (See Chapter 16 for more complete details.)

Mrs. Sutts said her relatives would "pull my hair out when they find out I've been talking about the Jersey Devil. But I know there is such a creature. I'll never forget how frightened I was when I saw him. I was so scared I thought I'd die."

Whether "it" was the Jersey Devil or not is really unimportant, for the kangaroos keep hopping down through history. Recent years have seen an outbreak of 'roo mania.

Reports of the giant kangaroo of South Pittsburg, Tennessee, made it all the way to the pages of New York's daily newspapers. During mid-January of 1934, a kangaroo spread terror among the Tennessee hill farmers. This extremely atypical 'roo was reported to have killed and partially devoured several German police dogs, geese and ducks. The Reverend W. J. Hancock saw the animal and described it as fast as lightning, and looking like a giant kangaroo as it ran and leapt across a field. Another witness, Frank Cobb quickly came upon more evidence of the kangaroo's activities. The head and shoulders of a large police dog were all that remained. A search party tracked the 'roo to a mountainside cave, but the prints disappeared.

In recent years, writers have tried to blame this Tennessee giant kangaroo story on the pen of the late Horace N. Minnis, a South Pittsburg correspondent of the *Chattanooga Times*. The only trouble with this "newspaper hoax" theory is that Minnis was not a newspaper correspondent for the area in 1934.

In 1949 the area surrounding Grove City, Ohio was experiencing a monster flap. Perhaps it was coincidence – or perhaps it wasn't – but during the creature wave another type of "monster" decided to show up – this time a phantom kangaroo. Mr. Louis Staub, while driving a Greyhound bus near Grove City in January of that year, encountered the marsupial when the vehicle's bright headlights illuminated it. He described it in the following terms:

"It's about 5½ feet high, hairy, and brownish in color. It has a long pointed head. It leaped a barbed wire fence and disappeared. it resembled a kangaroo, but it appeared to jump on all fours. I'm certain it wasn't a deer."

Sightings of kangaroos exploded all over the state of Nebraska in 1958, but these accounts are examined elsewhere in this book. (See Chapter 21).

A year before Nebraska's flap, strangeness would settle in Minnesota. From 1957 until about 1967, the woods around Coon Rapids, Minnesota, were frequently the site of many kangaroo reports. Mrs. Barbara Battmer first brought these cases to my attention when I interviewed that area's residents. Her two sons were seven and nine, when in 1957 they were playing near a forested area of Coon Rapids, off Highway 10. They claimed then, and have stuck to their story ever since, that they saw two kangaroos hopping together through the woods. The five-foot-tall animals hopped out of some trees, crossed a small clearing about fifty feet in front of the boys, and disappeared into another wooded area. This clear view of the creatures made them certain the color of the kangaroos was a blending of light tan to medium brown.

Because of Mrs. Battmer's efforts, more people came forth with their knowledge of Coon Rapids kangaroo stories. Linda Brodie is certain it was a kangaroo she saw in 1958. And Mrs. Gary Haider told me of her two brothers coming home in 1958 with reports of a "*Big* Rabbit." Mrs. Haider said the boys described the "enormous" rabbit as being as big as they were, and when seen it was just hopping around. Mr. and Mrs. Willard L. Hays of Coon Rapids testify to the fact they saw two oversized "bunnies" on the evening of April 24, in 1967. Hazel Hays told me that the kangaroos were in an open area approximately one mile west of Highway 47, near the Anoka County Fairgrounds.

During all this activity in Minnesota, kangaroos were making appearances elsewhere in the country. On July 26, 1965, Bert Radar spied a phantom 'roo east of Abilene, Kansas, on Interstate 70. Jerry L. Condray saw his mystery kangaroo on August 15, 1965, northeast of Wakefield, Kansas.

Sometime early in 1967, William Shearer encountered one of these critters in Puyallup, Washington, a town more well known for recurring reports of screaming Bigfeet than for hopping kangaroos.

Almost as if the kangaroos were again hopping their way across or around the Midwest, in 1968, they turned up in Michigan and Ohio. On the last day of May during that year, a motorist traveling along Ohio Route 63 reported to the Ohio State Patrol that he had seen a kangaroo hopping about near Monroe at 2:30 a.m. The radio dispatcher took the report lightly, but sent Patrolman James Patrick for a check. Patrick reported back within a matter of minutes.

"The thing hopped right across the road in front of my cruiser," Patrick said. "It sure looked like a kangaroo to me." He said the animal leaped off in the direction of Lebanon, Ohio.

Meanwhile, the Director of the Cincinnati Zoo, Ed Maruska, was telling the newspapers, "I doubt there's a kangaroo around here on the loose. We had a kangaroo story about two years ago. Never found one. Down the years we've chased after reported black leopards, panthers, and even a polar bear. Anyway," Maruska said, "Anyone seeing the kangaroo, which I doubt exists, should try to keep it is sight and call the Zoo."

But to keep *it* in sight, you would have had to have been in Lansing, Michigan. There on the 3rd of August, a citizen reported to state police that he had seen a kangaroo hopping around the campus of Michigan State University, near College and Jolly Roads.

November, 1971 was the month that "The Phenomenon" visited Kansas in two of its many guises; this time as kangaroos and those blasted UFOs. Mrs. Edward Johnson, who lives near Abilene, reported seeing a kangaroo not far from her home on the first of November. Synchronistically, the next day *another* Johnson family encountered the unknown. The Dural Johnson Family of Delphos, Kansas reported that on November 2nd a donut-shaped flying object landed. (And this was not to be all. Two days later a Manhattan, Kansas retired Army dentist reported seeing a cigar-shaped flying object near Welda. Dr. Dean H. Stewart said he saw the object which had an orange nose cone and a white body as he was duck hunting at a lake near Welda.)

The Dural Johnson family of Ottawa County were quite puzzled by their November 2nd expeiences. Ronnie Johnson, 13, was tending sheep when the blinding object landed in a field on the property, breaking several tree limbs. When Ronnie got his parents, the object made a rumble and a roar as it took off, leaving behind a classic landing spot for all to see. The Johnsons took a picture of the spot in the dark, and it revealed a fluorescent glow in the shape of the object where it had landed. Sheriff Ralph Enlow felt the Johnsons were quite sincere in what they reported to him. Not only was Sheriff Enlow impressed, but a panel of UFOlogical consultants to the *National Enquirer* were so intrigued by the physical and testimonial evidence that they awarded the incident their "Best Case of the Year" prize.

The fact that kangaroos and UFOs both decided to show up in the same state at the same time is interesting. The great German psychoanalyst Carl G. Jung pioneered the study of synchronicity, which involves the noncausal "production" of *meaningful coincidences*. (Jung's thesis was presented in his, *Synchronicity: An Acausal Connecting Principle*.) Are we dealing with a synchronicity . . . a meaningful coincidence? Synchronistically, did two *unrelated* Fortean phenomena – in this instance UFOs and kangaroos – manifest themselves in roughly the same time frame, *and* in the same state? Or, *are* the laws of causality at play? We can't ignore the hints that the various phenomena are singular aspects of something larger.

And as if UFOs and the Jersey Devil were not enough to get involved with kangaroos, even the lake monsters of Ireland sometimes reflect the kangaroo-itis. There was Gay Denver, a 16-year-old student who in 1968 was quietly pushing his bike up the rise overlooking Glendarry Lake near Achill Sound. Denver came upon a "lake monster" climbing a turf bank into the woods.

"It was moving in a jumpy way like a kangaroo," Denver breathlessly told the authorities. "It has a long head like a sheep and a long neck and tail. The hind legs were bigger than the front ones."

Kangaroo Mania was not realized by the vast majority of Americans until 1974. Needless to say, I had been following the reports for years. But the incident involving the Chicago police officers opened the floodgates and the Midwest experienced a kangaroo flap . . . a hectic period of increased activity which in turn is responsible for an increased public awareness.

Actually, the Chicago area had once before played host to the Unidentified Furry Objects even preceding 1974. In 1971, during the month of July, a mystery 'roo apparently turned up in Evanston, Illinois. The animal made its appearance on the grounds of Northwestern University, where it was spotted by an unnamed campus policeman. The incident was in turn reported to the Evanston police, who never caught up with the creature.

Like other types of mystery animals, the phantom kangaroos disappear into nothingness once the search parties arrive. They are never apprehended. As with other anomalous creatures, there is a strong possibility that the kangaroos are not real animals in the flesh-and-blood aspect of the word, but rather a transitional phenomenon—something only temporarily real.

On October 18, 1974—the same day Chicago patrolmen Byrne and Ciagi encountered the screaming marsupial—another sighting was made setting a standard for the days to follow. This time a four and a half foot tall kangaroo was seen hopping around Belmont and Oak Parks in the Windy City's Northwest Side.

The next day, Saturday, October 19, offered even more activity. It all began in the morning, around 7:00 a.m., when 13-year-old Kenneth Grieshamer was delivering newspapers. The boy, standing on the corner of Sunnyside and Mulligan Streets, heard the screech of brakes and spun around. Instead of seeing a car, Grieshamer saw a kangaroo standing a few feet away. "He looked at me, I looked at him, and then away he hopped," the boy said.

That same day, about an hour later, two boys saw a kangaroo near Austin and Eastwood Roads. And if two sightings weren't enough, an unidentified caller reported to the Chicago police that he had seen a kangaroo hopping around Belmont and Mango Avenues at about 6:00 p.m. that night. Apparently the kangaroo developed quite an appetite after making three appearances on Saturday because the next morning the Chicago police switchboard received calls from startled residents who claimed the creature was rummaging through their garbage cans.

On Wednesday, October 23, a kangaroo was seen roaming about Chicago's Schiller Woods, near Irving Park Road. This was to be the last date a kangaroo would be seen in Chicago until early November. From then on, things were pretty quiet all around until the marsupials started to pop up in other midwestern cities. It was on the first of November when the epidemic spread to Plano, Illinois . . . .

John Orr, an off-duty Plano, Illinois police officer spotted a kangaroo Friday evening while driving on Riverview Road, just outside the city limits. The animal leaped eight feet from a cornfield, landed in the middle of the road, and was caught in the bright lights of Orr's highbeams. "I'm positive I saw him," Orr said. "People don't believe you when you see things like that. I definitely know it was a kangaroo."

"If I hadn't slowed down, I would have hit him. My cousin was in the car behind me and when she saw him, she just plain ran off the road."

Orr told reporters that the kangaroo stood in the road for a few seconds and then hopped off into a wooded area.

Plano, Illinois is about 50 miles west of Chicago. The general assumption, up to the time of Orr's sighting, was that only one kangaroo was on the loose. But now with the Plano sighting a few folks began to have their doubts – either doubting the workings of the human mind or the assumption that there was only one kangaroo running around Illinois. However dramatic the Orr sighting might have been, it only served as a taste of things to come because the day afterward *kangaroos were seen in Chicago and Plano at approximately the same time.*

Jerry Wagner, Steve Morton, and Shawne Clark – all 17 – were driving along Plano's Shafer Road, around 9 p.m. on the night of November 2, 1974. Suddenly, the car's headlights picked up something in the middle of the raod. The something turned out to be – you guessed it – a full grown kangaroo!

"We almost ran over it. It jumped onto the road about 20 feet ahead of us," Jerry Wagner said. "I was on the passenger side in the front seat and I pointed it out to Shawne and Steve and all three of us saw it."

"It landed on the road near the intersection with the main road, and there was no traffic. It sat up on its haunches as kangaroos do and then jumped over a fence about five feet high and disappeared into the woods."

Wagner continued, telling reporters, "I never really believed those stories about people seeing a kangaroo around here, but I do now."

After the sighting the three youths reported the incident to the Kendall County Sheriff's Office. And while they were doing that, a similar scenario was being enacted in Chicago, some fifty miles away.

Cathy Battaglia, 17, and her boy friend, Len Zeglicz, 19, were out for a walk around 9:30 p.m. when they encountered a strange creature in the 5600 block of South New England Avenue. At first they thought the creature was a dog. However, when the animal looked at the couple, turned, and then hopped away down the street, the two knew for a fact they had seen a kangaroo.

If the two reports of November 2nd are accurate, it is obvious that more than one kangaroo was hopping around the Midwest in 1974. The possibility that one kangaroo – capable of doing 25 miles per hour (and then only for a short while) – traversed a distance of 50 or so miles in 30 minutes is simply too difficult to accept. The other sightings of November 1974 provide excellent evidence to confirm the general suspicion that more than one 'roo was on the loose.

On the morning of November 3rd, Frank Kocherver, 21, saw a kangaroo near a forest preserve on Chicago's Northwest Side. Kocherver reported that the animal leaped from a two-legged position into the woods.

Then on Monday, November 4th, a truck driver saw a deer and what he thought to be a kangaroo near Plano, Illinois. The driver pulled his rig over to the side of the road and tracked the deer and "another animal that definitely is not a deer – its prints in the mud of the field are different and I think it is a kangaroo."

And then the kangaroos *really* started to get around.

According to the *Wall Street Journal,* on November 6th near Lansing, Illinois a truck driver was forced to swerve off the road in order to avoid hitting one of our maverick marsupials.

Six days after the Lansing, Illinois encounter, Rensselaer, Indiana experienced a mini-flap of kangaroo sightings. It started when Alfred Hentschel, an employee of St. Joseph's College, saw one of the bounding phantoms come out of a cornfield bordering a drug store on Rensselaer's south edge around 8:30 a.m. From there, the kangaroo hopped down Charles Street, and then crossed over into another cornfield. When last seen by Hentschel, the animal was hopping west toward some trees on the distant edge of another cornfield. The sighting touched off a massive search, but not a trace of the animal was found.

"I hope some farmer or somebody else sees it, or everybody'll think I'm a nut," said Hentschel. "But it was a kangaroo . . . I know it was." Hentschel really didn't have long to wait because, later that day, two more sightings were made.

Around noon Charles James of Rensselaer saw what he thought was a kangaroo. He saw the animal bounding out of some woods near St. Joseph's College, after which it hopped over a hill about 1,000 feet from the witness. Following the sighting seven law enforcement units sped into the area only to find . . . no kangaroo.

Then about 5 p.m. that day, Bill Babcock, Sr. reported that he, too, had seen the animal. The kangaroo, he reported, was hopping around near a gravel pit located near his construction company office. Babcock stated he last saw the creature heading west.

Three days later on November 15, 1974, the kangaroo – or *a* kangaroo – was back in Chicago. Joe Bernotus was taking a train to work that Friday morning when he saw the creature through the vehicle's window.

"I'm sure that somebody else must have seen it because I was in an eight car-train. But when people see something like that they don't always want to say anything."

Bernotus reported that the animal was five feet tall and "black all over, except for the stomach and face, which were brown." He went on to say that the kangaroo was just standing in a vacant lot near Damen and Montrose Streets.

On Sunday, November 17th, a mystery kangaroo was seen in Carmel, Indiana which is located several miles north of Indianapolis. Amos Miller, his wife, and another couple spotted the animal while driving to church that Sunday morning. Those four people reported that the kangaroo was sitting on its haunches near the Cool Creek Bridge at Indiana 234 and Keystone. Later that afternoon police received a call from a woman who saw the marsupial hop off into some woods.

The police believed the kangaroo reports. "We don't doubt the story one bit," said a police spokesman. But officials never did catch up with the creature.

Actually, no one caught up with the kangaroo, or kangaroos, that were hopping around the countryside in 1974. The last sighting that year was made on the 25th of November, and the report comes from Sheridan, Indiana.

Donald Johnson, a Sheridan farmer, was driving his pickup truck down a deserted rural road when he encountered the creature. Johnson slowed down at the intersection and, looking to his right, saw a kangaroo "running on all four feet down the middle of the road." The animal spotted Johnson, jumped over a four foot tall barbed wire fence, and bounded across a field where he was lost to sight.

But even this was not to be the end of the kangaroo sightings. The marsupials, although fewer in number, decided to stage a few appearances in both 1975 and 1976.

It was a Monday morning, about 7 a.m. on the 14th of July 1975. Mrs. Rosemary Hopwood was winding her way along Illinois Route 128. South of Dalton City, near Decatur, she was startled to see an animal she first took to be a dog. Getting closer, she saw it was a kangaroo walking on all fours at the side of the road. Then, as she told me, the kangaroo moved across the road and sat up on its back legs. She described the animal as light beige in color, about five and a half feet long when it traveled on all fours, and about two and a half feet in height when sitting up. The thing had pointed ears and a long, thick tail. It hopped away into an Illinois cornfield – disappearing to join the many cases similar to it.

Three days later, a couple of other people saw a kangaroo in the same general area.

Rosemary Hopwood has encountered other denizens of the paranormal, and this fact makes her kangaroo story all the more interesting.

"Oh, I see them all the time!" That's how Mrs. Hopwood replied when asked whether or not she ever saw any strange lights near her St. Elmo, Illinois home. She quickly thought about such an open and frank response, and self-consciously added, "But maybe most of them are aircraft lights." Maybe most of them are, but as a Fortean I am forced to wonder.

Rosemary Hopwood was the recipient of much "ribbing," as she put it, because of her experience. A more positive side effect was that other people with weird tales to tell felt comfortable sharing them with Mrs. Hopwood. For example, one St. Elmo farmer told her about the time a black panther had paced his car. But still, all these stories, and her frequent feeling that she was seeing UFOs in the area, did not make Rosemary Hopwood think it was any less weird to say she saw a kangaroo in Illinois.

DuQuoin, Illinois, was the site of another July, 1975, 'roo encounter. Kevin Luthi was one of several people who saw a five foot kangaroo bound through some cornfields. Luthi was not quick to report his sighting, as he felt "everyone would think" he was "crazy."

In 1976 Illinois was once again the site of kangaroo activity. Harry Masterson, of Rock Island, spotted one of the animals near his home on Tuesday, April 6th. Masterson, 25, was out walking his dog at 6:30 a.m. when he encountered the animal.

"I looked across the street and there it was. A kangaroo. It was a big one. It came hopping through the yard. The kangaroo and I stood there looking at each other for about a minute. Then it turned around and went hopping away off to the north."

Masterson was sure the animal he had seen was a kangaroo. He told me that he had been to the Milwaukee Zoo and knew what a kangaroo looked like. More witnesses also chimed in with their testimony.

When the animal began its exit, Harry ran into the house and persuaded his wife, Barbara, and his mother-in-law to come outside and see the creature. By the time the others had made it outside the kangaroo was already on its way, hopping "faster than a dog" according to Barbara. With no alternatives, the trio just incredulously stood on the front lawn and watched the marsupial disappear into the rapidly rising sun.

Mrs. Masterson said that exactly one month to the day after their sighting an unnamed woman saw a kangaroo in Rock Island.

On August 17, 1976 a kangaroo was seen by a citizen's band radio operator near Golden, Colorado at 2:10 a.m. The radio operator's report was forwarded to the police and five law enforcement officers attempted to track the marsupial down with some measure of success. At 4:15 a.m. one of the group, Patrolman Donald Douglas, saw the kangaroo near some clay pits. He said the kangaroo was full grown and hopped away when he approached it.

After 1976, the kangaroos seemed to have literally leapt over 1977. The next big outbreak of sightings took place in Wisconsin in 1978. The most startling result of the Wisconsin drama was the first photograph of a phantom kangaroo – a mostly unheralded picture, published here for the first time. But prior to the photograph being taken, a series of kangaroo close encounters occurred.

The fifth of April, 1978, is the first recorded date of a Waukesha, Wisconsin, area sighting. On that day, at 6:45 a.m., east of Highway A, on East Moreland Blvd, witnesses Wilcox and Kroske saw a kangaroo. This was followed by the April 12th, sighting by members of the Haeselich family of nearby Pewaukee Township.

"It was going pretty quick. It was hopping. We knew it had to be a kangaroo," Jill Haeselich told a reporter at the time.

Jill, her husband Peter, and his mother, Esther, were sitting in the dining room eating supper about 6:15 p.m. when they spotted the kangaroo in their back yard. It disappeared over a hill as Peter tried to pursue it. "It was so fast," Jill recalled.

The next day, at 4:45 P.M., William J. Busch was returning home from his job as a social worker at a Waukesha County residential school when he saw his kangaroo. Busch was driving on Highway 83, when about 15 feet in front of him, a three foot tall creature with a "slightly odd-shaped" head, little front legs, and long back feet scampered across the road.

Three days later at 3 a.m. on April 16, Greg and Janet Napientek saw a kangaroo as they were driving home along Highway A, east of Waukesha.

"I've seen deer before. I know what a deer looks like. I know it was a kangaroo," Janet Napientek observed.

Up in their hilltop home on Sierra Drive in Brookfield Township, near Waukesha, the Nero family has a good view of the nearby wooded terrain. On the 23rd of April, around 10:45 a.m., Lance Nero was having toast and coffee when he glanced outside to see *two* kangaroos hop out of the woods, across a road, through part of a field, and across another road. Lance and Loretta Nero, plus members of the Waukesha County Sheriff's Department discovered tracks left behind by the animals. Some deputies tried to quickly debunk the tracks by saying they were made by deer or cows, in spite of their appearance.

Veteran cryptozoologist Mark A. Hall interviewed the Neros and found them to be bright and sincere people. They showed Hall five casts, and he described the tracks to me: "Generally the tracks have a two-pronged fork appearance with two knobs at the rear of the 'fork handle.' The tracks were impressed into mud at a new housing development which accounts somewhat for the depth of them." Measuring two of the casts, Mark Hall found this range in length, 5.75 inches to 6.0 inches; and width, 2.75 inches to 3.125 inches.

As if the tracks of a phantom kangaroo were not enough, on the 24th of April, 1978, a good photograph of one of the elusive beasts was taken. At 5:20 p.m. on that Monday, two 23 year old Menomonee Falls men spotted a kangaroo in the bush near Highway SS and Highway M. They took two SX-70 Polaroid color photographs. One photograph is blurry, but the other clearly shows a kangaroo-like animal (see accompanying photograph). The two men refused to give their identity to a reporter in 1978, fearing public ridicule.

The clear color Polaroid picture shows a tan animal with lighter brown front limbs, hints of a lighter brown hind limb, dark brown or black patches around the eyes, inside the two upright ears, and possibly surrounding the nose and upper mouth area. The animal compares favorably with Bennett's wallaby or brush Kangaroo, a native of Tasmania, found from snowy summits to lower valleys. The Waukeska phantom also looks like the black-tailed or swamp

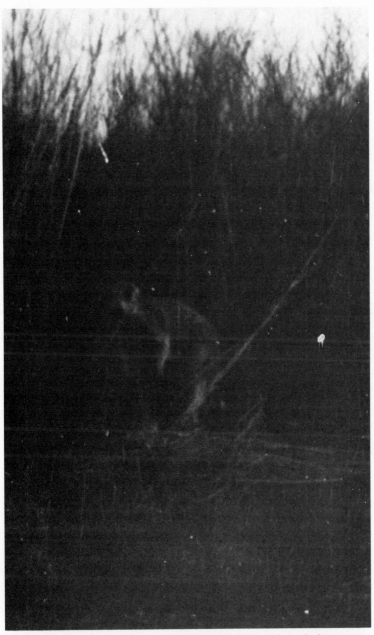

A black and white print of the original color Polaroid photo taken April 24, 1978, of a mystery kangaroo near Waukeska, Wisconsin.

wallaby, a marsupial inhabiting the wet dense gullies from Queensland to SE South Australia. Or, of course, it could be some undiscovered form of mammal we have as yet not imagined. Still, whatever they are, they continued to be seen in Wisconsin in 1978. At 2:30 a.m., on the 24th of April, Tom Frank saw one near Highway C in Merton Township. On the 9th of May, at the Camelot Forest housing development, Waukesha County's last kangaroo of 1978 was sighted.

Later in the month of May, some 185 miles northeast of Waukesha, in Eau Claire County, Wisconsin, another kangaroo was spied. On the 21st, a Sunday night, an Eau Claire woman was returning home, on Highway 12 betwen Augusta and Fall Creek, when she saw a creature the size of a man hopping across the road.

So ended the 1978 Wisconsin kangaroo accounts.

Canada was the site during the warm months of 1979 for some more mystery kangaroo visitations. Early on the morning of the 31st of May, a police officer radioed the station to report he had sighted a kangaroo in the Markham Road–Finch Avenue area of Scarboro, a section of Toronto, Ontario. A Metro Toronto Zoo official, when asked for his opinion, said: "We're definitely not missing any wallabies or any other kind of creature and we haven't sent anyone out to look for anything. It's likely just a rabbit with long ears."

A few days later and several hundred miles to the northeast, another kangaroo popped up. Roy Hanley, a guard at the Acadia Forest Products, Ltd. mill in Nelson–Miramichi, New Brunswick, saw a kangaroo at 3 a.m. on the 5th of June, 1979. Hanley was on duty at the time when he came upon the creature. "I was standing no more than 10 feet from him. As far as I'm concerned it was a baby kangaroo," Hanley told reporters. "It was about 3 to 3½ feet in height, had large powerful looking hind legs, small front paws, a long large tail, big droopy ears, and a greyish-brown coat."

A taxi driver and her passenger also had seen a kangaroo near the mill, and other encounters were reported from Millton and Douglasville, New Brunswick, near the Maine border.

The Hanley sighting stimulated interest in the folk collection of the "Songs of the Miramichi." Folksong No. 47 is entitled, "The

Wild Cat Back on the Pipe Line," and tells of the many people who saw a strange animal on the pipeline. One passage goes:

The next one that saw it, his name was LeClair.
He said 'twas no monkey, nor neither a bear,
For he came from Australia and knows it is true,
For he saw many like it, 'twas a big kangaroo.

This song, written by Jared MacLean, is dated 1948, and gives a good deal of historical backdrop to the recent kangaroo reports out of New Brunswick. The title of the song, "The Wild Cat Back on the Pipe Line," further demonstrates how the kangaroo and phantom panther accounts often merge. Along with the reported encounter between Herman Belyea and an erect panther in 1951 in New Brunswick, strange, upright, kangaroo-like animals appear to have a lengthy history in this part of Canada, separate from the eastern Bigfoot/Windigo lore.

In September, 1979, the action was back in the United States. A dark colored leaping kangaroo was seen near Delaware's tiny village of Concord. Police found a six inch lock of hair and 4 x 4½ inch tracks.

1980 was an uneventful phantom kangaroo year. Ed Barker of KGO radio, San Francisco, recently told me that a crew of his searched Golden Gate Park, probably in 1980, after some San Franciscans reported they spotted a kangaroo there. Even the 1980 accounts are phantoms.

1981 produced a bumper crop of kangaroo stories. Beginning in June, they stretched into October, from the Rockies to Appalachia.

Ray Ault saw the year's first 'roo early in June. Rancher Ault was out with his sheep near Cedar Fort, Utah County, Utah, when he was spooked by an animal jumping six feet straight in the air. "I was checking the sheep up the canyon and off to the side of them I saw something jump straight up. I thought that was a little strange. I got closer to the animal that jumped and it looked me right in the eye. Then jump . . . jump . . . jump . . . off it went," Ault said.

Ray Ault was certain it was a kangaroo, and commented, "I've seen kangaroos in the movies and on TV and there was no mistaking it. It looked like a big kangaroo rat, kind of yellowish with some dark on the ears. Who knows where the thing came from?"

The Utah rancher was frightened at first, but then began to worry about what his friends would think. "Of course they all thought I was crazy and they said I'd been hanging around in the sheep pen too long. But after I described everything they finally believed me," Ault said later.

From Tulsa, Oklahoma, a new twist was added to the usual mystery kangaroo tales. On Monday, the 31st of August 1981, a blond bearded man went into a Tulsa cafe, ordered a coffee, and told the waitress, Marilyn Hollenback, he had just hit a kangaroo. She laughed for 20 minutes, she later said. The unidentified man also told Tulsa Police officers, patrolman Ed Compos and his partner Sgt. Lynn Jones. The officers and the waitress then looked in the back of the man's truck and saw a 3½ foot kangaroo. The skeptical cafe patrons were convinced. But there is more. The man told them there were two kangaroos because he swerved and missed one. The man, his dead kangaroo and his truck drove away, never to be seen again. Officer Ed Compos told reporters, "I wish I had taken a picture of it. I told the whole squad and they are laughing about it. There was a dead kangaroo! Everyone saw it."

An Owasso, Oklahoma family came forth later in the week insisting they frequently had to dodge three foot tall kangaroos while making early morning rounds delivering newspapers.

Finally late in September 1981, something happened which frequently occurs in the midst of a mystery animal flap. Namely an exotic animal which could not realistically be confused for the reported creature is captured, and the media/officialdom uses the alien animal to "explain away" the mystery beast sighting. Just such an event occurred on the 27th of September, 1981, a Sunday, when a 25 pound Patagonian Cavy or Mara was caught. What this particular South American rodent was doing in Tulsa, Oklahoma, no one could guess, but it fits well into the pattern of such Fortean things.

Reflecting historically for a moment, we only have to go back to 1974 to find two good examples of this. During the Chicago kangaroo flap, a kinkajou was seized. This wee South American procyonid was exploited by the skeptics, and immediately utilized as a convenient candidate to debunk the widespread series of kangaroo reports. During the same year, an incredible something attacked and killed dogs, cats and rabbits in Arlington County, Virginia. This mystery beast flap was detoured by the capture of a palm civet. Exotics appearing in the middle of monster sighting waves have become a classic trait I have begun to observe more and more frequently. Not too surprising, then, that a Patagonian cavy should turn up in Oklahoma when the news began to talk of kangaroo capers.

From Oklahoma, the kangaroos next made an appearance in North Carolina. Near Asheville, home of the famed Brown Mountain Lights, a kangaroo was seen on Friday, the 9th of October 1981, near a Biltmore, North Carolina motel. Police and reporters gave chase.

"I was afraid someone might shoot it!" exclaimed motel desk clerk Jeff Greene.

The kangaroo was neither shot nor caught. It, like the scores before it, disappeared into the morning dew, and this one was not seen again around the motel.

Mystery animals take many forms. Phantom kangaroos are apparently the latest incarnation, and just as surely as I put these words to paper, there is another one out there ready to bound into our consciousness. Perhaps we should pause a moment and consider the little joke these newest members of the cryptozoological tribe may be playing on us. For, you see, the zoological genus to which the flesh and blood wallabies and kangaroos belong is termed "Macropus," and that literally means "Big Foots"!

14

BIGFEET, UFOs, and MOMO

Reports of hairy anthropoidal creatures comparable to the legendary *yetis* of Tibet are older than American history. Mark Hall and I in a study published in *The INFO Journal,* noted "A vast folklore and a belief in a race of very primitive people with revolting habits is found from northern California up into the Arctic lands themselves. This tradition covers not only the whole stretch of the Pacific coast, but much of the rugged territory to the east, even into Greenland. Generally, these subhominids are described as very tall, fully haired and retiring. Sometimes they are described as carnivorous."

The first known written account of such a creature in America dates back to 1811 and appears in the journal of one David Thompson, surveyor and trader for the Northwest Company of Canada. The *Memphis Enquirer* of May 9, 1851, reported an Arkansas sighting of the previous March, noting, "This singular creature has long been known traditionally in St. Francis, Greene and Poinsett counties, Arkansas sportsmen and hunters having described him so long as 17 years since."

Sightings of these anthropoids have continued up to the present day. The Bigfoot/Sasquatch of the American Northwest and British Columbia is only the most famous such creature, and practically every state and province in North America has logged its share of reports. In the past several years sightings have increased dramatically and probably will continue to grow. In 1970 Illinois experienced a prolonged anthropoid scare, complicated by repeated stories of large, mysterious felines allegedly seen in some of the same areas. The trend continued on into the 1970's, and during the early 1980's anthropoids appeared in many parts of mysterious America.

What has this to do with UFOs? A great deal, apparently.

Consider the following:

On the evening of May 18, 1969, a power blackout blanketed a small rural area outside Rising Sun, Indiana. For two hours the home of Mr. and Mrs. Lester Kaiser was without electricity. The Kaisers did not connect the blackout with sightings of mysterious lights along a nearby ridge which had been made during previous weeks.

The next evening, around 7:30, the Kaisers' son George was walking through the farmyard on his way to a tractor when he was startled to see a weird figure standing about 25 feet away.

"I watched it for about two minutes before it saw me," young Kaiser said later. "It stood in a fairly upright position although it was bent over about in the middle of its back, with arms about the same height as a normal human being. I'd say it was about five-eight or so and it had a very muscular structure. The head sat directly on the shoulder and the face was black, with hair that stuck out on the back of its head; it had eyes set close together and a very short forehead. It was covered with hair except for the back of the hands and the face. The hands looked like normal hands, not claws."

When Kaiser, who had been standing transfixed, finally moved, the creature made "a strange grunting-like sound," turned, leaped over a ditch, ran down the road at great speed, and disappeared. Investigators subsequently made plaster casts of footprints found in the dirt by the ditch. These casts show three toes plus a big toe.

The following evening, around 10:15, neighbor Charles Rolfing watched a glowing greenish-white object for eight minutes as it maneuvered in the sky above him.

A power blackout, an anthropoid and a UFO on three successive evenings. An interesting coincidence, at the very least.

A remarkable incident from Vader, Washington, a year and a half later adds a fourth piece to the puzzle.

On December 4, 1970, Mrs. Wallace Bowers heard her children calling for her to come outside. Stepping out the door, she was astounded to discover huge footprints in the inch-deep snow covering her yard. When she looked at them closely, she found that the tracks sank all the way through the snow to crush the gravel underneath down about an inch and a half. The prints measured fifteen inches in length and nearly six inches across. She called the sheriff's office immediately. Vader, Washington, is in the middle of Bigfoot country and Mrs. Bowers was uneasily recalling how strangely the family dog had behaved the night before.

At 7:15 a.m. three days later, on the seventh, Mrs. Bowers again heard her children calling, "Mommy, come look!" The children were at the window staring out at something moving across the sky. At first, according to their mother, it "looked like a bright star" but then it got closer and for ten minutes the observers were able to view it carefully.

The object appeared to be centered by a dome around which a larger circle seemed to be revolving. It was deeper orange in the center, with the light diffusing toward the outer edge, but with a definite bright rim.

Mrs. Bowers said it seemed slightly tilted to one side, rather like an airplane banking, and hovered briefly over the nearby Bonneville power lines. After it left the power lines, it changed from orange to a bright clear light and at one time seemed to make one last sweep closer, again turning orange. The children thought they saw a "gray shape" drop away from the UFO just before it vanished in the distance.

During the sighting Mrs. Bowers switched on the intercom in the house only to hear a peculiar "sharp" sound. "And the funny

The famous frame of Bigfoot from the 1967 Patterson film,
now owned by Rene Dahinden of British Columbia.

thing is," she told a reporter for the *Centralia-Chehalis Chronicle,* "we tried to use the intercom the night before and we got that same sharp sound."

But that was not to be all. Later in the week (the UFO sighting occurred on a Monday) Mrs. Bowers was putting a log in the living room fireplace when she saw the curtains moving in the boys' bedroom.

"All the children were in the living room with me," she said. "And all I could think of was getting them safely out of there. So I loaded them into the car and we left, but I definitely saw a shape in the bedroom as we drove away." They returned only after Mr. Bowers had come home from work.

"I feel sure that was probably a prowler," Mrs. Bowers remarked. "We've had trouble in our neighborhood and I don't think it's related to the others. But the footprints and the saucer – I don't know . . ."

Nonetheless the "prowler" was a strange one: he took nothing. He rummaged through the bedrooms but afterwards the Bowers could find nothing missing. While it is of course impossible to prove anything, I cannot help thinking of the mysterious "gray shape" the children thought they saw and then of those enigmatic entities John Keel has called "bedroom invaders," and their close kin, the madgassers and Springheel jacks (See Chapter 18).

Two other incidents briefly noted:

First Monongahela National Forest, near Marlinton, West Virginia, October 1960. W.C. "Doc" Priestley was driving along a road behind a group of friends in a bus when he encountered an eight-foot hairy ape-like "monster with long hair standing straight up." Just moments before he saw the "monster," his car engine suddenly had ceased working. "I don't know how long I sat there," Priestley said, "until the boys missed me and backed up the bus to where I was. It seemed the monster was very much afraid of the bus and dropped his hair and to my surprise, as soon as he did this, my car started to run again. I didn't tell the boys what I had seen. The thing took off when the bus started."

Priestley and the bus resumed their journey. Soon, however, the car began to sputter again. "I could see the sparks flying from under the hood of my car as if it had a very bad short. And sure enough, there beside the road stood the monster again. The points were completely burned out of my car." The bus backed up again and the creature fled into the forest.

Priestley's was only one of a number of anthropoid sightings made in West Virginia that year.

Second, Erie, Pennsylvania, July 31, 1966. Five persons in a car parked on a Presque Isle beach saw a UFO land; shortly afterwards a tall, evidently anthropoidal figure shambled up to the car in the dark, terrifying the witnesses and leaving large footprints in the sand. The incident by now is a well-known one and has been reported in *Flying Saucer Review* and in several UFO books. A few days later a large hairy biped appeared near Edinboro, a city 18 miles from Erie.

Northeastern Missouri has had its share of mysteries. "Momo," as the monster of July–August 1972 was to be called, is only the most famous.

Along River Road, which stretches north from Highway 54 along the Mississippi River and past the mouth of the Salt River, there is a longstanding tradition about a phantom man who walks across the road and vanishes. In the 1940s travellers and residents repeatedly heard what sounded like a woman's screams emanating from the general vicinity of an abandoned lime kiln. The screams always came around midnight; they were never explained.

In addition to recurring reports of fireballs or spook lights, there have been a number of mysterious deaths in the area. The strangest of all occurred during the winter of 1954, when a man and a woman were found dead in a car along the roadside. The woman sat on the passenger side and seemed to be asleep. The man lay crouched under the steering wheel completely nude, his clothing piled neatly 20 feet behind the car. The coroner listed the deaths as caused by "asphyxiation" even though the window on the driver's side was open all the way – this in ten-degree-below-zero weather.

Joan Mills and Mary Ryan were not on River Road that day in July 1971, but they were not far from it. Highway 79 is a backwoods road which runs north of Louisiana, Missouri, a place that a year later would achieve a measure of immortality in Fortean annals. Mills and Ryan had taken the highway on their way back to St. Louis because they were looking for a picturesque spot for a picnic. When they found a promising spot, they turned off on a dirt road, put out a blanket and brought out the food. "We were eating lunch," Miss Ryan recalled, "when we both wrinkled up our noses at the same time. I never smelled anything as bad in my life."

Her friend suggested they were smelling a whole family of skunks. Suddenly her jaw dropped and she pointed toward a brushy thicket behind her companion.

"I turned around and this thing was standing there in the thicket," Miss Mills said. "The weeds were pretty high and I just saw the top part of this creature. It was staring down at us."

Miss Ryan added, "It was half-ape and half-man. I've been reading up on the abominable snowman since then, and from stories and articles, you get the idea that these things are more like gorillas. This thing was not like that at all. It had hair over the body as if it was an ape. Yet, the face was definitely human. It was more like a hairy human."

"Then it made a little gurgling sound like someone trying to whistle under water," according to Miss Mills.

The hairy creature stepped out of the brush and proceeded to walk toward the young women, who dashed for their Volkswagen and locked the doors. The beast, continuing to gurgle, caressed the hood of the car and then, in a clear demonstration of intelligent behavior, tried to open the doors.

"It walked upright on two feet and its arms dangled way down," Miss Ryan stated. "The arms were partially covered with hair but the hands and the palms were hairless. We had plenty of time to see this . . ."

The women were terrified – all the more so because Miss Mills had left her car keys in her purse, which she had abandoned outside in the flight to the safety of the automobile. "Finally," said Miss Mills, "my arm hit the horn ring and the thing jumped straight in the air and moved back." She kept on beeping the horn.

"It stayed at a safe distance, then seemed to realize that the noise was not dangerous," Mary Ryan said. "It stopped where we had been eating, picked up my peanut butter sandwich, smelled it, then devoured it in one gulp. It started to pick up Joan's purse, dropped it and then disappeared back into the woods."

Joan Mills ran out of the car to retrieve her purse and returned to roar on down the highway at 90 m.p.h. Once back in St. Louis, the two women submitted a report to the Missouri State Patrol.

"We'd have difficulty proving that the experience occurred," Miss Mills wrote, "but all you have to do is go into those hills to realize that an army of those things could live there undetected."

A dramatic enough introduction to the events scheduled to erupt exactly a year later. Joan Mills and Mary Ryan were due to have their story confirmed in startling fashion.

The "Momo" (after "Missouri monster") scare began on Tuesday, July 11, 1972, at 3:30 p.m. on the outskirts of the city of Louisiana (pop. 4600). Terry Harrison, 8, and his brother Wally, 5, were playing in their yard, which sits at the foot of Marzolf Hill. The two boys had gone off by some old rabbit pens in the woods next to the Harrison property. Suddenly an older sister, Doris, who was inside, heard them scream and looked out the bathroom window. She saw something standing by a tree – "six or seven feet tall, black and hairy. It stood like a man but it didn't look like one to me."

The thing was flecked with blood, probably from the dead dog it carried under its arm. Its face could not be seen under the mass of hair covering it, and it seemed to be without a neck.

The Harrisons' dog got very sick shortly after the incident. Its eyes grew red and it vomited for hours afterwards, finally recovering after a meal of bread and milk.

That same afternoon Mrs. Clarence Lee, who lives half a block away, heard animal sounds, growling and "carrying on something terrible." Not long afterwards she talked with a farmer whose dog, a recent gift, had disappeared. He wondered if the "monster" had taken it.

Three days later, on July 14, Edgar Harrison, Terry and Doris' father and a deacon in the Pentecostal Church, conducted the

(left) Louisiana, Missouri, creature observed by Doris and Terry Harrison on July 11, 1982.

(below) A: Position when first observed by Terry (aged 8 years).
B: Position when observed by Doris and Terry from within the house.

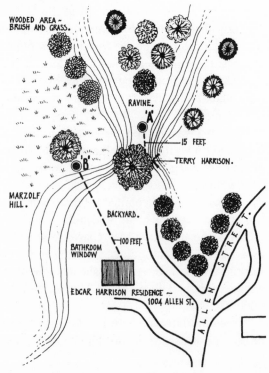

WOODED AREA ~ BRUSH AND GRASS.

RAVINE.

'A'

15 FEET.

TERRY HARRISON.

MARZOLF HILL.

BACKYARD.

BATHROOM WINDOW

100 FEET.

EDGAR HARRISON RESIDENCE ~ 1004 ALLEN ST.

ALLEN STREET.

regular Friday evening prayer meeting at his house. Around 8:30 the meeting began to break up, and as Harrison and a dozen or so of his congregation lingered, talking, they sighted two "fireballs" soaring from over Marzolf Hill and descending into the trees behind an abandoned school across the street. The objects appeared at five-minute intervals. The first was white and the second green.

About 9:15 Harrison heard ringing noises such as might be caused by the throwing of stones onto the metal water reservoir which stands at the top of the hill. The reservoir, which holds a million and a half gallons of water, is in an area where neighborhood children often play. After one especially loud ring, "I heard something that sounded like a loud growl. It got louder and louder and kept coming closer. At that time my family came running from the house. They began urging me to drive off.

"I wanted to wait and see what it was that was making this noise. My family insisted that I drive away and so I drove down Allen Street across the Town Branch."

"I stopped the car and my wife and family told the congregation, 'Here it comes!' And those forty people turned and ran down the street."

Police officers Jerry Floyd and John Whitaker went to the Harrison home, searched the residence but found nothing. That night, however, UFOs were reported in nearby New Canton, Illinois.

Late that evening Harrison, along with several others, explored Marzolf Hill and came to an old building from which a pungent, unpleasant odor was emanating. Harrison subsequently described it as "a moldy, horse smell or a strong garbage smell." This was not to be the only time he encountered the odor – in the days ahead he would find it whenever he approached an area where the strange noises seemed to be coming from.

Around 5:00 the following morning Pat Howard of Louisiana saw "a dark object" walking like a man cross the road near the hill.

On the 19th Police Chief Shelby Ward led a search through Marzolf Hill, accompanied by Harrison, State Conservation officer Gus Artus and seventeen others. Nothing was uncovered.

But the next day Richard Crowe, a reporter for Chicago's *Irish*

Times and for *Fate* magazine, and Loren Smith went up the hill
with Harrison for another look. Near the tree where Doris had
seen the monster, Crowe was to write, "There was a circular spot
in the brush where leaves and twigs had been stripped from the
branches." Further along Crowe found evidence that someone or
something had been digging in an old garbage dump, and not far
away Harrison showed him two disinterred dog graves with the
bones scattered about. Higher up the hill they came upon two
tracks some distance from each other. The first, over ten inches
long and five inches wide, appeared to be a footprint; the other,
five inches long and curved, was evidently the print of a hand.
The prints had been made in hard soil (there had been no rain
for ten days), and Crowe estimated that it would take a minimum
of two hundred pounds of pressure to create such impressions.

Harrison led Crowe to an abandoned shack which Harrison
thought might serve as a resting place for the monster. While they
were there, Harrison's dog Chubby suddenly ran away; "then,"
Crowe wrote, "we smelled an overwhelming stench that could
only be described as resembling rotten flesh or foul, stagnant
water."

"That's him, boys!" Harrison exclaimed. "He's around here
somewhere."

They shone their flashlights through the surrounding trees but
saw nothing. In the distance they could hear dogs barking furi-
ously. (While the monster was about, dogs would refuse to go up
the hill but would run up and down the street in agitated fashion.)
Within five minutes the odor had subsided. Harrison, Smith and
Crowe smelled it twice more before the night was over.

On Friday, July 21, Ellis Minor, who lives along River Road,
was sitting home alone around 10:00 or 10:30 p.m. when he heard
his bird dog start to growl. At first Minor thought the stimulus
was another dog passing through the yard, but when the dog
growled again, Minor snapped on a powerful flashlight and
stepped outside – where he saw a six-foot-tall creature with long
black hair standing erect. As soon as the light hit it, the thing
turned around and dashed across the road, past the railroad tracks
and into the woods.

For his part, Edgar Harrison by now had become obsessed with finding the solution to the monster mystery. His family had refused to come home again after the howling incident on the night of the 14th, they had taken up residence in the restaurant the family runs in the downtown section of the city. Harrison took a leave of absence from his job at the water works to devote his full attention to the monster; in the company of assorted friends, reporters and curiosity seekers he camped out at the foot of the hill for twenty-one straight nights. Evidently even the negative report of Oklahoma City's zoo director Lawrence Curtis on the plastercasts of the prints did not shake Harrison's firm conviction that something very strange was taking place. "It does not seem to be an actual print made by a natural living animal," Curtis said on the 25th. "It appears to have been made by one of those rubber-type gloves women use to wash dishes with – either that or a snow mitten."

Though he never saw the monster himself, Harrison did succeed in making two startling discoveries which add a whole new dimension to the riddle. First, he noted that the notorious odor always appeared just when searchers appeared to be on to something, leading him to believe the odor was really a stink gas used to distract the searchers' attention. On several occasions witnesses reported seeing a small glowing light which would explode leaving the stench in its wake.

On the night of the 29th Harrison and a group of college students, standing on top of the hill, heard what sounded like a shot from near the road. They rushed down the hill until they got near the road, where they all distinctly heard an old man's voice saying, "You boys stay out of these woods."

The voice seemed to come from a nearby clump of trees no more than 20 feet wide by 50 feet, but an immediate and thorough search of the small area failed to turn up anything.

A week later, on August 5th, another evidently disembodied voice spoke to Pat Howard and a friend, who were camped out in Harrison's back yard. The two were drinking coffee when someone – or something – said, "I'll take a cup of your coffee." Again a search produced no results.

Late in July mysterious three-toed tracks made by something with an oval foot appeared on the Freddie Robbins farm eight miles south of Louisiana. On August 3rd, just before dawn, Mr. and Mrs. Bill Suddarth, who farm northwest of the town, heard a high-pitched howl in their yard, grabbed flashlights and headed outside. In the middle of the garden mud they observed four tracks of some three-toed creature.

Suddarth quickly phoned Clyd Penrod, a hunting buddy, who drove over to make a plaster cast of the best print. Penrod was puzzled by the whole affair. "It was 20 to 25 feet from the tracks to anything else," he said. "I can't understand how they were made." They began nowhere and ended nowhere, and no other tracks were to be found anywhere else on the property.

The Suddarth prints were different from the ones discovered at the Robbins' farm; these second prints were narrower, longer and more perfectly formed.

Crowe's investigation uncovered a number of Louisiana UFO sightings which did not make the papers, presumably because reporters were already busy enough running down monster stories and rumors. Nonetheless, on the night of the 26th, a "fireball" alighted on top of a large cottonwood tree at the first railroad crossing on River Road. It shot out two spurts of red light and then zoomed out of sight. On the following three nights colored lights were observed along the top of the limestone bluff at the northern end of River Road. The witnesses, the Harrison and Shade families (Mrs. Shade is Mrs. Harrison's sister), thought the lights were signalling back and forth to each other. Sunday night, the 30th, at 9:00, an orange, glowing UFO with lighted "windows" landed in the thicket at the top of the bluff and sat there for five hours before it "went straight up into the air and disappeared," in Mrs. Lois Shade's words.

That week the Shades' seven-year-old son Rossie came home with two pieces of paper with writing on them. He said to his mother that "something in my head told me" to pick them up and take them with him.

The first message, written with blue ballpoint on good quality white paper, read:

Explain away my fears, answer my questions and relieve my heart. I ask, I want, I seek and I punish. The sweet, good delightful, beautiful are destroyed as I see only devastion (sic) and feel sorrow for myself & bitterness. Is askance the answer? I don't know? *I'm lost* & forlorn though I desperately try to see the good. Turning to God to music & love I feel releif (sic) & I feel guilt What is it?

And the second:

I can't realize the finality of the affair I don't realize the futility of my fondness My adoration is wanted but not myself as a whole, and as someone said "you can't have the cake & the icing too." Making the cake the good part and the icing: although not bad, the show, it's hard to see why you can't have both! Only on rare *occasions* I've been told do both come together. For the icing though by far the most romantic & sweet looking is very deceptive for it has a bitter taste if not taken in stride. Oh, but I feel like turning away the cake too. I've been advised and I've sought many answers from other mens words but the decision is mine. Yeah, you who read this, only I shall understand my writings take from me not the pleasure of my work, leave it still.

Both were written by the same hand. Mrs. Shade searched for other possible messages but found no others. Both she and her brother-in-law, Harrison, believed they were penned by either the monster or the intelligence controlling it. To an outside observer, however, the "messages" sound like nothing so much as the ravings of a deranged, rejected lover.

The Shades not long before had been subjected to an equally strange experience: The evening of the partial eclipse (July 26th) the entire family had seen "a perfect gold cross on the moon," Mrs. Shade said. "The road was lit up as bright as day from the cross." They interpreted the sight as an omen from heaven.

"Momo" was not the only monster to frighten Middle America that summer of 1972. In the extreme northwestern part of Arkansas, a state which borders Missouri from the south, the summer brought several reports of an imperfectly-observed, vaguely-described "creature." It first appeared, according to an article in Fayetteville's *Northwest Arkansas Times,* some time in January, when on two occasions Mrs. C.W. Humphrey of Springdale heard dogs barking loudly, looked out the door of her trailer home and saw a "creature" strolling on by. In the following months several other persons in the neighborhood caught a glimpse of the thing, but only in the dark, and so they did not get a good look at it. Early in July Pete Ragland shot at the creature with a .22 pistol.

Then, starting at 10:15 on the evening of July 20th, the climactic events took place. Mrs. Humphrey, her three sons and a daughter-in-law were sleeping when they were awakened by pounding on the trailer. Mrs. Humphrey quieted one of the children and went outside to find the cause. There she encountered the "biggest looking thing I ever saw" – something that alternately walked upright and crawled on all fours.

Shortly afterwards Bill Hurst, who lives just south of the Humphrey residence, sighted the creature in his garden. It was staring at him with "two great big eyes." He was sure it was some sort of animal (others had thought it might be a huge man). When he yelled at it, it took off running.

The night of September 6th Mrs. Barbara Robinson of Springdale called police to report that a prowler had peered through a bedroom window of her house. The policeman who investigated remarked that the prowler "had to be at least seven feet tall" since the window was that high and there was nothing in the immediate area on which he could have stood.

The *Peoria* (Illinois) *Journal-Star* for July 26th relates the claim of Randy Emert, 18, who reportedly saw a monster two different times over the previous two months. Emert said the thing resembled the Missouri beast in most particulars although its height was between 8 and 12 feet, and it was "kind of white and moves quick." When it appeared, it brought with it Momo's rancid odor and also seemed to scare the animals living in the woods near Cole Hollow Road. Emert said, "It lets out a long screech – like an old steam-engine whistle, only more human."

Emert asserted that a number of friends had seen either the creature or its footprints. "I'm kind of a spokesman for the group," he said. "The only one who has guts, I guess."

Mrs. Ann Kammerer of Peoria corroborated Emert's story, stating that all of her children, friends of Emert's, had seen the thing. "It sounds kind of weird," she admitted. "At first I didn't believe it, but then my daughter-in-law saw it."

According to Emert, there was an old abandoned house in the woods with large footprints all around it and a hole dug under the basement. Readers will recall the empty shack in Louisiana where Edgar Harrison thought Momo might be staying. Another turns up in the next chapter with reference to the Enfield accounts.

Two days later, on July 25th, the *Pekin* (Illinois) *Daily Times* announced that "Creve Coeur authorities said a witness reported seeing 'something big' swimming in the Illinois River." The Illinois River flows through Peoria. On the night of the 27th "two reliable citizens" told police they had seen a ten-foot-tall something that "looked like a cross between an ape and a cave man." A United Press International account describes it as having "a face with long gray U-shaped ears, a red mouth with sharp teeth, [and] thumbs with long second joints . . ." It smelled, said a witness, like a "musky wet down dog." The East Peoria Police Department reported it had received more than 200 calls about the monster the following evening.

Leroy Summers of Cairo, Illinois, saw a 10-foot, white, hairy creature standing erect near the Ohio River levee during the evening hours of July 25th. The cairo police found nothing when they came to investigate and Police Commissioner James Dale warned that henceforth anyone making a monster report would have his breath tested for alcoholic content.

A series of several "monster" reports in the Vineland, New Jersey, area apparently were caused by the sight of a 6'5" bearded swimmer as observed by a group of excitable teenagers. Or so the local police would have us believe. By the fourth week of July "monstermania" evidently had taken a grip on the consciousness of many Americans.

It is not my purpose here to analyze the many strange stories recounted above, but some brief observations might be in order.

I am confronted with three presumably separate questions: mysterious anthropoids, UFOs and, perhaps most important, psychic phenomena. Clearly, the answers do not lie in conventional flying saucer buff theorizing, and Hayden Hewes' much-publicized theory that Momo and his relatives might be experimental animals dropped by extraterrestrials from their saucer-spaceships proves only that there is much of which many ufologists are unaware.

For example, there are the many folk traditions about "Wild Men and Women." The legends remind me unmistakably of some anthropoids – up to a point – when suddenly I discover that the other half of the traditions are just as unmistakably out of the fairy-faith. Using Hewe's logic, might I then assume that anthropoids are a kind of fairies? Of course not. Not any more than I can assume, because in recent years Irish peasants have reported viewing "leprechauns" stepping out of flying saucers, that fairies are really UFO beings.

Fairies, some anthropoids, some UFOs. In a sense all are the same, each no more and no less real than the others, and all are part of a vast riddle whose answers do not wait on another planet but much, much closer to home.

15
The North American Ape

"It is difficult to determine just where a story of this sort has its beginning," *Hoosier Folklore* notes in a March 1946 article on "strange beast" legends. The journal then abitrarily picks a story from Mt. Vernon, Illinois. It is here that I, too, shall begin.

During the summer of 1941 Reverend Marsh Harpole was hunting squirrels along the Gum Creek bottom near Mt. Vernon, a small city in the southeastern county of Jefferson, when "a large animal that looked something like a baboon" leaped out of a tree and walked upright toward the startled hunter. Harpole in turn struck the creature with his barrel and then frightened it away by firing a couple of shots into the air.

In the months that followed this incident, rural families would report hearing terrifying screams at night in the wooded bottom lands along the creeks. Hunters sometimes found mysterious tracks. By early spring of the next year, after the killing of a farm dog near Bonnie, large parties of volunteers—some with rifles and shotguns, others with nets and ropes—scoured the creek bottoms. But the creature easily evaded them—perhaps because of its reputed ability to leap from 20 to 40 feet in a single bound – and in fact appeared as much as 40 or 50 miles from the location of the original sighting, in Jackson and Okaw Counties. Finally it disappeared and was not seen again – for a time, at any rate.

Hoosier Folklore concluded:

> About 25 years ago, a 'coon hunter from Hecker one night heard a strange beast screaming up ahead on Prairie du Long Creek. Hunters chased this phantom from time to time all one winter. Their dogs would get the trail, then lose it, and they would hear it screaming down the creek in the opposite direction. It was that kind of creature: you'd hear it up creek, but when you set out in that direction you'd hear it a mile down creek.

Enfield, Illinois, less than 40 miles to the southeast of Mt. Vernon, is a sleepy little village of some 800 residents which 31 years after the 1941-42 "monster" scare would play host to what must have been, if not the same animal, at least an awfully close relative.

About 9:30 p.m. on April 25, 1973, Mr. and Mrs. Henry McDaniel of Enfield returned to their home in the northwest section of town, where they were greeted by two of their children, Henry and Lil, with a fantastic story about how a "thing" had tried to get into the house by scratching on the door and the window air conditioner.

Not long afterwards the thing was back. McDaniel greeted it with a flashlight and a .22 pistol, firing at it four times as it sprinted across the yard and covered, so he would assert, 50 feet in three jumps. It ran north through brush along the L&N railroad tracks which pass near McDaniel's residence, and vanished from sight.

"It had three legs on it," McDaniel reported, " a short body, two little short arms, and two pink eyes as big as flashlights. It stood four and a half feet tall and was grayish-colored . . . When I fired that first shot, I know I hit." The creature had given out a hiss rather like a wildcat's.

McDaniel's sighting provided the impetus for a media-created "panic" which brought hordes of unwelcome visitors to Enfield, including curiosity seekers whom an angry White County Sheriff Roy Poshard, Jr., promptly jailed. Two of those incarcerated, however, Roger Tappy and Mike Mogle of Elwood, Indiana, swore they had seen a "gray monkey" moving faster than a man through some underbrush. Tappy, Mogle and two companions opened fire on the animal with a .22 rifle and three shotguns but it got away.

On Sunday, May 6th, Rick Rainbow, News Director of WWKI, Kokomo, Indiana, in the company of three friends from Kokomo, encountered the creature near an old abandoned house close to McDaniel's residence. The thing stood about five and a half feet tall and was gray and stooped over. When it saw the men, it fled. Because its back was to the observers and it was in the shadows, they were unable to get a very good look at the creature. However, as it ran, it uttered a high-pitched cry which Rainbow recorded on his tape machine.

Just hours before, at 3:00 a.m., McDaniel had seen the creature once again. Awakened by the howling of neighborhood dogs, he looked out the front door.

"I seen something moving out on the railroad track, and there it stood," he said later. "I didn't shoot at it or anything. It started on down the railroad track. It wasn't in a hurry or nothing."

About this time I visited Enfield. Near McDaniel's place I heard a high-pitched loud screech which I could not identify.

Something that walks upright, leaps incredible distances and makes eerie cries—just what have we here? Mystery Kangaroos? Apes? But of course there are no apes in southern Illinois, or anywhere else on the North American continent for that matter.

Or are there?

Stretching all through the Mississippi Valley and the valleys of its tributaries is a vast network of closed-canopy deciduous and mixed forests. The gallery forests of the Mississippi Waterweb consist mainly of oak, gum and cypress trees in the southern portions, and elm, ash and cottonwood in the northern branches. These Bottomlands, as they are technically termed, cover a good deal of the South and are more or less unexplored and ignored— most unfortunately, for hidden deep in the Bottomlands waits what could be the zoological discovery of the century.

The record begins, so far as written accounts go, back in 1869, on the western fringes of the Bottomlands, along the Osage River of Missouri and Kansas, where in the latter state's Crawford County residents reported seeing a "wild man" or "gorilla." The creature allegedly had a stooping gait, very long arms and immense hands. It walked on its hind legs but sometimes went on all fours. Then, as is often the case in our time, local opinion held that the thing was a gorilla or large orangutan which had escaped from some menagerie.

Such "gorilla" reports span over a century. The word "gorilla" crops up often in more recent accounts of beasts observed in the creek bottoms. At Hamburg, Arkansas, in 1968, the *Arkansas Gazette* noted stories of a prowling "gorilla." In 1962 farmer Owen Powell of Trimble County, Kentucky, spotted what he called a "gorilla," about six feet tall, black, walking on its hind legs, and having front legs or arms hanging down to its knees. A boy was snatched up in the back yard of his home in Kinloch, Missouri, in 1968, by what he would call a "gorilla." The screaming of his aunt and the barking of the family dog encouraged the "gorilla" to drop the boy. In Boone County, Indiana, in 1949 fishermen Charles Jones and George Coffman were chased from the banks of Sugar Creek by a brown "gorilla."

At least one Bottomlands resident believes the animal he has seen is a "chimpanzee." Over a three-year period, from 1967-70, Howard Dreeson of Calumet, Oklahoma, left out bananas and oranges for the animal, which he hoped eventually to capture.

Now what we must remember here, obviously, is that all these things are "impossible" according to virtually unanimous zoological opinion. Apes, the primates most closely related to man, exist only in Southern Asia and tropical Africa. Specifically, gibbons and orangutans are Asian and chimpanzees and gorillas are African.

But quite aside from this highly important consideration, our North American apes (which for purposes of convenience I shall call NAPES hereafter) are "impossible" for another reason: they usually walk and run upright.

It is true, as we all know, that most monkeys and all apes are *capable* of assuming an erect posture. But that is not quite the point. Monkeys such as the rhesus or the baboon stand erect only as a means of looking about or as a threatening gesture. Apes occasionally walk or run bipedally to free the hands for fighting or to carry food or offspring. Clearly, however, these are unusual situations. NAPES, though able to move quadrupedally, are *habitually* bipedal as part of their natural mode.

In general the American apes *appear* to be chimpanzees. Ape-like, hairy and tailless, they range in height from four to six feet, though now and then some very scared person reports a seven-footer. ("A creature covered with long hair always looks bigger than it really is," zoologist Bernard Heuvelmans writes in *Personality* [South Africa, June 5, 1969] in reference to reports of seven-foot-tall creatures with 10-inch footprints.) The hair color seems to be brown to black, but there are reports of gray or white individuals. This color variation in pelage may be the result of age differences. Certainly a 1971 report from Broward County, Florida, that a small brown-black "skunk ape" (so called because of its foul smell) and a larger gray one with splotches and sores all over it were seen in each other's company suggests this. The foul odor (sometimes called "musky") is a fairly common feature of NAPE reports. The eyes are often said to be green. The creatures seem most often to be nocturnal in their activity and to possess tremendous abilities to leap great distances.

NAPES appear so radically out of place that those rare individuals who encounter them never forget the experience. Sometimes sightings even leave a lasting impression on the geography of an area.

One such place is in Allen County, Kentucky, where, according to folklorist Harold Holland:

> The name "Monkey Cave Hollow" apparently was given to one locality about four miles northeast of [Scottsville, Kentucky] by the earliest settlers for the simple reason a forested valley was inhabited by a tribe of what the pioneers identified as some sort of monkeys. These creatures foraged in the woods and took refuge in small caves.

Holland mentions that he once talked with an old-timer who when a boy of seven or eight

> saw the carcass of the last "monkey." He stated that a hunter came by his father's house and displayed the dead beast. He said that he could not recall exactly what it looked like (after all, it had been 80 years or thereabouts) but the creature had hands and feet "like a person," was about the same size as he himself was, had no tail and was covered with brown hair.

Travelling circuses and carnivals play an important role in the story of the North American ape. The "gorilla sideshows" of the circus and carnival lots are, says former circus man and animal trainer Robert Barbour Johnson, all populated by old chimpanzees. Inevitably the question arises: Are escaped old chimps the source of the ape population in America's Bottomlands? The answer very probably is no, for reasons I shall explain later. What in fact may be happening is the reverse: Perhaps in past days clever circus managers might have added to their exhibits members of this American species and claimed they were theirs all along!

Take, for example, an incident from the Hannibal, Missouri, region. Mainland residents one day around the turn of the century noticed a mysterious animal moving about on a large wooded island in the Mississippi River near that city and notified the sheriff, who subsequently saw it and thought it might be a hyena, except that it was eating grass. When the sheriff and others managed to capture it, it turned out to be "the man from Borneo," allegedly escaped from a circus. Said circus was most happy to get him "back."

Fine. Unfortunately we must once again complicate things by pointing out that the orangutan of Borneo and Sumatra is constitutionally incapable of swimming the Mississippi (or any other) River, while our primate friends from the Bottomlands seem to be able to do so without inordinate difficulty.

Which leads us to another more complex capture report:

On August 16, 1926, according to the *New York Times* of the next day, one J. Blanchard, a watchman at the New Jersey Power and Light Company, at Booton, caught an ape by knocking it off a power line with a pole. A *Times* story on August 18th reports some apparently contradictory details: it alleges that a chimpanzee was recovered at Booton after it escaped from a travelling zoo at Rockaway. The chimp, the article says, slipped from its cage and *swam* the Rockaway River. An attendant pursued it into a grove of trees but it evaded him. On August 17th Francis Murphy, proprietor of the zoo, found the animal in the woods, called to it and received it into his open arms.

Is this a case of two different apes being caught in the space of as many days near Booton, New Jersey? What are we to surmise from the travelling zoo's claim that their chimpanzee escaped by *swimming* the Rockaway River? Was this "swimming chimpanzee" instead one of the North American variety? What are we to deduce from such reports of swimming "chimpanzees" and island-stranded "orangutans"?

Most primates swim remarkably well, but authorities agree that anthropoid apes avoid water and cannot swim. For example:

The famous gorilla Mokoko of the Bronx Zoo, the first male of its species ever to reach sexual maturity in captivity, was tragically drowned in a waterfilled barrier in 1951. (Heini Hediger, *Man and Animal in the Zoo.)*

A chimpanzee drowned quickly in the moat of the new apehouse of the Antwerp Zoo, and a gibbon in the London Zoo drowned even in very shallow water at the bottom of its large cage. (Adolph H. Schultz, *The Life of the Primates.)*

During the summer that we had Bobby and the little female chimpanzee Jenera on an island in the lake in front of the house of Emory's president, they would go into the water, on many occasions up about waist high, but they never made any attempt to go any deeper or to swim away from the island. (Geoffrey H. Bourne, *The Ape People.)*

Cyclone fencing was placed in the moat (at the Chimpanzee Consortium at Holloman Air Force Base in New Mexico) as a protective device to prevent drownings . . . The drowning of a female chimpanzee in 1966 might have been prevented if the fence had extended to the point where she slipped into the moat. (Wendell and Carolyn Wilson, Aeromedical Research Laboratory, New Mexico.)

Only in one rather vague case has any evidence for swimming ability among known apes been suggested. Vernon Reynolds, the British primatologist, examined that case, writing in *The Apes*:

A report from Spanish Guinea states that four chimpanzees were observed swimming across the 60 to 65-meter-wide Benito River. They made swimming motions like dogs . . . I am inclined to think that the "chimpanzees" seen swimming in the above report were some other species. The general response of chimpanzees is universally agreed to be one of avoidance and even fear. I have myself on two occasions helped to pull chimpanzees out of a water-filled moat in which they were quite clearly drowning, and I am convinced they cannot swim.

Plainly, then, known species of apes do not swim. But from all indications, NAPES do – their range up and down the Mississippi Waterweb implies water dispersal as well as the use of the gallery forests bordering the river systems. Even a cursory examination of NAPE accounts, taking place in locations with such revealing names as Gum Creek (Illinois), Sugar Creek (Indiana), Walnut Creek (Alabama) and the Anclote River (Florida), reveals a high percentage of sightings along the creek bottoms of rural America. The documentary movie about Fouke, Arkansas's, ape-like "monster" *The Legend of Boggy Creek*, notes several times that "he always travels the creeks."

The sighting of a swimming ape by Charles Buchanan serves as an illustration. On November 7, 1969, Buchanan, camped out on the shore of Lake Worth, Texas, awoke about 2:00 a.m. to find a hairy creature that looked "like a cross between a human being and a gorilla or an ape" towering above him. Buchanan had been sleeping in the bed of his pickup truck when the thing had suddenly jerked him to the ground, sleeping bag and all. Gagging from the stench of the beast, the camper did the only thing he could think of: he grabbed for a bag of leftover chicken and shoved it into the long-armed beast's face. It took the sack in its mouth, made some gutteral sounds and then loped off through the trees, splashed in the water and began swimming with powerful strokes toward Greer Island.

Bears are good swimmers and no doubt some few accounts of the North American ape may arise from misidentifications of bears. But from the overall descriptions, as well as the evidence of the footprints, there are some powerful reasons to question the across-the-board bear explanations sometimes used in attempts to debunk appearances of wild apes in America.

The evidence of footprints, more than anything else right now, strongly supports the notion that an undiscovered species of apes exists on our continent.

All primates are pentadactyl – five-toed. Among the higher primates, hominids (men) and pongids (apes) have a foot that is plantigrade. Both hominids and ursids (bears) leave behind a footprint clearly showing the foot is plantigrade and has an apposable big toe. One of the great differences between the foot (and thus the footprints) of men and apes is the existence in humans of a great toe that lies alongside and points in the same direction as the other toes. Among the apes the first or great toe is opposed to the other toes. Because of this easily discernible feature in the track of a pongid, the record of an ape in America is quite certain.

As far back as pre–Columbian times, America's native inhabitants were apparently noting appearances of tracks of this type. The Indians often made stone carvings of items common in their environment, and perhaps an ape track was one such item. According to John W. Allen's *Legends and Lore of Southern Illinois,* in Jackson County there are "carvings . . . in the bed of Rock Creek . . . Here are *the footprints with the great toes turned at right angles,* arms, hands, face profiles, snakes lizards, and chiseled trenches." (Author's emphasis.)

Curiously, as our survey of footprints moves into historic times, we again find ourselves in southern Illinois. In 1942, as already mentioned, strange footprints were found in Jefferson County while some persons were reporting upright apes or "baboons." These tracks allegedly resembled those of a raccoon – but were four times as large.

Increasing the track of a raccoon by four would give us a track measuring from 10 to 12 inches in length. So this track compares favorably in size and general shape to that of the wild apes in America. The similarity of the anthropoid ape track to that of a raccoon may not be apparent at first glance, but a likeness does exist.

Evidence for the North American Ape takes many forms, but
possibly the best is the evidence of footprints. This track,
which I found in Decatur, Illinois, in 1962, is typical of the
ape-like prints being left by an undiscovered creature
throughout the Bottomlands of America.

In the spring of 1962 I came upon an ape-like footprint in a dry creek bed near Decatur, Illinois. The print was about 10 inches long, with a clearly visible large opposed toe sticking out to the right of a left foot impression. About 13 inches in front of this print was a partial footprint. The complete track is very much like ones found throughout the South. This Illinois track seems to record the most northern of the NAPES' recent appearance.

Moving from the fringes of the apes' range, let us consider the footprint evidence from the deep South.

An ape observed near Clanton, Alabama, in 1960* left a track, preserved in a cement cast, which was "about the size of a person's foot but looking more like a hand," according to comments made to me by *Clanton Union-Banner* editor T.E. Wyatt. Of course, the pongid foot does resemble a hominid hand more than a hominid foot.

Farther south, in Florida, the ichnological finds are overwhelming. In 1965, following the late-night visit of a stooping figure in Hernando County, investigators discovered rounded tracks with "one big toe stuck out to the side like a thumb on the hand."

In 1971 a "skunk ape" prowled through the Big Cypress Swamp, producing footprints from which casts were made. These casts show a footprint about 9 inches in length, with an opposed great toe. Arguing most convincingly for the pongid nature of the "skunk ape," however, is the existence of *knuckle* prints.

Broward County (Florida) Rabies Control Officer Henry Ring, investigating sightings of two apes by the residents of the King's Manor Estates Trailer Court during August 1971, reported that he had "found nothing but a bunch of strange tracks, like someone was walking around on his knuckles." What Ring discovered was

---

* An interesting facet of this report is witnesses' comparing the sound this animal was making to that of an elephant. A tape of the Enfield, Illinois, creature's cry reminds me of the short trumpeting of an elephant, or the howling of the siamang. Commenting on the Alabama case, Ivan T. Sanderson remarks "that a herd of elephants in a forest can sound exactly like a troop of chimps having a ball."

hardly "nothing" – to the contrary, it was striking evidence of the presence of anthropoid apes in Florida. Whereas most quadrupedal mammals, as well as monkeys, "walk" on the flats of the hands, the gorilla, chimpanzee and orangutan use the backs of the fingers to "knuckle-walk." Officer Ring's finding of knuckle prints is a vital clue in any effort to piece together the NAPE puzzle.

Handprints resembling those of a gorilla-like man or man-like gorilla are also part of the puzzle. Near El Reno, Oklahoma, in December 1970, something which moved on all fours raided a chicken coop, leaving a handprint on the door. The door and the 7"x5" handprint were taken to Lawrence Curtis, Director of the Oklahoma City Zoo, for an opinion. Curtis was frankly baffled. He found the thumb of the print quite unusual – it was crooked as if deformed or injured. Curtis thought it was from a primate but was uncertain of what kind. (Howard Dreson, it will be re-called, said he had fed a "chimpanzee" in the same area from 1967 to 1970.)

So what kind of primates do we have living in the wilds of North America? Are these Bottomlands apes circus-carnival-zoo escapees?

Ten years ago, I conducted a survey of all information relating to feral or introduced primates in the United States and Canada. I made contact with all continental state fish and game agencies, all primate research centers, various humane societies and selected zoological garden and wildlife authorities. From this research some brief observations can be made with relationship to the question of apes in America and their origin.

Some pet monkeys do escape and usually are recaptured, or die in the wild. A few have gone entirely feral. Examples from In-diana, where rhesus lived for 10 years in the wild, or from Nova Scotia, where Ralph Marr shot at a monkey and later collected hair, skin and blood samples, illustrate the point that scattered escapees are successful. However, breeding feral populations are rare. To date there are "officially" only three such feral monkey populations of importance to the NAPE question. One is a squirrel monkey group near Coral Gables/Miami, Florida. Another collection of about two hundred rhesus monkeys lives along the Silver River near Ocala, Florida. In Texas, a recently discovered band of baboons has been sighted along the Trinity River.

All of the known feral monkey populations in Florida and Texas are the result of probable introductions by human beings within the last fifty years. Other evidence of such introductions and their resulting feral populations may be found in the Ozarks, Appalachia and perhaps Mississippi.

It is clear, though, that these feral monkeys are not the large apes seen in the Bottomlands. What then of anthropoid ape escapees?

Escapes of higher primates from zoological gardens are very rare. In October, 1970 one gorilla and five chimpanzees escaped from the Los Angeles Zoo but were recaptured within a very few minutes with tranquilizer guns. Marvin Jones, the foremost compiler of zoological park longevity records, observes, "Few zoos have had escapes that I know of, and having looked close at many zoo files, I am sure that they would have been noted. In most cases these were caught."

The deliberate releasing of four chimpanzees on the uninhabited Bear Island off the coast of Georgia is apparently the first attempt at establishing a free-ranging North American chimpanzee population.

But a rather free-ranging, swimming, nocturnal ape already exists in many parts of the southern United States. Historic America's awareness of the apes goes back to at least 1869. Prehistorically, the American Indians seem to have known it also, giving it in the name *memegwicio* in their folk tales. If we consider only the historical written records, however, the appearance of the ape in these sources may be significant in the context of their possible introduction from Africa.

While slave-trading between Africa and the United States began in the early 1600s, it did not become routine until after the invention of the cotton gin in the 1790s. It is possible that some chimpanzees, or a subspecies, might have been brought over then, since slave ship captains often kept chimps as pets. In fact, the

Ufiti

first chimpanzee to reach a zoo in England was brought to Bristol in the autumn of 1834 by a Captain Wood, who had picked it up on the Gambia Coast.

But for many reasons, particularly the behavioral differences I have described, I think it unlikely that the source of the American apes might have been chimpanzees or gorillas brought over on slave ships.

Much confusion, however, does exist in Africa about just what kinds of apes live there. In 1967, for example, the Basle zoo received an alleged Koolokamba or gorilla-like chimpanzee (*Pan troglodytes koolokamba*) which turned out to be a red-backed female gorilla. The problem of "Ufiti" is also worth noting.

"Ufiti" was first seen near Lake Nyasa in 1959. The Nyasaland Information Department recounts that first sighting in melodramatic fashion: "The first white man to see the strange monster opened fire with a revolver as it slunk eerily along the road in the misty moonlight." When Ufiti was finally photographed, experts could see that she was a chimpanzee, though a very out-of-place one. But then she was no typical chimpanzee: she was almost six feet tall and had a gray lumbar saddle which is found among mature male gorillas, but unknown (until Ufiti) in chimpanzees. Ufiti finally was captured and sent to the Chester Zoo in March 1964; there she lived for a little over a month before her deteriorating health caused her to be euthenised.

Besides events like the Ufiti affair, there is some slight evidence that something like the NAPES have been reported in Africa. Animal collector Charles Cordier has found a footprint which compares favorably with ones found in southern America.

My own belief is that a wide-ranging, supposedly prehistoric subfamily of the pongids, the Dryopithecinae, which paleontologists tell us existed in Africa, China and Europe, may be the source of the giant apes of Africa and the Bottomlands of the United States. This idea, I realize, is heretical enough, since the generalized pongids of the Dryopithecinae are supposed to have lived only from the Miocene to Pleistocene times.

The obvious immediate objection is that the geological evidence for New World monkeys is "very scanty," in Le Gros Clark's words,

and is represented by three genera from the Miocene in Columbia and Patagonia. But if the Dryopithecinae subfamily members
appeared in the Nearctic in Recent times in conjunction with the
appearance of prehistoric man, the lack of fossil finds is not startling. In addition to the probably low numbers of specimens, the
Bottomlands of the Nearctic are likely just as unfossiliferous as
the forests of South America.

The dryopithecines seem to be the perfect candidates to explain
the North American apes. Napier writes that they were "a highly
successful family living in both temperate and subtropical
woodlands." Theodosius Dobzhansky, remarks that it is not surprising that fossil apes have been found in Europe "since that continent, together with North America, enjoyed warm temperate to
tropical climates during the Tertiary period."

Even the name *Dryopithecus* furnishes a clue. It means "oak ape,"
and was so called, Alfred Sherwood Romer wrote in *Man and the
Vertebrates*, "because of the presence of oak leaves in the deposits
from which the first remains of this form were obtained."

The occurrence of the "oak apes" in North American swampy
habitats and temperate Bottomland hollows seems beyond question. I do not know whether they are recent arrivals brought over
from Africa or Pleistocene immigrants from Asia. But however
they got here, they are here – wild apes which have adapted to
the American environment, habitually bipedal, nocturnal and able
to swim, and now await the attention of zoologists. They are
merely another important part of the countryside's unusual
wildlife to be found in Mysterious America.

16
The Jersey Devil

One January night in 1909, E. P. Weeden of the Trenton, New Jersey City Council bolted upright in bed when he heard someone trying to break down his door—a most unusual "someone," apparently, because Weeden also heard distinctly the sound of flapping wings.

Councilman Weeden rushed to his second-floor window and looked outside. He did not see the intruder, but the sight that greeted his eyes chilled him far more than the icy temperature ever could have: In the snow on the roof of his house something had left a line of tracks. And whatever that "something" was, it had hoofs.

On the same night "it" left hoofprints in the snow at the State Arsenal in Trenton. And shortly afterwards John Hartman of Centre Street caught a full view of it as it circled his yard and then vanished into the night. Trenton residents living near the Delaware River were shaken by loud screeching sounds, like the cries of a giant cat, and stayed in their homes that night too frightened to venture out.

"It" reappeared in Bristol during the early morning hours of January 17th. The first person to observe it, a police officer named

Major Recorded Sightings of the Jersey Devil

(courtesy of Middle Atlantic Press)

Sackville, was patrolling along Buckley Street around 2:00 a.m. Officer Sackville was alerted by the barking of dogs in the neighborhood that something was amiss. Feeling increasingly uneasy, he reached the race bridge when a sudden movement from the path below caught his eye. Carefully he turned his head. When he saw it, he was so stunned that for a moment he could not move.

Gathering his wits, Sackville drew his revolver and plunged toward "it." It let out an eerie cry and hopped rapidly away, with the officer in hot pursuit. Suddenly it raised its wings and flew above the path, and Sackville, afraid that it would get away, fired his gun. He missed. By the time he got off a second shot, the thing was gone.

The second witness was Bristol postmaster E. W. Minster, who the next day told this story to reporters:

"I awoke about two o'clock in the morning . . . and finding myself unable to sleep, I arose and wet my head with cold water as a cure for insomnia.

"As I got up I heard an eerie, almost supernatural sound from the direction of the river . . . I looked out upon the Delaware and saw flying diagonally across what appeared to be a large crane but which was emitting a glow like a firefly.

"Its head resembled that of a ram, with curled horns, and its long thin neck was thrust forward in flight. It had long thin wings and short legs, the front legs shorter than the hind. Again, it uttered its mournful and awful call—a combination of a squawk and a whistle, the beginning very high and piercing and ending very low and hoarse. . . ."

John McOwen, a liquor dealer who lived on Bath Street with the back of his house facing the Delaware Division Canal, heard his infant daughter crying and went into her room to see what was wrong. It was about 2:00 a.m. A "strange noise" brought him to the window, which overlooked the canal.

"It sounded like the scratching of a phonograph before the music begins," he said later, "and yet it also had something of a whistle to it. You know how the factory whistle sounds? Well, it was something like that. I looked from the window and was astonished to see a large creature standing on the banks of the canal. It looked something like an eagle . . . and it hopped along the tow path."

The next day Mrs. Thomas Holland discovered hoofmarks in her snow-covered yard, as did other residents of Buckley and Bath Streets.

And Trenton and Bristol were not the only places where the creature was seen. At Camden twelve men at work in the Hilltown clay bank took one glance at the thing as it descended toward them, and then, as one account wryly notes, they "were off to set an unofficial record for the three-mile run in working clothes."

Other New Jersey towns and cities reporting visitations were Wycombe, Swedesboro, Huffville, Mantua, Woodbury, Mount Ephraim, Haddonfield and Mount Holly. Said a contemporary news story, "Hoofprints have been noticed in hundreds of places over a strip of country at least 16 miles long and three miles wide."

What was it? It was the "Jersey Devil." Whatever the Jersey Devil is.

The Jersey Devil, sometimes called the Leeds Devil, has been the state's "official demon" since the 1930s, but long before that a great body of folklore had grown up around the elusive beast. Some versions of the legend—folklorists claim there are over thirty variants of the tale in circulation—list the creature's alleged birth as having taken place in 1887. However, the Gloucester Historical Society has traced the tale back as far as 1790, and there is every reason to believe it was around before then.

The most frequently related account of the Devil's origins goes like this:

In 1735 a Mrs. Leeds of Estellville, N.J., upon finding she was pregnant for the thirteenth time and less than exhilarated about it, snorted that if she was going to have another child it might just as well be a devil—and it was. It was born with an animal's head, a bird's body, and cloven hoofs instead of feet. Cursing its mother (it could speak at birth) it promptly flew up the chimney and took up residence in the swamps and pine barrens of southern New Jersey, where it has lived ever since.

(American folklore is filled with similar stories about a pregnant mother's careless words backfiring on her. As late as 1908 a tale circulating through rural Alabama had it that a Birmingham baby was born "with horns like a devil." During her pregnancy the mother had remarked, "I'd as soon have a devil in the house as a baby!")

Over the years the story, like all good stories, grew in the telling. Eventually the Devil was held responsible for every major calamity that befell the state, and some people even maintained that its appearance presaged the coming of war. On a less cosmic scale it was said that its breath could sour milk, kill fish and dry up cornfields. The late Rev. Henry Carlton Beck recounted another part of the myth in his *Jersey Genesis*:

> Accompanied, as it usually is, by the howling of dogs and the hooting of owls, there can be no surer forerunner of disaster. Where the barrens line the shore it flits from one desolate grass-grown dune to another and is especially watchful upon those wild heights when coasting schooners, driving their prows into the sand, pound to splinters upon the bars and distribute upon the waves their freight of good and human lives.
>
> Upon such occasions Leeds' Devil is seen in the companionship of a beautiful golden-haired woman in white, or yet of some fierce-eyed, cutlass-bearing disembodied spirit of a buccaneer whose galleon, centuries ago, was wrecked upon the shore of Cape May County.

How seriously anyone took these yarns is hard to say, though some Jerseyites must have at least half-believed them. Most people probably treasured the story for its quaint and amusing character and kept it alive chiefly as a story to entertain their children with on Halloween.

Certainly Jersey citizens and others as well have had their share of fun with the beastie. In 1906 huckster Norman Jefferies, publicity manager for C. A. Brandenburgh's Arch Street Museum in Philadelphia, came upon an old book which mentioned Mrs. Leeds' curious offspring, and it gave him an idea. With attendance at his shows declining, Jefferies had been on the lookout for a stunt to bring the crowds back. Unfortunately for him, the Philadelphia papers, having been taken in by earlier Jefferies tricks, were not about to offer him any cooperation. So he planted this story in a South Jersey small-town weekly:

> The "Jersey Devil," which has not been seen in these parts for nearly a hundred years, has again put in its appearance. Mrs. J. H. Hopkins, wife of a worthy farmer of our county, distinctly saw the creature near the barn on Saturday last and afterwards examined its tracks in the snow.

The report created a sensation. All over the state men and women started glancing over their shoulders and bolting doors and windows. While always taking care publicly to profess skepticism, Jerseyites steadfastly refused to take any chances. What if the monster was real after all? Had not an "expert" from the Smithsonian Institution said that it "bore out his long cherished theory that there still existed in hidden caverns and caves, deep in the interior of the earth, survivors of those prehistoric animals and fossilized remains . . ."? The expert was sure the Devil was a pterodactyl.

Shortly thereafter the animal was captured by a group of farmers. After making sure every paper around got the news, Jefferies took the "Devil" with him to Philadelphia and placed it on exhibition in the Arch Street Museum. The crowds, huge and mostly uncritical, gazed in wonder at the thing – which was actually a kangaroo with bronze wings fastened to its back and green stripes painted the length of its body.

Jefferies confessed in 1929 that he had bought the animal from a dealer in Buffalo, N.Y. and let it loose in a wooded area of South Jersey where it was certain to be caught without difficulty.

The *Woodbury Daily Times* got into the act, too, reporting in its December 15, 1925, issue that farmer "William Hyman" had killed an unknown animal after it raided his chicken coop. "Hyman describes the beast," the paper said, "as being as big as a grown Airedale with black fur resembling Astrakhan; having a kangaroo-fashioned hop; forequarters higher than its rear, which were always crouched; and hind feet of four webbed toes."

Fine, except that "William Hyman" never existed. And neither, needless to say, did his specimen of the Jersey Devil.

But is there more to the Jersey Devil than mere folklore and fabrication? The question is certainly heretical enough. Even Charles Fort drew the line here, writing in *Lo!* that "though I should not like to be so dogmatic as to say there are no 'Jersey Devils,' I have had no encouragement investigating them." But Fort's knowledge of the phenomenon seems to have been confined to the Jefferies and "Hyman" hoaxes and evidently he was unread in the vast literature of the subject.

The problem is complicated by the virtually absolute refusal of journalists to take the Devil at all seriously, even though some commentators have admitted rather uneasily that there are portions of the legend that are, well, odd. Like, for example, the sterling characters of some of those individuals who insist they saw a mysterious thing with wings hopping and/or flying through the pine barrens. Like the persistent discoveries of unusual tracks and the unexplained disappearances of livestock. Like the haunting cries sometimes heard emanating from the woods. But reporters, perhaps understandably, would rather have the Devil be a charming, harmless piece of Halloween lore than an annoying puzzle for which there may be no ready answers. As a consequence, their treatment of even apparently authentic reports of unknown animals in New Jersey is almost invariably flippant, dotted with references to such obvious nonsense as Mrs. Leeds' baby, and ultimately confusing to anyone who endeavors to separate fact from fiction.

If the Jersey Devil is no more than a creation of the folk imagination, then what was it that a city councilman, a policeman, a postmaster and many other reputable people encountered in January 1909? What made the tracks on Weeden's roof and all along the Delaware River?

Perhaps it was the same thing Mrs. Amanda Sutts saw on her family's farm in 1900. She recalled the incident for the *Trenton Evening Times* sixty years later, still convinced that the creature was the Jersey Devil. At the time of the incident she was ten years old and living on a farm near Mays Landing in the heart of Devil country.

"We heard a scream near the barn one night and ran out of our house," she said. "We saw this thing that looked like a kangaroo. It wasn't such a great big animal – it was about the size of a small calf and weighed about 150 pounds. But the noise it made is what scared us. It sounded like a woman screaming in an awful lot of agony."

Mrs. Sutts said that was the only time she ever actually viewed the creature, but her family often heard it and would follow its tracks, which were 8 to 10 feet apart and led to a large cedar swamp at the rear of the farm. Her father had seen the thing once before, when he was sixteen years old.

"When the horses heard the Devil scream," she observed, "they would carry on so you'd think they were going to tear the barn down. You could hear the Devil scream a long way off when the horses would quiet down.

"People may say there's nothing to it but I know darned well there is. Some might say I'm an old crank but when you know a thing you know it."

The first persons to note the presence of a peculiar animal in the area were the Indians, who said it originally appeared in what is now Bucks County (where many alleged sightings of the Devil have been made in recent years), near the boundary line of Philadelphia. In fact they named the creek there *Popuessing,* meaning "place of the dragon." In 1677 Swedish explorers examined some weird footprints in the rocks near the same creek and re-named it "Drake Kill," which also refers to the dragon.

The legend claims that by the mid-1700s the Devil had become such a nuisance that a clergyman was called in to exorcise it. A century later, in 1840, a strange animal went on a rampage, slaughtering livestock, attempting to seize children and generally terrorizing the area. In the course of one foray it supposedly killed two large dogs, three geese, four cats and thirty-one ducks. (If that sounds incredible to you, consider the case of an enigmatic marauder that destroyed *51 sheep* in a single night on a farm near Guildford, England, in March 1906.)

During the winter of 1873-74 the Devil was seen prowling in the vicinity of Bridgeton; in 1894-95 a trail of unidentifiable footprints around Leeds Point excited speculation that the beastie had returned to the place of its birth. Near Vincentown in 1899 farmers reported losing livestock to some kind of mystery animal.

After the 1909 flap the Devil went back into hiding and did not reappear until June 1926, when two 10-year-old boys in West Orange reportedly saw what news accounts refer to vaguely as a "flying lion." A large posse scoured the area in search of the creature but found nothing.

About August 1st of the following year huckleberry pickers near Bridgeport startled an animal resting in a cedar swamp and chased it until it outdistanced them, hooting angrily all the while. A *New York Times* dispatch describes the animal "as large and as speedy as a fox and with four legs, but also having feathers and a cry that is partly bark and partly the hoot of an owl."

Almost exactly a year later berry pickers at Mays Landing and Leeds Point allegedly encountered a similar creature. Another witness was Mrs. William Sutton, a farmer's wife, who said she saw it in her cornfield. An unidentified man flagged down a car driven by Charles Mathis and pleaded to be taken from the scene of his meeting with "a horrible monster." A thirteen-year-old boy said he had seen the Devil gazing at him through his bedroom window.

A badly shaken John McCandless reported a terrifying experience which he said occurred on January 21, 1932, while he was passing through an area five miles north of Dowington, Pa. Hearing a moaning sound in the brush, McCandless spotted "a hideous form, half-man, half-beast, on all fours and covered with dirt or hair." After others told of seeing the figure, McCandless and a group of friends armed with rifles and shotguns plowed through the trees and fields every day for a week, but by this time the thing had disappeared.

In 1935 Philip Smith, "a sober gentleman of honest reputation," claimed he saw the Devil walking down a Woodstown street and the next year, following an outbreak of alleged sightings, a posse of farmers searched neighboring forests and swamps without success.

It may be no more than a part of the legend that has the Devil popping up on December 7, 1941, but perhaps I should take a bit more seriously a report of its appearance in Mount Holly in 1948. In 1949 a "green male monster" supposedly was seen at Somerville; unfortunately that is the extent of my information. In 1952 something killed large numbers of chickens on Atlantic County farms. Since Atlantic County is in Devil territory, locals held the beast responsible.

On October 31, 1957, state newspapers asked in the headlines of front page stories: "Is Jersey's 'Devil' Dead? Skeleton Baffles Experts." Said the stories, "The Jersey Devil may have met his final end this summer in the depths of the Wharton Tract down in the pine barrens of central South Jersey. Foresters and other members of the New Jersey Department of Conservation and Economic Development at work on the state-owned property report the finding of a partial skeleton, half-bird and half-beast, and impossible of conventional identifications." It was a Halloween gag, of course.

But five students from the Spring Garden Institute at Philadelphia were not amused when "unearthly screams" kept them awake one night in 1960 as they camped near Lake Atsion in Burlington County, N.J. "We were pretty much on edge," said Bert Schwed, one of the group, "after finding four large tracks earlier in the underbrush near our camp. They were about 11 inches long and they looked something like a large bird print with the heel dug in and the toes spread out."

Over in Dorothy, near Mays Landing, in October of the same year, residents complained to Game Warden Joseph Gallo that they were hearing weird cries in the night and discovering unusual tracks in the ground in the morning. After a brief investigation Gallo and State Game Trapper Carlton Adams concluded the tracks were caused by a large hopping rabbit whose feet touched the ground together to form one print and the noises were made by owls. Not terribly impressed by this official conclusion, locals said they know an owl's screech when they heard it.

Shortly afterwards the Broadway Improvement Association of Camden offered a $10,000 reward to anyone who could catch the Devil alive. "They do not seem worried about the prospect of having to pay up," the *Trenton Times* noted sardonically.

Toward dusk on May 21, 1966, a creature "at least seven feet tall" ambled through the Morristown, N.J., National Historical Park and left in its wake four hysterical witnesses who had viewed it from a parked car. They said the creature was "faceless," covered with long black hair, and had scaly skin. It had broad shoulders and walked on two legs with stiff, rocking movement.

The four drove to the park entrance and stopped approaching cars to warn people that a "monster" lurked inside. Raymond Todd, one of the witnesses, caught a ride with a young lady who took him to the Municipal Hall in Morristown, where he blurted out his story to the police.

Oddly enough, the girl had seen a similar entity a year before. She told police that she and several friends had been parked one night in the park when a huge, broad-shouldered something had loomed up in their rear window and thumped on the back of the car. Her mother had asked her not to report the incident, she said.

Is there a Jersey Devil?

Well, there is *something*. Or perhaps a number of somethings. Underneath all the myth, all the nonsense, all the fabrication, is a small core of truth out of which the legends have grown. There are just too many loose ends – like tracks and sightings by reliable witnesses – that can no longer be glossed over.

But it is difficult to move beyond these simple (and by now, fairly obvious) conclusions. To start with, nothing *precisely* like a "Jersey Devil" has ever been reported elsewhere. But then the same is true of those entities called "Mothman," whose activities seem confined generally to certain southeastern states.

Mothman and the Jersey Devil share other traits as well. For one thing both supposedly possess wings; they also sometimes "glow" or "flicker" in the dark. The differences, however, are greater. Witnesses have reported three Mothman types; one a winged quasi-humanoid, another an enormous bird, and the last a mechanical contrivance. None bears much resemblance to the ram-headed Jersey Devil. Moreover, Mothman glides through the air with the greatest of ease; the Devil on the other hand flies clumsily and close to ground level and can negotiate only short distances at a time.

Of course, there is no shortage of winged weirdies of all sizes and varieties around the world, so we should not hold the Devil's distinctive shape against the poor fellow. But just what *is* that distinctive shape?

Assuming for the moment the Devil exists at all, the creature probably most resembles what was observed in January 1909. At any rate these reports are more detailed than most others and for once the press treated them with reasonable objectivity.

Perhaps *several* Jersey Devils haunt the pine barrens region, including "flying lions" and "kangaroos," or in any case creatures which looked like that to flustered individuals seeing them in less than ideal light conditions. Most of the folklore, though, clearly takes its inspiration from alleged run-ins with a beastie of the 1909 variety.

Not everything that gets shoved under the "Jersey Devil" banner really belongs there. Like other states, New Jersey harbors more than one mystery animal, but whenever one appears, inevitably it gets hailed, usually for purposes of ridicule, as the latest manifestation of the Devil and so joins the great body of myth, legend and lore.

The Morristown creature might be more closely related to Bigfoot than to the Devil, but its lack of facial features and its scaly skin are not characteristic of Bigfeet sighted in other parts of the country. Possibly pumas or phantom panthers deserve blame for at least some of the stock kills. 1840 was the last year of normal *Felis concolor* abundance in New Jersey but the behavior of the rampaging creature of that year suggests that it could have been a phantom panther.

Is there a Jersey Devil?

I remain open-mindedly skeptical and hope that in the future someone will make a discovery or a sighting that will settle the question for once and for all.

But in the meantime I am convinced of this much: The Jersey Devil is more than just a legend, more than a centuries-old folk tale, more than a convenient gimmick for hucksters to use in fooling the unsuspecting. It is all these things, true, but it is also one thing more: a mystery.

Phantoms
Afield . . .

17
Kelly's Little Men

Some UFO investigators call this event the "granddaddy" of all flying saucer occupant stories. This incident in Kentucky, indeed, is one of the most thoroughly investigated and documented in the annals of modern mysteries. The individuals who extensively looked into the accounts within the first few hours included local police and sheriff officials, state police, Air Force and Army personnel, radio station and newspaper reporters and photographers, and various civilian investigators from as far away as New York City. The in-depth examination of the unsophisticated witnesses, the early nature of the mid-1950s date of the sightings, and the fantastic details of this truly close encounter have led to this occurrence being revered as one of the few "classics" in ufological literature.

In the popular mind, Hopkinsville, Kentucky, is the site of the 1955 happenings, but actually, they occurred in the small community of Kelly (population 150), located seven miles north of Hopkinsville. At the time, the specific location of the "invasion" was the Kentucky farmhouse of the Sutton family, a modest one-story frame structure with a corrugated iron roof. The house had electricity, but did not have a telephone, television or radio. The farmhouse was occupied by eight adults and three children, who maintained a rural and limited lifestyle. The residents consisted of members of the Sutton/Lankford family, and Elmer "Lucky" Sutton's friend, Billy Ray Taylor and his wife.

Billy Ray Taylor was the first to have a strange experience that hot, mosquito-filled night of August 21, 1955. Because of the new moon and the clarity of the sky, it was rapidly getting dark when Billy Ray went to the backyard well for a drink of water. He quickly ran inside, telling everyone about having seen a silver flying saucer that was shooting out flames "all the colors of the rainbow." Billy Ray said it had passed overhead, stopped dead in the air, and dropped straight down into a gully about three hundred feet behind the Sutton farm. Everyone in the house did not take Billy Ray seriously, and they all thought he was pulling their collective leg, or merely had seen a shooting star. No one gave it much thought, and no one thought it was important enough to even venture out into the backyard to look around.

An hour later, at about eight o'clock, the family dog started barking violently. Lucky Sutton, Mrs. Lankford's oldest son from a previous marriage and the no-nonsense head of the household, noticed a strange glowing globe moving towards the house. The dog yelped away, apparently quite scared by the apparition. Soon Lucky Sutton and Billy Ray Taylor saw the glow was from a little man who was holding both of its extremely thin arms up over its head. The little man was about three and a half feet tall, had huge eyes with no pupils or eyelids, and large pointed, crinkly ears. Its skin was silvery and metallic when in the glare of the outside electric lightbulb, but its body seemed to glow when in a darker area near the house. And they noted it liked to stay in the shadows. As the features of the little man grew clearer, they saw its body was very thin and the arms ended in talon-like claws. The thing was bald, appeared to have a straight slit from ear to ear for its mouth, and completely lacked a nose. It was the most frightening and strangest creature the two men had ever seen.

Confronted with this terrifying situation, the men reacted quickly and decisively. They both reached for their guns – a .22 rifle for Billy Ray and a twenty gauge shotgun for Lucky – and blasted away at the little man when it was less than twenty feet from the house. As the visitor was hit, what occurred surprised the two men. As they described it, the little man was apparently not hurt but "flipped over" backwards and scurried off into the shadows. Lucky and Billy Ray went inside and soon another (or the same?) little man appeared at a side window. The men again shot right through a screen at the entity. Again it flipped over and vanished into the night. Since the women were beginning to scream, and things were getting rather frightening, the men decided to go outside to see if they had actually killed one of the little men, so then all could be reassured.

Cautiously and quietly, Billy Ray moved through the darkened house, towards the screen door that faced the backyard. He was followed closely by Lucky Sutton, and the rest of the adults and children. Going through the door, standing under the small roof over the step, Billy Ray was about ready to go into the backyard when it happened. Lucky Sutton and the others saw a claw-like hand grab Billy Ray Taylor's hair. Instantly, Alene Sutton pulled Billy Ray back into the farmhouse, and Lucky ran into the yard, blasting at the thing on the roof. The little man was knocked off the roof, but floated to the ground. Before they knew where it had actually landed, the group saw another little man in a tree near the house. Billy Ray rushed back outside and joined Lucky in firing on this one. This creature, too, floated to the earth. And everytime one of them was shot at, or shouted at, they glowed brighter. As the little man in the tree hightailed it from the scene, another one came from around a corner of the house and dashed in front of Lucky.

In all, the residents of the Sutton farmhouse said they had to drive off six separate advances. By eleven o'clock, after several harrowing hours of claws scratching on the roof, shotgun blasts, creature faces at the windows, and crying children, the Suttons decided to abandon the farm. All eight adults and three children piled into two automobiles, and sped down US Route 41, to Hopkinsville. Once in town, the Suttons, Lankfords, and Taylors went straight to the police station.

Police Chief Russell Greenwell would later describe the Kelly

(© Philip Hemstreet and Beth Fideler, 1983)

One of the most terrifying incidents occurred when Billy Ray
Taylor stepped outside and one of the little men grabbed his
hair.

witnesses as genuinely terrified. To one investigator, Chief Green-well said: "Something scared those people. Something beyond reason – nothing ordinary."

The police were very struck by the sincerity of these frightened folks. Soon a caravan of local and state police cars roared off at high speed towards Kelly. Before long, the farm was flooded with authorities and investigators – from the local police to the military police from Fort Campbell, from a big city news photographer to a local radio station's newsman. It was about 11:30 p.m. by now, and tension filled the air as the various investigators attempted to assess the situation. At one point, as everyone probed around (possibly destroying evidence of the encounter), someone stepped on a cat's tail and it let out a screech that had everybody's nerves jumping. The skeptics looked for evidence of drinking and could find none. Others looked for the little men and none were seen. Nothing unusual was found. Well, almost nothing. Police Chief Greenwell and a group of other men reported they saw a luminous patch in some grass near the house, but as they went closer to it, it seemed to disappear.

Slowly, one by one, the investigators left. By about 2:30 a.m., having found little and promising to come back after dawn, the crowd was gone. The only people remaining at the farmhouse were the Suttons, Lankfords and Taylors. And the little men!!! For after the residents of the farmhouse had tried to settle down, turned all the lights out, and gone to bed, one of the creatures' clawed hands reached up on the screen. Noticing a glow at the window, Mrs. Glennie Lankford, 50, was the first to see it. She alerted the rest of the family. Lucky, as he had done before, grabbed his shotgun and fired at the little man. Although the creatures were seen off and on until just before dawn, the events of the second visitation were not as dramatic as those of the first.

As the sun rose, the "invasion" of the little men at Kelly, Ken-tucky, was over, and the onslaught of investigators and media had just begun. Despite the efforts of many skeptics, the testimony of the Suttons, the Taylors and the Lankfords was never con-tradicted, or proven false. Interviewers have come away from

Kelly convinced these people had a very real experience. What the true nature of that experience was, and who the little men were is one of the deepest mysteries in ufology.

18
The Mad Gasser
of Mattoon
and His Kin

Some very strange entities haunt some rural towns in America.

Following the Civil War and for the next seventy years, a strange something dubbed the "Ghost of Paris" frequently terrorized Paris, Missouri. In October, 1934, a wave of sightings of the "Ghost of Paris" occurred. Local residents were frantically telephoning the City Marshal and demanding he drive the "Ghost" away. The poor marshal was at his wits' end as to how to handle the situation. The phantom was described as tall, dressed in black, and carrying some sort of wand in "her" hand. According to local tradition, "she" appeared in Paris, Missouri, every year about October, and then was seen sporadically until Spring. The "Ghost of Paris" was said to frighten children, and cause grown men to run down the middle of the main street, yelling for help. Whatever "she" was, the "Ghost" certainly seems to be the Midwest's precursor to, and female relative of the Mad Gasser of Mattoon.

Until the late summer of 1944, Mattoon, Illinois, had nothing in its history to distinguish itself beyond the fact that in 1861

General Ulysses S. Grant had arrived there to muster the 21st Illinois Infantry into state service. Other than that, Mattoon was a typical, peaceful little Midwestern city (population 15,827 in the 1940 census), depending for its livelihood on the railroads and the prosperous farm lands that surrounds it.

Then one night the first of a series of events would occur which would shake Mattoon out of its complacent anonymity and draw to it the attention of the entire nation. And within two weeks its citizens would be the objects of ridicule for falling victim, so it was said, to classic mass hysteria, because they insisted something was happening to them that authorities said could not be taking place. In the end Mattoon, and perhaps the truth as well, would lose.

During the early morning hours of August 31st, a resident of the city woke up feeling ill. He tottered out of bed, stumbled into the bathroom and vomited. Then he roused his wife to ask her if she had left on the gas.

"I don't think so," she said, "but I'll check." When she tried to get up, she discovered that she was paralyzed.

Shortly after this incident, a housewife in another part of town awoke when she heard her daughter coughing. She got up to find that she could barely walk.

The next evening, about 11:00 p.m., Mrs. Bert Kearney, asleep in a bedroom shared with her three-year-old daughter Dorothy, was stirred from slumber at the sudden appearance of a peculiar smell.

"I first noticed a sickening sweet odor in the bedroom," she later told a reporter for the local newspaper, "but at the time I thought that it might be from flowers outside the window. But the odor grew stronger and I began to feel a paralysis of my legs and lower body. I got frightened and screamed."

Mrs. Kearney's neighbors searched the yard and the rest of the neighborhood without finding any clues to the origin of the mysterious gas. Police investigation proved similarly unproductive. But at 12:30 a.m., as he arrived home from work, Mr. Kearney caught a glimpse of someone who matched the later descriptions of the "mad gasser of Mattoon" as the newspapers would call him.

From the shadowy world beyond the nightmares of the citizenry of Mattoon, Illinois, the Mad Gasser burst on the scene to terrorize the bedrooms of that sleeping town in 1944.

The stranger, who was, in Kearney's words, "tall, dressed in dark clothing and wearing a tight-fitting cap," was standing at the window. When he saw Kearney approaching he fled. Kearney pursued him but could not catch him.

The next day Mrs. Kearney complained of having burned lips and a parched mouth and throat.

It was the Kearney report that brought the *Mattoon Journal-Gazette* into the picture. The *Journal-Gazette*, by handling the events in an extremely sensationalistic manner (its initial story refers to Mrs. Kearney as the "first victim" strongly implying that there would be more "victims"), would open itself to controversy and severe criticism. Several years later a writer for the *Journal of Abnormal and Social Psychology* would blame the paper for in effect "manufacturing" the scare and frightening citizens to the extent that they took leave of their senses enough to spend the next fourteen days imagining that a "mad gasser" was prowling the streets. That particular approach to the Mattoon affair has become the standard one, but as we shall see – tempting as it might be from some points of view – it does not quite explain everything.

By September 5th police had received four more reports of "gas attacks." Each time the individuals concerned said they first had sniffed a "sickly sweet odor," then become nauseated and partially paralyzed for from thirty to ninety minutes. During the afternoon of September 5th, according to a news account, police "checked what they thought might be a hideout for the anesthetic prowler but found nothing to bear out the theory." That same evening a woman named Mrs. Beulah Cordes handed over to police the first concrete physical traces of the gasser's existence.

Mrs. Cordes and her husband Carl had returned home, entering their house through the back door, about 10:30 that night. Mrs. Cordes proceeded to the front door and while unlocking it she spotted a white cloth on the porch. Curious, she picked it up and noticed that it had been soaked in some kind of liquid.

"When I inhaled the fumes from the cloth," she related subsequently, "I had a sensation similar to coming in contact with a strong electric current. The feeling raced down my body to my feet and then seemed to settle in my knees. It was a feeling of paralysis."

She suddenly vomited. Several minutes later her lips and face swelled and burned, her mouth began to bleed and she lost her ability to speak. Two hours later the condition was gone.

Police found a skeleton key and an empty lipstick tube on the porch where Mrs. Cordes had seen the cloth. These two items led them to suggest that a prowler had been trying to break into the house when he heard the couple approaching.

As public alarm mounted – spurred in part by the *Journal-Gazette's* lurid accounts of the "fiendish prowler" (who in fact had neither robbed nor molested anyone) – Police Chief E. C. Cole ordered the ten men on the force on twenty-four-hour duty, and Thomas V. Wright, City Commissioner of Public Health, appealed to the State Department of Public Safety to dispatch investigators to the city. Mrs. Cordes' cloth was passed on to chemists at the University of Illinois for analysis.

The same night of the Cordes report a Mattoon housewife heard someone at the bedroom window but before she could act gas had seeped into the room and she was partially paralyzed for several minutes.

"This is one of the strangest cases I have ever encountered in many years of police work," Richard T. Piper, a crime specialist with the State Department of Public Safety, told reporters. His mystification is not hard to understand. The weird attacks, which were rising in intensity, seemed senseless and random. The only "pattern," a pretty dubious one, was that most of the victims were women – not necessarily significant since a large percentage of the city's male population was in uniform and fighting overseas. The lack of any obvious "motive" would prove a major factor in dismissing the attacks as hysterical imaginings.

On Wednesday night, the sixth, the gasser struck three times. At 10:00 Mrs. Ardell Spangler smelled a sickly sweet odor, felt a peculiar dryness in her throat and lips and suffered from nausea. Mrs. Laura Junken reported a similar experience shortly after midnight and Fred Goble told of one at 1:00 a.m. Robert Daniels, a neighbor of Goble, saw a "tall man" fleeing from the house.

The *Decatur Herald* for September 8th summarized the events of the preceding several days:

"Twelve persons in the last week have been visited by the nocturnal prowler who shoots an unidentified chemical into bed chambers through open windows. Cases have been reported in all sections of Mattoon.

"Victims report that the first symptom is an electric shock which passes completely through the body. Later nausea develops, followed by partial paralysis. They also suffer burned mouths and throats and their faces become swollen.

"Mattoon police advanced the theory yesterday that the marauder was a young person experimenting with a chemistry set. . .

"Mayor E. E. Richardson said he planned to call a meeting of the city council to authorize a reward for the capture of the prowler if he is not found soon."

Other victims, whose stories were not released until Friday, included Mrs. Cordie Taylor and Glenda Hendershott, an 11-year-old girl who was discovered unconscious in her bedroom.

Thursday night was relatively calm in Mattoon, making it the first community breathing spell since the beginning of the month. Police took calls from three persons who said they had seen a strange man in their neighborhoods but these reports may have been the products of conclusion-jumping by anxious citizens. Mrs. Mae Williams' story may have been more than that, however. Mrs. Williams notified police that at midnight a tall, dark man answering the gasser's description had attempted to force her door but her screams drove him away.

The *Journal-Gazette,* while taking note of the seeming de-escalation of attacks, still managed to strike a note of alarm. "Mattoon's 'Mad Anesthetist' apparently took a respite from his maniacal forays Thursday night," John Miller observed in the Friday issue, "and while many terror-stricken people were somewhat relieved they were inclined to hold their breath and wonder when and where he might strike again."

And the citizenry were not taking any chances. If the police could not catch the elusive prowler, they would do it themselves, they decided – and they took to the streets with rifles and shotguns looking for suspects. For their part the police, recipients of considerable public abuse for their failure to stop the attacks, succeeded only in collaring one lowly suspect whom they were forced to release after he passed a lie-detector test. All the while anti-police, anti-city hall feeling grew by leaps and bounds as the helplessness of officialdom became increasingly clear. Businessmen announced that on Saturday afternoon they would lead a mass protest rally to put additional pressure on the already-harried Mattoon force (who, it must be said in fairness, were doing the best they could under impossible circumstances). To local officials the gasser now was more than a menace to public safety – he was rapidly evolving into a political liability as well.

That night the gasser resumed his attacks, hitting first at the residence of Mrs. Violet Driskell. Mrs. Driskell and her daughter Romona, 11, awoke late in the evening to the sounds of someone trying to remove the storm sash from their bedroom window. They dashed outside to the porch to call for help but fumes overcame Romona and she vomited. At the same moment her mother sighted a man sprinting away.

Shortly afterwards, at 1:45 a.m., the prowler sprayed gas through a partly-opened window into a bedroom where Mrs. Russell Bailey, Katherine Tuzzo, and Mrs. Genevieve Haskell and her seven-year-old son lay sleeping. Elsewhere, Miss Frances Smith, principal of the Columbian Grade School, and her sister Maxine sniffed the mysterious gas and fell ill – or, as the *Journal-Gazette* had it:

"The first infiltration of gas caught them in their beds. Gasping and choking they awoke and soon felt partial paralysis grip their legs and arms. Later, while awake, the other attacks came and they saw a thin blue smoke-like vapor spreading throughout the room.

"Just before the gas with its flower-like odor came pouring into the room they heard a strange 'buzzing' sound outside the house and expressed the belief that the sound was made by the 'madman's spraying apparatus' in operation."

By now the town was beside itself with fear. At the last moment state authorities succeeded in talking organizers of the protest out of having their meeting, arguing that it would serve no purpose but to increase the hysteria and promising to bring in a large force of state police. Two FBI agents from Springfield already had slipped quietly into Mattoon. Their chief interest, according to rumor, was in trying to identify the type of gas the prowler was using; presumably, once the identification had been made, it could be traced to its source. Mrs. Cordes' cloth had been of no help in that respect, for the State Crime Bureau's analysis had revealed nothing. In the meantime authorities worked with only limited success to keep the vigilante bands off the streets.

While solid evidence was lacking, there was no shortage of guesses. Most theories, taking cognizance of the apparent sense-lessness of the whole affair, centered on the possibility that the gasser was a lunatic. State's Attorney W. K. Kidwell even checked with Illinois mental hospitals for information on individuals they had released recently. Police Commissioner Wright opined that the anesthetist might be an "eccentric inventor" who had devised a new weapon which he was testing on local people. The wildest story of all, whose origins are unfortunately obscure, contended that the culprit was really an "apeman," a most interesting idea in view of the tradition of "man-ape" reports in central and southern Illinois.

Saturday night dozens of armed farmers from the surrounding area joined citizens and police in patrolling Mattoon, but still at least six alleged attacks took place. One of these was reported by the Smith sisters, who had been victimized just the night before. Another couple, Mr. and Mrs. Stewart B. Scott, returned late in the evening to their farm on the southern edge of Mattoon to find it filled with the by-now-familiar sickly sweet gas.

The next morning Commissioner Wright issued a statement urging residents to get a grip on themselves.

"There is no doubt but [sic] that a gas maniac exists and has made a number of attacks," he said. "But many of the reported attacks are nothing more than hysteria.

"Fear of the gas man is entirely out of proportion to the menace of the relatively harmless gas he is spraying. The whole town is sick with hysteria and last night it spread out into the country."

Wright's remarks were aimed obliquely at discouraging further reports, the only way city officials could see out of a situation that was at once dangerous to the public and embarrassing to them politically. The police commissioner's directive ordering those making reports to submit to examination at Mattoon Memorial Hospital was even more to the point. Since analysis of the Cordes cloth already had shown that the "gas" left no traces, its victims risked looking like fools. The city fathers had carefully shifted the burden of responsibility from themselves to those whose safety they had failed to protect. And now the victims, in a dilemma worthy of Kafka, had to answer for their own victimization.

Most of the gasser's activities took place on the northwest side of town, one of the city's better residential districts, and Sunday night he struck there again, spraying gas into the kitchen of the Kenneth Fitzpatrick residence. Mrs. Fitzpatrick nearly collapsed, and when her husband came to her rescue he was almost overcome himself.

A short time later three sisters, two of them young girls aged twelve and eight, smelled a sickly sweet gas in their living room. The oldest, Mrs. Richard Daniels, was affected seriously enough for a physician to order her to bed.

That night was the climax of Mattoon's mad gasser scare and after that events moved rapidly to denouement. Newspaper accounts affected increasingly skeptical tones and the police now openly suggested to those who reported being attacked that they were imagining things. To those who had not smelled the gas, seen the gasser or chased him through their neighborhoods, the possibility that he might exist at all seemed more and more remote. After all, how could anyone have so completely escaped detection when all the resources of the city and the state were mobilized against him? And besides, none of it made any sense.

On the evening of the eleventh police received numerous calls but dismissed them all as false alarms with only the most perfunctory investigation. But in one case a physician who appeared on the scene shortly after an attack, while finding no evidence of gas on the victim's person, conceded that there was a "peculiar odor" in the room.

But officialdom was not impressed. Anxious to wrap everything up as quickly as possible, Police Chief Cole called a press conference the next day and said that he and his men had cracked the case. "It was a mistake from beginning to end," he asserted.

"Local police, in cooperation with state officers, have checked and rechecked all reported cases," he said, "and we find absolutely no evidence to support stories that have been told. Hysteria must be blamed for such seemingly accurate accounts of supposed victims.

"However, we have found that large quantities of carbon tetrachloride are used in war work done at the Atlas Imperial Diesel Engine Company plant and that it is an odor which can be carried to all parts of the city as the wind shifts. It also leaves stains on cloth such as those found on a rag at a Mattoon home."

A spokesman for the plant was quick to reply. W. J. Webster, works manager, said, "We use tetrachloride at the Atlas plant only in fire extinguishers. Trichlorethylene gas is used in our work and it is odorless and produces no ill effects in the air."

The *Decatur Review* added its own objections to the police claims: "There was no explanation of why several screens had been cut prior to reported gassing by several persons . . . Many persons wondered why the odor from the Atlas Diesel plant hadn't caused illness among the townspeople before. . . ."

Nor of course did the official explanation account for the sightings of the man believed to be the gasser, the same one who was seen fleeing from houses shortly after attacks sometimes by persons who did not know that an attack was taking place at the moment. One such witness, who chased the stranger several blocks, sticks to his story even today. So do the gas victims I was able to interview in preparing this chapter. And there is still the concrete testimony of Mrs. Cordes' cloth.

The last recorded attack was made on September 13th, when a "woman dressed in man's clothing" sprayed gas into Mrs. Bertha Bench's bedroom. The next morning she and her son Orville, 20, found imprints of high-heeled shoes on the ground by the bedroom window.

And so, as the saying goes, the mad gasser of Mattoon passed into history.

The whole truth about Mattoon probably will never be known. First and most obvious, the genuine hysteria of the period helped to create a confusion of its own and it is likely that some of the reports, especially those made in the last few days, may have described occurrences real only in the minds of the persons involved. Second, most of the principals are either dead or impossible to locate, and in any case memories of the event have dimmed over the years though they have not faded altogether. At best we can only guess what really happened – and point to parallel phenomena of which the Mattoon citizens could not have been aware.

It is noteworthy, for example, that on February 1, 1944, three persons living in a house in Coatesville, Pa., died after inhaling a mysterious "sweet-smelling gas" of unknown origin. Neighbors fell ill and had to seek medical attention.

And in December 1961, at a Baptist church in Houston, Tex., a "sickening sweet gas" disrupted a Christmas program, sending a hundred persons reeling outside into the fresh air. The victims complained of nausea, headaches, vomiting and sweating, and eight individuals, mostly children, were admitted to the hospital for oxygen treatment. Firemen could find no cause. Perhaps someone suggested "mass hysteria."

The mad gasser of Mattoon was not the first of his kind either. Victorian England knew a peculiar character dubbed "Springheel Jack." In the 1961 article "The Mystery of Springheel Jack," J. Vyner wrote:

> The intruder was tall, thin and powerful. He had a prominent nose, and bony fingers of immense power which resembled claws. He was incredibly agile. He wore a long, flowing cloak, of the sort affected by opera-goers, soldiers and strolling actors. On his head was a tall, metallic-seeming helmet. Beneath the cloak were close-fitting garments of some glittering material like oil-skin or metallic mesh. There was a lamp strapped to his chest. Oddest of all: the creature's ears were cropped or pointed like those of an animal.

His name was "Springheel Jack," or at least that is what people called him. On the heels of his boots he supposedly wore springs – hence his name – which enabled him to jump great distances, clearing roads and eight-foot walls without difficulty. (One hundred years later, when German parachutists tried to ease the shock of landing with sprung boots, they discovered that it didn't work; all they got for their troubles were broken ankles.)

When the *London Times* called him an "unmanly brute," the newspaper was referring to his conduct, not his biological composition. But there is something decidedly unearthly about this Victorian denizen who, from his first appearance in the dark lanes of Middlesex, England, in November 1837 to his last forty years later, behaved in a manner so bizarre and so without apparent motivation that the only parallel events seem to be two weird series of incidents that took place in Illinois a century afterwards.

Like the Illinois mad gasser whose depredations have been examined herein, Jack was vicious but not deadly. His victims suffered fear and discomfort but they survived, never understanding exactly what happened to them or why. His operation, whatever it was, began in Middlesex where he frightened and sometimes assaulted lone nocturnal wayfarers, some of them public officials who complained to the Lord Mayor of London, who in his turn set up horse patrols to scour the suburban areas of the city. That did not stop Jack. Moving from village to village, for a time he took up residence on the grounds of Kensington Palace, where he was seen climbing over the park wall at midnight and bouncing across the lawns. He appeared to prefer private parks, where he rested before setting out to commit fresh outrages.

The *Times* for February 22, 1838, details one such "outrage." Two days before, at 8:45 in the evening, a violent ringing of the bell summoned Jane Alsop, 18, to the front door of her home in the village of Old Ford. When she saw a man standing outside, she asked him what he wanted. "For God's sake bring me a light," he snapped, "for we have caught Springheel Jack here in the lane!" Immediately Miss Alsop left to find a candle; when she returned, she handed it to the stranger. In the *Times'* words:

> The instant she had done so . . . he threw off his outer garment [a large cloak], and applying the lighted candle to his breast, presented a most hideous and frightful appearance,

and vomited forth a quantity of blue and white flame from his mouth, and his eyes resembled red balls of fire. From the hasty glance which her fright enabled her to get at his person, she observed that he wore a large helmet, and his dress, which appeared to fit him very tight, seemed to her to resemble white oil skin. Without uttering a sentence he darted at her, and catching her partly by her dress and the back part of her neck, placed her head under one of his arms, and commenced tearing her dress with his claws, which she was certain were of some metallic substance, and by considerable exertion got away from him and ran towards the house to get in. Her assailant, however, followed her, and caught her on the steps leading to the hall-door, when he again used considerable violence, tore her neck and arms with his claws, as well as a quantity of hair from her head; but she was at length rescued from his grasp by one of her sisters. Miss Alsop added that she had suffered considerably all night from the shock she had sustained, and was then in extreme pain, both from the injury done to her arm, and the wounds and scratches inflicted by the miscreant about her shoulders and neck with his claws or hands.

Within a day or two of the Old Ford incident, according to the 1838 *Annual Register*, two sisters named Scales, while passing along Green Dragon-alley in Limehouse, spotted a strange-looking man lurking nearby. He suddenly stepped up to one of them, "spurted a quantity of blue flame right in her face" and walked away. Lucy Scales dropped to the ground, unable to see, and fell into a violent fit which did not subside until several hours later.

Their brother, whose house they had left just prior to the attack, heard his sisters screaming and rushed to the scene. His other sister described the assailant as "tall, thin and of gentlemanly appearance," covered with a cloak and carrying in front of him a small lamp. He had remained silent during the entire incident.

Theories about Springheel Jack's identity were legion. One had it that he was a dressed-up kangaroo which had escaped from a circus act. Another held the Marquis of Waterford, a deranged peer whose activities had let to his arrest on several occasions, responsible for the scare.

There was no accounting, however, for Jack's apparent return in 1872, this time in the Peckham area of southeast London. Said the *News of the World* for November 17, 1872: "We can hardly be expected to credit that the figure is eight feet in height, springs over stone walls and lofty hedges, and on nearing a victim changes from grim blackness to luminous white." But the reports, some of them involving several witnesses, were hard to dismiss. The *News* recounted an incident which allegedly occurred to two teen-aged daughters of the head master of Dulwich College and their governess, who had seen "a figure enveloped in white and with arms extended" moving toward them from across the road. Their screams frightened it away.

But in 1877 Jack was back. From the April 28, 1877, *Illustrated Police News:*

> A curious story comes from Aldershot. For some time past, the sentries on two outlying posts have been frightened by the appearance at night of two spectral figures. The figures, glowing with phosphorous are in the habit of suddenly manifesting themselves, making tremendous springs of 10 or 12 yards at a time and upsetting the sentry before he had been able to collect himself sufficiently to oppose earthly arms to his ghostly visitants. The latter do him no bodily injury, contenting themselves with upsetting the poor man, after which they mysteriously disappear. So great has been the alarm that it has been found necessary to post double sentries.

Later, sentries did, indeed, fire on Jack.

And in its November 3rd issue the same paper lists this curious item: "For some time Newport, near Lincoln, has been disturbed by a man dressed in a sheepskin or something of the kind. The man has springs on his boots and can jump a height of 15 feet. The other night he jumped on a college, got into a window by the roof and so frightened the ladies that one has not yet recovered."

All of this is unlikely enough, but not nearly so unlikely – or so discomforting – as the affair of the "Houston Bat Man," which carries the activities of Springheel Jack, or someone much like him, into our own time and links them with the great 20th Cen-

Springheel Jack, with chest aglow, eludes the bullets of Aldershot's sentries in 1877.

tury riddle of the flying saucers. The "Houston Bat Man" also discourages us from treating the legend of Springheel Jack as no more than a bit of Victorian folklore.

According to the witnesses' testimony, at 2:30 a.m. on June 18, 1953, Mrs. Hilda Walker, Judy Meyers and Howard Phillips were sitting on the front porch of an apartment building seeking relief from the summer heat which was robbing them of sleep, when suddenly Mrs. Walker glanced up.

"About 25 feet away I saw a huge shadow cross the lawn," she said. "I thought at first it was the magnified reflection of a big moth caught in the nearby street light. Then the shadow seemed to bounce upward into a pecan tree. We all looked up.

"That's when we saw it. It was the figure of a man with wings like a bat. He was dressed in gray or black tight-fitting clothes. He stood there for about 30 seconds, swaying on the branch of the old pecan tree. Suddenly the light began to fade slowly. Little Judy screamed as the light died out and the figure disappeared.

"Immediately afterwards we heard a loud swoosh over the housetops across the street. It was like a white flash of a torpedo-shaped object."

Phillips told the *Houston Chronicle* that the figure "was encased in a halo of light" and dressed in what looked like a paratrooper uniform. He stood about six-and-a-half feet tall and was framed in a dim gray light.

Springheel Jack one hundred years after his time? We have all the details we need – the "bouncing" motion, the luminosity, even the "wings," which could have been a cloak imperfectly observed in the half-light – except one, and that is the peculiar gas-like substance Jack allegedly sprayed in the faces of his victims. It would take the mad gasser of Mattoon to supply that last dangerous item.

Meanwhile, back in Illinois, by 1952 Mattoon's mad gasser was only a memory. Chief Cole had first officially disposed of his presence, and two years later, in a 1954 issue of *The Journal of Abnormal and Social Psychology*, Donald M. Johnson – arguing that even the supposed gas existed only in the minds of hapless hysterics scared out of their senses by the *Journal-Gazette's* sen-

(© Philip Hemstreet and Beth Fideler, 1983)

The Blue Phantom of Route 66.

sationalistic reporting – did it scientifically. No one betrayed any willingness to consider the disquieting alternative: that the mad gasser might have been a real if shadowy manifestation of some unimaginable Unknown. If his motives were incomprehensible, if he inexplicably evaded capture, if he did not behave as some good earth-bound criminal should – then, why, he could not have been at all. And so neither, as it turned out, could the "blue phantom" of 1952.

The blue phantom first showed up, it is said, on U.S. Highway 66 near Joliet, Illinois, late in May. Two drivers independently reported that someone had fired at them from a moving blue car. One of them was wounded, though not seriously. Later the same day another driver said a man in a blue automobile had taken a shot at him, this time three miles south of Lincoln on 66.

On the afternoon of June 2nd the phantom chose a new tactic: ambush. Edward Smith of St. Louis, Illinois, was driving just south of the Sangamon River when something hit his car. He slowed down and glanced back in time to see a man jump from bushes beside the road, hop into a big blue car and speed north on Route 48. Police interviewed an eleven-year-old girl who had watched the sniper make his escape in what she thought was either a Ford or Buick sedan. Highway patrolmen speculated that a .38 caliber bullet had caused the crease in Smith's back window.

By June 8th there had been ten reported shootings along central Illinois highways, including one in which the sniper's bullet shattered a windshield. State police and sheriff's deputies set up roadblocks along a seventy-mile area and even employed the services of a low-flying airplane in an attempt to nab the gunman — all, however, to no avail. On June 10th the phantom, as if to thumb his nose at those so desperately trying to stop him, chose as his fifteenth target a Marengo squad car. Police officer Lawrence Brown, who had been patrolling the streets at dawn when the incident occurred, chased his assailant's car at speeds up to 90 m.p.h. but could not overtake it.

The same day, though, State Police Chief Thomas J. O'Donnell was telling reporters, "We have not relaxed our search and we are investigating every case but we are not convinced there is a phantom gunman or that any shots were fired in most of the 'shooting incidents' reported.

"We have yet to find anyone who saw a gun or who could give anything definite about the description of the sniper. On the other hand, we have a maze of vague and conflicting information that does not add up to the conclusion that one gunman is causing all these reports."

Perhaps not. On June 9th, on Route 66 east of Springfield, William Moffit's car window was struck by a bullet fired from a *dark green* automobile speeding by in the opposite direction. But it is unlikely that Moffit took seriously O'Donnell's theory that nearly all the "sniping" incidents resulted from stones hitting cars or from the setting off of "torpedo" firecrackers. Neither, one suspects, did a truck driver in the Clinton area who early in the morning of June 17th saw two bullets penetrate his windshield. Police officers who inspected the holes concluded they were made by .22 caliber slugs fired from an automatic rifle. Nothing was said about stones or firecrackers.

The previous evening—in fact just a matter of hours before the Clinton incident—D. L. Weatherford had observed someone standing on a bridge on Route 121 north of Mount Pulaski. The "someone," a man who wore khaki shirt and trousers, held a revolver and stood close to a parked blue Chrysler sedan. Weatherford did not stop to ask questions.

It was a blue Ford, however, which a Decatur couple pursued through the city the evening of June 19th after its occupant ungraciously took a pot shot at them. And at Mattoon (of all places) the same night police investigated a report from Fred Manley who said a man in a yellow Chevrolet panel truck had fired at him with a shotgun about 7:30 p.m. as he was driving on Route 16 between Charleston and Ashmore.

Near Champaign on June 24th, in what seems to have been the last appearance of the phantom sniper—or at least *a* phantom sniper—a man in a black sedan pulled up alongside a car driven by L. J. Wiles and let loose a volley of four shots, one of which crashed through Wiles' right window. Wiles, understandably shaken, still managed to collect his wits enough to chase the gunman's car into Champaign but lost it in the city traffic.

The phantom was lost to history as well apparently, for that was the last anyone saw of him, or them, or whomever—unless we count the epidemic of cracked windshields in Bellingham, Washington, during the spring of 1954, which really is something else altogether.

Conceivably some "phantom snipings" were not that at all but the work of demented individuals taking advantage of the publicity in order to commit vicious "practical jokes" of their own. Fred Wanley's attacker may have been one of those.

But the real phantom comes out of the same eerie mold as Mattoon's mad gasser (and probably England's Springheel Jack, too)—a weird entity that leaves traces but remains curiously untraceable. The bullets the sniper shoots into windows do not pass through the car and out the windows on the other side, yet they cannot be found inside the vehicle; and he escapes a police dragnet sufficiently extensive to snare a more mundane lawbreaker. But we have physical evidence—wounds and shattered glass—that he, or at any rate *something*, does exist, Chief O'Donnell to the contrary

Like the other phenomena in Mysterious America, the Mad Gasser and his various kin are tangible but intangible, real but unreal. Certainly nothing the conventional mind, given the choice, would prefer to have to deal with. Forced to, it will opt inevitably for the easy, irrelevant answer.

Fort summed it all up in his inimitable way when he wrote, "In hosts of minds, today, are impressions that the word 'eerie' means nothing except convenience to makers of crossword puzzles. There are gulfs of the unaccountable but they are bridged by terminology . . . Probably vast holes of ignorance always will be bridged by very slender pedantries."

19
The Phantom
Clowns

The new multicolored clothing on the stranger made people feel
slightly uneasy. The man's name, Bunting, was a reflection of his
attire, the residents of the small Westphalian town were soon to
learn. The tall, thin newcomer offered his services to the town
council, and they readily accepted. Pest control was a serious problem in 1284 and this fellow Bunting said he could get rid of all
the rats in town. Thus the beginnings of the legend of the Pied
Piper of Hamelin were born. Bunting did lure the rats with his
mystical music into drowning in the Weser River, but the
townspeople refused to pay him. The Pied Piper decided to collect in another fashion. On St. John's Day, June 24th, Bunting
returned to Hamelin and piped his haunting tune. Soon all one
hundred and thirty children were enchanted into following him
out of the town and into a cave in the Koppenberg Mountain. The
entrance was sealed and the children were trapped forever.

The legend of the Pied Piper of Hamelin is said by some scholars
to be based on the truth. Others feel the story grew out of the
Children's Crusade of 1212 in which 20,000 young crusaders

marched towards the East and were never seen again. Whatever its origin, the tale is a well known one, having been retold in many ways at various times. Robert Browning's poem, for example, was written in the 1800's, and places the events of the Piper's last visit to Hamelin on July 22nd, 1376. The town of Hamelin does exist, and perhaps the sinister character and deeds of Bunting may have as well.

In the Spring of 1981, Boston, Massachusetts appears to have been the port of entry for a new version of the Pied Piper story. During the first week of May some individuals in multicolored clothes just like Bunting's began trying to entice school children into coming along with them. The reports of clowns in vans bothering children were openly discussed in the newspapers, by the School Committee, the area police and scores of parents and children.

On May 6, 1981, the Boston police, responding to persistent complaints, warned that men in clown suits were harassing elementary schoolchildren. One of the men was seen wearing a clown suit only from the waist up, from the waist down he was naked. According to reports, the clown had driven a black van near the recreational-horseshoe site of Franklin Park in the Roxbury area of Boston between 4:00 and 6:00 p.m. He also appeared in the Jamaica Plain neighborhood of Boston near the Mary E. Curley School.

A day earlier, in the adjoining city of Brookline, two clown men reportedly had tried to lure children into their van with offers of candy. The Brookline police had a good description of the van: older model, black, with ladders on the side, a broken front headlight and no hubcaps. After the clown men and van had been seen near the Lawrence Elementary School on Longwood Avenue in Brookline, the police told school administrators to be "extra cautious."

The previous week Investigative Counselor Daniel O'Connell of the Boston Public School District had sent a memo to the district's elementary and middle school principals. He wrote, "It has been brought to the attention of the police department and the district office that adults dressed as clowns have been bothering children to and from school. Please advise all students that they must stay away from strangers, especially ones dressed as clowns."

By May 8th reports of clown men in vans harassing children had come in from East Boston, Charlestown, Cambridge, Canton, Randolph and other cities near Boston. Police were stopping pickup trucks and vans with clowns delivering birthday greetings and "clown-a-grams" but no child molesters were arrested.

Frustrated policemen pointed out that virtually all of the reported sightings originated with children aged five to seven. The headlines in the May 9th issue of the *Boston Globe* told the story: "Police discount reports of clowns bothering kids." The public had been calmed and that was the end of the story. Or so the papers would have had us believe.

However, 50 miles south, in Providence, R.I., reports of clown men disturbing children were coming to the attention of psychiatric social workers counseling the city's youth. Perhaps these sightings can be explained as spillovers from Boston. But the reports since Providence are more difficult to dismiss.

The focus of activity shifted 1000 miles west – to Kansas City, Kansas, and Kansas City, Missouri. On the afternoon of May 22nd police cruisers on the Missouri side crisscrossed the city chasing a knife-wielding clown in a yellow van reported at six different elementary schools. Earlier in the day, at 8:30, a mother had watched a yellow van approach her children as they walked to a school bus stop. The van stopped and someone inside spoke to her two girls who then screamed and fled; the vehicle sped away. The children told their mother that a man dressed as a clown and carrying a knife had ordered them inside. By noon the police had received dozens of similar reports – of a clown in a yellow van. The calls did not taper off until five o'clock that afternoon.

The previous week in Kansas, school children said a clown had chased them home from school and threatened them if they didn't get into his van. Some reports claimed the clown brandished a sword instead of a knife.

Residents of the two Kansas Cities called it the "Killer Clown" affair. Some parents in Kansas were even keeping their children out of school.

Before long "group hysteria" was touted as the explanation for the reports. But still firsthand accounts continued to be reported.

LaTanya Johnson, a sixth-grade student at Fairfax Elementary School, said she saw the clown near the school. "He was by the fence and ran down through the big yard when some of the kids ran over there. He ran toward a yellow van. He was dressed in a black shirt with a devil on the front.* He had two candy canes down each side of his pants. The pants were black too, I think; I don't remember much about his face," she told a *Kansas City Star* reporter.

"These kids are terrified," one school principal remarked.

And Kansas City, Mo., and Kansas City, Kans., were not the only mid-western cities in which children were terrified. Omaha also had reports of clowns bothering children, as did Denver.

In Pennsylvania during the first week of June 1981, children in the Hill District of Pittsburgh said two men dressed in clown suits and driving in a van had bothered them. These were the first of a series of peculiar reports of costumed figures in the Pittsburgh area.

In the Garfield neighborhood of the city someone wearing a pink and white rabbit costume reportedly frightened children and eluded capture by hopping from his blue van and scampering into an East Liberty bar. Later in the week police got a report of a "rabbit" in Allegheny Cemetery.

Some of the other weird stories involving costumed persons included accounts of "Spiderman" joining forces with a "gorilla" and a "clown" in Arlington Heights, Pa., and trying to entice a boy into a vehicle. During the last week in May, Police Inspector William Moore said the department was getting 15 such reports every day. After a sighting of a clown on Bentley Drive in Terrace Village, police conducted a search with the help of two canine patrols and 100 kids with clubs.

Police and volunteers never were able to capture any clowns but witnesses insisted the costumed figures they had seen were real and not imaginary.

---

* One of the major origins of modern white-faced clowns with their traditional black and red clothing is the devil in "Miracle Plays" of the middle ages.

(© Beth Fideler and Philip Hemstreet, 1983)

The Phantom Clowns appeared in attire filled with the symbols of their demonic origins. The wave of elusive clown-in-van sightings certainly had more sinister connotations than humorous ones.

The story of the phantom clowns went unnoticed on a national scale until I began getting a hint we were in the midst of a major flap of a new phenomenon. Slowly, through contacting fellow researchers did I discover the phantom clown enigma went beyond Boston, Kansas City, and Omaha. Indeed, the reports filtering into me demonstrated a far reaching mystery was developing. In the individual cities, the local media were not aware they were living through a series of puzzling events which were occurring nationwide. Only through the Fortean underground was I able to ascertain the depth and breadth of the phantom clown drama. Something quite unusual was happening in America in the Spring of 1981.

So what is going on here? Group hysteria, as one newsman would have us believe? Or more? Phantom clowns in at least six major cities spanning over a thousand miles of America in the space of one month is quite a mystery. Were the "clowns in vans" being sighted elsewhere in the United States? Are they still being seen? Only time will tell, but something strange happened earlier in the year in Mineral Point, Wisconsin, which served as a precursor.

During the last week in March, the small village of Mineral Point was swamped with sightings of a strange entity which terrorized teenagers. This phantom was labeled a "vampire" and seemed to haunt the Graceland Cemetery.

One police officer actually saw the "vampire." Officer Jon Pepper described the being as a "huge person with a white-painted face" wearing a dark cape. (Strangely, the Mineral Point Vampire's white-face seems to be almost derisively related to the greasepaint of clowns!) As the events unfolded in Wisconsin, an incident in Washington D.C. would distract the media's attention from the vampire's terror. The sightings quickly faded from the press' and public's consciousness when President Ronald Reagan was nearly assassinated on March 30th.

The Mineral Point Vampire seems to have a host of deadringers in the Fortean and occult literature. Springheel Jack of Victorian England had pointed ears, was tall and thin, and wore a long, flowing cloak. Springheel Jack terrorized women of his day with a mysterious blue light he shone from his chest, and the weird mist that issued from this "lantern." Closely allied to the Mineral Point Vampire, also, seems to be the Mad Gasser of Mattoon who sent fear into the heart of that Illinois community in 1944. And then there is the strange story of the dark-coated, tall "grinning man" that stepped out of a UFO on a rainy night in 1966, and into the life of Woody Derenberger of Mineral Wells, West Virginia. Woody Derenberger's encounter propelled him into the world of contactees. From Mineral Point, Wisconsin to Mineral Wells, West Virginia, the connectiveness between these mysterious beings does exist.

Perhaps the caped entities and phantom clowns have something to tell us. Certainly the shadowy monk-like figures and checker-shirted characters mentioned so often in the occult and contactee literature have become almost too commonplace and familiar. Even reports from the 1970s told of plaid shirted Bigfoots being seen. The denizens of the netherworld apparently have had to dream up a new nightmare that would shock us. The scores of Fortean, ufological, and flying saucer "people," thus, have now been joined by leagues of phantom clowns in vans. The Men in Black terrorizing UFO witnesses from their Black Cadillacs may be too obviously sinister compared to this new chapter of the story. The cosmic joker is alive and well, and living in a clown suit. The masquerade of the elementals is taking on a new multicolored phase. After all, can you think of anything more frightening than "Ronald McDonald," a modern Pied Piper, with a mission?

20
Strange Appearances of the Wandering Nephites

The story begins, for our purposes at least, in the summer of 1494, on the occasion of Christopher Columbus' second voyage to the Americas. One day, while exploring the West Indies, Columbus anchored his ships off the coast of Cuba near a beautiful palm grove and sent a landing party to shore to get a fresh supply of wood and water.

As others in the group cut wood and filled their water casks, an archer strayed into the forest with his cross-bow in search of game, only to return a few minutes later to relate a baffling and frightening experience. The man, clearly shaken, reported that just a few moments before he had suddenly come upon a band of about thirty well-armed Indians, which was unsettling enough, but nothing compared to the sight of three white men who were in the company of the natives.

The white men, who wore white tunics that reached to their knees, immediately spotted the intruder and as the Indians watched impassively one of the three stepped toward the hunter

and started to speak when the hunter, giving vent to an understandable impulse, took to his heels and ran.

Upon hearing the story, Columbus' men — like their informant
more frightened of the Indians than curious about the enigmatic
white men — got on their boat and made with all haste back to the
fleet. The next day Columbus dispatched another party to search
for the strangers and the following day still another, but no trace
of them was ever found, much to the admiral's frustration. Columbus was still laboring under the delusion that he was cruising
the shoreline of Asia and believed that the three men might be
inhabitants of the province Mangon.

Washington Irving, who recorded this peculiar incident in his
Life and Voyages of Christopher Columbus, felt compelled to
apologize for including it in his book and then, perhaps by way
of pennance, went on to offer his own imaginative explanation.
"As no tribe of Indians was ever discovered in Cuba wearing
clothing," he wrote, "it is possible that the story of the men in white
originated in some error of the archer, who, full of the ideas of
the mysterious inhabitants of Mangon, may have been startled
in the course of his lonely wandering in the forest by one of those
flocks of cranes which it seems abounded in the neighborhood."

Well, one can hardly blame Irving for trying, since there is no
room in our conventional understanding of history for caucasians
co-existing with American Indians before Columbus' arrival. It is
easier to believe in cranes that look like men than it is to deal
with disquieting notions suggested by a number of unacceptable
yet oddly consistent yarns, claims and folk tales about a trio of
decidedly unusual gentlemen usually called the Three Nephites.

Let us skip over three centuries and move from Christopher Columbus in Cuba to one Joseph Smith of Palmyra, New York.

Smith, born in 1805, died young (he and his brother Hyrum were
done in by a lynch mob in Carthage, Illinois on June 27, 1844)
but distinguished himself, and also brought on his murder, by
founding the Church of the Latter-Day Saints, better known as
the Mormon Church, under the alleged direction of angelic beings. The first supposed meeting with angels took place in 1820,
when Smith was only 14. Several other visions occured over the

next few years, according to Smith, and led to his discovery on a hillside near Palmyra of gold plates which detailed the alleged history of the former inhabitants of the North American continent. The plates disappeared after Smith "translated" them, but not before he had produced eleven witnesses to swear to their existence.

Whatever the truth about Smith's visions and the gold plates, there is no question that the resulting *Book of Mormon,* based on the prophet's translation, is a remarkable document probably quite beyond the inventive powers of the young man who was poorly educated and consequently not terribly literate. Attempts by skeptics since then to attribute the document to a reworking of an early 19th century romance by Solomon Spaulding have not been particularly successful. Moreover, Smith's sincerity is attested to by his refusal to recant his beliefs even in the face of the kind of savage persecution that finally ended in his death.

The Book of Mormon claims to be the record of the first inhabitants of the Western Hemisphere and covers a period from 600 B.C. to 400 A.D. It is made up of fourteen books and is over five hundred pages long. The first two of these books, *I* and *II Nephi,* trace the flight of Lehi, a descendant of Joseph who was sold into Egypt by his brothers, and his family and followers from Jerusalem to a land of promise across the sea. Once there, two of the sons, Laman and Lemuel, led a rebellion against their father and were punished by being cursed with dark skin. From these Lamanites, says Mormon doctrine, the American Indians descended.

Another son, Nephi, remained faithful, however, and the major books of the *Book* follow the fortunes of the Nephites up to and beyond the coming of Christ to the continent after the Resurrection. The chronicle concludes with the final battle between the Nephites and the Lamanites, which resulted in the decimation of the Nephites and in the prophet Moroni, Mormon's son, placing the gold plates at the site of the struggle, from there to be recovered centuries later by Joseph Smith.

Just how one chooses to take these revelations depends on how seriously one takes the doctrine of Mormonism. This author, who is not Mormon, has his reservations. On the other hand, for reasons I am about to explain, I believe the answers – whatever and wherever they may be – are not likely to be simple; in fact, they may even be downright hair-raising. For Mormonism has given rise to one of the weirdest mysteries of American folklore.

In the book of *III Nephi* we are told the story of Christ's ministry in the New World, which in at least one important detail parallels the *New Testament's* account; namely, in Jesus' gathering about him twelve apostles. In the Book, however, three of these Nephite disciples ask that they be allowed to remain on earth to continue their ministry until his return. Mormon makes reference to having seen these three (325 A.D.) and in the final part of the work, Moroni says that he too had dealings with them before the Lord withdrew them from the company of the later Nephites, who had degenerated into sinful unbelievers. "Whether they be upon the face of the land no man knoweth," Moroni wrote (Mormon 8:11).

In the famous Christian legend of the Wandering Jew we also encounter the motif of the man who has traveled the world over preaching the gospel and whose labors will cease only at the Second Coming. Only in this case, the traveler has not made the choice; it has been forced on him by way of punishment because he scorned Jesus as he carried the cross to Calvary.

A related legend, this one concerning St. John the Beloved, is apparently based on Christ's remark in Matthew 16:28: "Verily I say unto you, There be some standing here, which shall not taste of death, till they see the Son of man coming in his kingdom." As George K. Anderson observes in his definitive *The Legend of the Wandering Jew*, "Christ's statement seems to indicate his belief that the kingdom of God is to come within the lifetime of many in Christ's audience; it is not to be some divine, far-off event, but something to take place in the not distant future. If we leave aside this theological point, however, the actual interpretation of this remark by certain followers of Christ made it possible to read into the verse a promise of immortality, although this immortality might mean only a continuance on earth until such time as Christ returned with God's kingdom."

Out of these two traditions grew a large body of myth, lore and

literature which has fascinated students of human belief for centuries. In its usual form, tales of St. John and the Wandering Jew
recount the appearance of a venerable old man with a long beard,
a staff and tattered clothes who preaches the word of God, effects miraculous cures and rescues people in time of danger. These
stories are incredibly widespread, or rather were, since they seem
no longer to exist in folk tradition (the last recorded tale goes back
to Utah of 1900). But in their time they ranged from Asia Minor
to the New World.

An Indian legend from upstate New York serves as a bridge between the older myth and the relatively more recent Three
Nephites tradition we are about to explore. The incident in question is supposed to have occurred in the late 18th or early 19th
century at Hector Falls, near the town of Watkins.

For some time the Indians had noted the presence of a
mysterious figure, a white man, who was often seen traveling
alone among the ravines and woodlands of the lake country. The
Indians stayed out of his way, suspecting that he might be some
kind of supernatural being who, if disturbed, could bring harm
to the tribe. Finally one of them discovered that the man was a
Jew. Not long afterwards the chiefs called a tribal council to
discuss what they might do about the unwanted visitor. By now
their uneasiness about his presence had led to paranoid fears that
he might be plotting to assassinate their queen, the semi-legendary
Katharene, so they agreed to drive him out of the neighborhood.

The next time they saw him, a group of warriors set off in hot
pursuit and chased him until they had him cornered. Or so they
thought. The stranger suddenly darted off in the direction of Hector Falls, but caught between the darkness and his own panic he
fell off a precipice, grasping at the last moment at the branches
of a small tree to prevent him from plunging into the waters below.
Unfortunately for him, the tree could not sustain his weight; it
and he went down.

Though they searched for years, the Indians never found his
body. To commemorate the event they marked the site of his fall
with a white spot, known to this day as the "Painted Rock."

A legend, of course, and perhaps nothing more, but an interesting one in view of the fact that Mormonism in later years would take root in upstate New York, in the same area where, according to *The Book of Mormon,* the last battle between the Nephites and the Lamanites had taken place. The tale is all the more fascinating because, like the Cuban encounter discussed earlier, it predates Mormonism.

But if the story is only legend, the peculiar affair of Robert Edge is something more than that. That someone who called himself Edge actually existed is hardly open to doubt, since many people saw him and his activities were reported in local newspapers. But the implications may be a bit more than a 20th century skeptic might feel comfortable having to contemplate.

On a calm, sunny day in May, 1878, a clap of thunder resounded over a thirty-five-mile area encompassing Lexington, Tennessee, and the surrounding countryside. There was not a cloud in the sky and when no storm followed the thunder, residents of Henderson county were nonplussed. That afternoon, a stranger, described as about thirty years old, slender, of medium height, with fair skin, dark-brown curly hair and a light reddish beard, wandered into town and announced he would hold a religious service that night. By evening the visitor had excited considerable controversy because even though no one had ever seen him before he seemed to know the area intimately. Rumors circulated that this man, who gave his name as Robert Edge, was someone special and so when the time came Lexington residents flocked to the meeting, hardly knowing what to expect.

What they got from Edge was a sermon unlike any they had heard before. Attacking the organized Christian churches as the "mother of harlots" (Smith's angelic informants called other churches "an abomination in his sight"), he called for a return to the principles of the primitive church, condemned secret societies, explained Biblical prophecies and called on his listeners to prepare for the imminent Second Coming by abandoning all earthly concerns and giving themselves to Christ.

Many in the audience were deeply moved and before long Edge

had gathered around him a respectable following. He roamed the country going to homes, farms and towns without ever having to ask for directions, a talent which contributed considerably to the aura of mystery around him. Individuals assigned to watch him complained that they could not keep track of him. Further, according to one account, "It was discovered that no one had ever seen him at any distance from a place of worship, and he was never seen until he arrived in the crowd or assumed his place in the pulpit." One rumor, which Edge would neither confirm nor deny, alleged that the enigmatic evangelist was a Mormon.

Determined to uncover the truth, a local Baptist deacon, named Jones, went to a house where Edge was eating and confronted him.

"My friend," Jones asked, "where are you from?"

"From about six miles," Edge answered evasively. He was referring to the town where he had been earlier in the day.

"What church do you belong to?"

"The church of God, sir."

"Where is it?"

"In the United States." (Mormons believe that America is the chosen land of God.)

"You have been speaking about one being ordained before he had the right to preach. By whom were you ordained?"

"By Jesus Christ, Sir."

"Where?"

"In Eternity."

"How long have you been preaching?"

"About 1,800 years."

At this point Jones left in disgust.

Edge is said to have had advance knowledge of dangers about to befall him and he managed to disappear somehow before an angry mob could locate him. He was never seen or heard from again. Later his followers joined the Mormon Church and, heeding Edge's advice to move West if they were subjected to persecution, escaped Henderson County and settled in Colorado.

Another mysterious stranger figures in an Augusta, Georgia legend. Around 1890, Augusta citizens discovered a remarkable evangelist in their midst, an elderly man with neatly-trimmed white hair and of stately appearance, with a clear, pleasant voice that was "yet incisive even to the piercing of the human heart." Like Edge he revealed little if anything about himself and preached like the prophets of old, doing most of his speaking in the Market Place, a construction composed of two large sheds that extended about a hundred feet across the street and about two hundred feet in length. The sheds, known as the Upper and Lower Markets, were supported by pillars. Here farmers brought in food from their fields, and townspeople came to purchase their daily groceries.

One day the old man announced that a storm would destroy the Lower Market and leave only the southwest pillar standing to prove that he was a prophet of God. Anyone who tried to move the pillar would die, he said. Not long afterward, an electrical storm erupted; the Lower Market burned to the ground and only the southwest pillar remained.

Later the evangelist visited at the home of Mr. and Mrs. Mack Little of Groveland, Georgia, fifteen miles west of Augusta. He repeated the prophecy once more before he left. Descendants of the Little family swore to the truth of the story many years later. The "Pillar of Prophecy" survived the great Augusta fire of 1916 and was still there as late as 1920.

Mormon patriarch David F. Fawns of Canada supplied his own footnote to the legend by claiming that on two occasions in 1900, as he stood by the pillar, the mysterious old man appeared to him. Fawns thought he might be one of the Three Nephites.

Now let us turn our attention to Utah, where in 1847 the Mormons established themselves after being driven out of the more settled regions of the country, and consider briefly what the participants took to be a miraculous visitation by a Nephite. The incident supposedly occured in April, 1852, in Salt Lake City.

One day during a long period of particular hardship for the newly-arrived Mormons, an aged man knocked at the door of a local family and asked if he could eat with them. Food was scarce, but the wife gave him what she had, namely water, bread, and onions, which the stranger consumed quickly. When he had

(© Beth Fideler and Philip Hemstreet, 1983)

Frightened and apprehensive, this turn-of-the-century Utah farmer's wife provides food for her uninvited guests, The Three Nephites, little realizing that good fortune will be her reward.

finished, he asked how much he owed her, jingling coins in his pocket to prove he could pay well. She refused the offer, at which point the stranger took two or three measured steps toward her and spoke in a voice so powerful that she almost fainted and had to sit down when she heard it. "Well" he said, "if you charge me nothing for my dinner, may God bless you and peace be with you."

The stranger turned and walked out. The wife asked a Mrs. Dunsdon, a neighbor who was there visiting at the time, to look out and see where the man was going. However, he had already disappeared and could not be found, even though in those early days there were no houses around, "not even an outhouse," the woman later wrote, "nor fence of any kind to intercept the eye." Still more oddly, when she returned to clear the table, the food was still there as if it had not been touched at all!

She subsequently recalled how her family had survived the famine even when her neighbors were starving. She said they had even had enough food left over to feed others who were less fortunate. "I gave in the day of my poverty, of the scanty store I had to the man of God," she remarked, "and it seems that ever after, my meal sack was never empty."

During the summer of 1874, Mrs. Edwin Squires of Wa Wa Springs, Utah, played host to a mysterious visitor who appeared out of nowhere to ask for a meal. Before his arrival she had gone to the spring for water and studied the desolate area for signs of her husband, who was due at any moment. She saw no one coming, so she went inside, put the water down, turned around and was stunned to see a man with gray hair and a long white beard standing there. When he requested something to eat, she uneasily prepared him a meal, which he ate as though very hungry.

In the course of the meal he commented that she was not well. "That's true" she said. "I have had a pain under my shoulder that has bothered me a great deal."

To which the old man replied, "Your liver is responsible for that, but it won't be bothering you any longer." Then he rose, thanked her and said, "God bless you, sister. You will never want for anything again. You will always be blessed with plenty."

Moments after he had walked out the door, Mrs. Squires stepped outside to see in which direction he had gone – only to discover that he had disappeared as suddenly as he had appeared.

Mrs. Squires came to believe her visitor was one of the Three Nephites. Her health problems ceased soon after her experience, as did the family's financial difficulties. When she died at the age of 89, her wealth was able to set all her children up in business.

So far, not one of our supposed Nephites has identified himself as such, unless one counts Edge's claim to having been around for 1,800 years as something as good as an admission. But in the summer of 1876 a peculiar white man named Nephi ministered to the Indians at Duck Creek, west of St. George, Utah. Nephi, who sported a long white beard and dressed himself entirely in white, told the Indians that the Mormons were their friends and would show them a better life. He also maintained that he was one of their forefathers and had been on earth for hundreds and hundreds of years. During the whole of his stay not a single Indian was seen along the nearby Virgin River or any of its tributaries.

Two women, one a Mormon, the other an atheist, who joined the Latter-Day Saints after the experience, credited one of the Three Nephites with saving their lives. One evening in the summer of 1900 they became trapped on a mountainside when their horses refused to cross a crevice filled with shale. The animals had panicked when the shale began to slide and would move neither backward nor forward. Maud May Babcock, the Mormon lady, dismounted and crawled over the mountaintop in hopes of running into a wandering prospecter. When that did not happen, she made her way back with a small willow and tried to drive the horse with it, but he still would not move. Finally, every other option exhausted, she prayed.

Suddenly a voice from above her asked, "How did you come here, my daughter?"

As Miss Babcock was to write, "I jabbered in my relief and excitement, trying to explain our predicament, and before my explanation was finished I was standing on the top with Miss Carrie Helen Lamson and both our horses in a circle facing the stranger." She had no idea how they had gotten there.

Their mysterious helper had a gray Vandyke beard, wore a cap on his head and was dressed in blue overalls. He looked well-scrubbed and his soft white hands appeared unused to hard manual labor. When he spoke he addressed Miss Babcock as "my daughter," when Miss Lamson, the non-Mormon, would ask him a question, he would direct his answer to her companion.

As they talked with him, the two women mounted their horses and prepared to resume their journey. They set off and had not gone more than twenty feet when Miss Babcock realized she had not thanked him for his help. She turned around and discovered, much to her astonishment, that he was gone. Since they had clear vision for at least a mile in every direction she could only conclude that he had vanished.

"He was one of the Three Nephites," she exclaimed suddenly.

Another, more circumstantial tale was told by John Alfred of Salt Lake City, who recounted an alleged experience that took place as he lay under an elm tree waiting for services to begin at the Mormon Temple. I mention it not because it is documented (it isn't) but because it has a Nephite identifying himself as such and also because it connects the Nephite tradition with a legend discussed earlier.

"A man came walking up – a long, white-bearded man," Alfred said. "He walked up to me and shook hands with me. He said, 'I want you to know you have met and shaken hands with one of the Apostles of Jesus Christ, ordained by the hand of Jesus Christ himself more than 2,000 years ago.' He told me the various things he had seen, the places he had been, things that had transpired over a period of 2,000 years. He had thrilled as he saw the church grow, and told me what it had meant to him personally because of the many defenses that had been given. He mentioned a pillar in Augusta, Georgia."

These incidents, or alleged incidents, are fairly typical of the hundreds told in past years about the Nephites. As a general rule, the three were not seen together, did not identify themselves directly (although in rare instances one would say, "I am one of the Three"), appeared and disappeared miraculously, made prophecies and seemed to know all things. Usually it was Mormons who encountered them – though, as shown, that was not invariably the case.

In some few instances only certain persons saw them. They appeared to all kinds of people, not just the gullible and superstitious. A. E. Fife, who collected a large variety of Nephite stories for a study of the subject in *The Journal of American Folk-Lore,* noted that a number of those he interviewed "were trained college people, among whom were medical men, college professors, and other professional people."

The problem folklorists have encountered in attempting to explain the persistent Nephite legends and reports is suggested by the conclusion Fife drew: "From the facts that we have gathered," he wrote, "it would seem that the Mormon converts who had certainly brought popular versions of the Wandering Jew legend to Utah with them, soon transformed them into Three Nephites legends once they had been exposed to the theology of Joseph Smith."

That would be true if the Three Nephites existed only as yarns passed from person to person and from generation to generation. But, when one has to deal with personal experiences of others, then the question becomes infinitely more difficult. Fife does not dispute the sincerity of his informants, many of them devout Mormons, nor does he explain just how they managed to delude themselves into believing they had experienced something they hadn't. Hector Lee, another student of the legend, begs the question when he dismisses first-hand testimony as, although not deliberately fabricated, "somehow psychic" – presumably meaning psychological.

Without committing myself to belief in 2,000-year old apostles (in which, lest readers mistake my meaning, I wish to emphasize I most decidedly do not believe), I think it is fairly obvious that folklorists simply do not care to confront the dazzling paranormal implications of the legend. The probably feel much the same way as the astronomer who a few years ago advanced a rather improbable "natural" explanation for a UFO sighting, remarking that while his theory might sound implausible it would have to do since flying saucers do not exist.

I would suggest a third alternative: namely, that Nephites as such do not exist, but that manifestations calling themselves or being taken for Nephites do. Thus, they join the ranks of supposed spirits of the dead, Venusians, visions of the Virgin Mary which apparently exist but not as what they appear to be or say they are. What the purpose of this deception might be, I hesitate to speculate.

The Swedish mystic Emanuel Swedenborg, who recognized the illusory nature of these elemental forces in the 18th century, wrote the following from his own experience:

"When spirits begin to speak with a man, he must beware that he believe nothing that they say. For nearly everything they say is fabricated by them, and they lie: for if they are permitted to narrate anything, as what heaven is and how things in the heavens are to be understood, they would tell so many lies that a man would be astonished. This they would do with solemn affirmation. . . Wherefore men must beware and not believe them. It is on this account that the state of speaking with spirits on this earth is most perilous."

Whatever the real story behind American manifestations of the Three Nephites, there can be no doubt that the many reports of these mysterious wanderers force us to have questions.

Fireside Thinking

21
The Name Game

As you travel about in this Mysterious America, be it on your way to work or play, or to some vacation destination, you pass many streets, or transit many towns with names we all have come to take for granted. How often have we paused to think about the meaning behind the names? Was the word of some special significance? Was this location named for a person, another place or an event? And if it was named for a person, what did their name originally mean? And who and why was it tacked on to *this* place? Are their some harmonic insights we can gain from looking a little deeper? Why do some places or even people seem to be the focus of inexplicable events while others are the host of more mundane incidents?

In Chapter 3, I have discussed devils' names and Fortean places. The fact that some areas had strange and weird vibrations or events connected to them gave native Americans and later settlers enough evidence to actually label these locales after the Ruler of Hell. In America, the use of the name "devil" regarding certain geographical fixtures, therefore, gives some indication of a history of mystery surrounding these spots.

An interesting English science fiction film illustrates this process, plus the hidden meanings behind names on which this chapter will concentrate. In the 1967 movie *Five Million Years to Earth,* a new subway excavation in the Hobbs End section of London unearths an apparent extraterrestrial craft. The scientists involved in the unraveling of this drama soon discover this part of London on Hobbs Lane has a long history of poltergeist, haunting and apparition activities. One keen young researcher discovers an old street sign near the diggings, and she notes the spelling is "Hob's Lane," not "Hobbs Lane." "Hob," it turns out, is another name for "devil," or the "Devil", if you prefer.

Some words do not appear to be what they so calmly convey. "Hob," for example, is an alteration of Robin or Robert, as in Robin Goodfellow, a rustic, a clown (lest we get too far from the phantom clowns). Robin Goodfellow, sometimes called Puck, was/is a tricksy house sprite or elf in popular English fairy lore. And Puck is sometimes called hobgoblin. Even the descriptive verb "hobble" refers to the word's origins, as the classic view of the Devil shows cloven hooves.

In the United States, consequently, Hobbs, New Mexico, and Hobbs, Indiana, have "devil's names." Although the local folks know a great deal about the strange things happening thereabouts, most probably do not know the etymological origins of their towns' names flash back to a demonic past. In Indiana, Hobbs had been the location of UFO sightings in the 1950s and 1960s. Hobbs, New Mexico, near the 33° latitude (another power point), has experienced a never ending stream of UFO encounters since Bill Watson's April 1955 sighting became known in ufology as the "Hobbs Incident." Indeed, this Southwest corner of New Mexico is a hotbed of so-called flying saucer activity with the most famous event being the "Roswell Incident" detailed in a best-selling book of the same name. Allegedly, in nearby Roswell, New Mexico, on July 8, 1947, a UFO crashed, and the US Air Force recovered small bodies from the craft, according to researchers Leonard Stringfield, William Moore, and Dr. Bruce Maccabee. The whole use of the term "little green men" appears to have been added to American slang by way of the incidents taking place in the

Hobbs–Roswell area in 1947. Considering the background to the name "Hobbs," such events are not too surprising.

But then, name selectivity is the name of the game being played. According to that profound student of American place names, George R. Stewart, approximately 3,500,000 named places – about one to the square mile – exist in the United States of America, with another million recorded but no longer in use. As I have plied the byways of this country and have blackened my hands on newsprint, I have been struck by how over and over again the same town or ones with similar names appear to get all the mysterious action. Or that same named witnesses continually pop up in the Fortean reports. Against the percentages, a name game is occuring.

Fortean author Jim Brandon has done considerable thinking and writing about the correlation of place names and weird phenomena. He has come forth with some rather interesting findings. Brandon, writing in the thoroughly enjoyable *The Rebirth of Pan* chooses, as his peculiar candidate for this game, the name Fayette and its variants Lafayette and Fayetteville which appear in 18 counties and 28 towns or cities across the USA. He gives scores of examples, and I refer the reader to his book for the details of the weird stories Brandon weaves. I shall give a few illustrations of this "Fayette" pattern from my files.

Near Mt. Diablo, California, site of the Black Mountain Lion of Devil's Hole are the haunts of the "Beast of Lafayette Lake." The search was on for this creature from boats, helicopters and horseback during October of 1975. James Lattie of the East Bay Regional Park District told the news media at the time: "You won't believe this but our men reported a most unusual occurence. That is an alligator, you know, the kind with jaws and long teeth – well, you won't believe it. Well, here goes our image but two of our patrolmen were sitting on the dam; they were looking in the water. Now they noticed this long shape moving along the water, sort of like a log and slow-like. And one of these patrolmen, he hails from Florida, says to his buddy: 'Hey, you know, if I wasn't in California, I'd swear that that's a gator trying to make the other side. Matter of fact, that is an alligator.' "

(courtesy of *San Francisco Examiner*)

Lafayette Lake, an elusive alligator, and a police helicopter
in pursuit – the beat goes on.

The patrolmen could not locate the eight foot alligator, the Regional Park district closed the lake, and the search parties were sent in. As with some errant 'gators, at last word, this Lafayette croc was never found.

An old clipping about the "Headless Horseman" of Fayette County, Ohio's "Haunted Hill" was recently passed on by Mark A. Hall. Apparently in June, 1953, diggings at Cherry Hill, known thereabouts as "Haunted Hill," revealed a headless skeleton. Fayette County legend tells of a man on horseback coming to the hill. His saddlebags were filled with gold. The man was murdered but his body was never found, although his horse was recovered. Folklore then developed about the "Headless Horseman of Haunted Hill." The 1953 skeleton was quickly reburied as Fayette County officialdom said the bones were Amerindian in origin.

My 1977 black panther investigations in Ohio were concentrated around the northeastern town of La Fayette. Fayette County, Pennsylvania, has some peculiar petroglyphs, lots of Bigfoot reports, and was visited by UFO occupants in 1973. Lafayette Hill, Pennsylvania, had a UFO swing by there in August 1975. Fayetteville, New York experienced a strange skyquake on April 17, 1968. Lafayette, Wisconsin, was visited by a phantom panther in November, 1977. Fayette, Indiana, had a UFO encounter, October, 1966. Fayette, Maine, is five miles from the haunted location of Devil's Den. Fayetteville, Arkansas, near Decatur, was noted by Jim Brandon as a hotspot of oddities. To his list of UFOs, water monsters, and mad gasser-types from there, I can add a fall of metal, a mystery skyquake, Bigfeet, phantom panthers, bizarre electromagnetic effects to cars, and frequent train derailings.

With amazing regularity the newspapers carry offbeat stories originating from a town or county with the Fayette root. In 1980, you could read the Associated Press wire stories on Friday, August 8th, about the escape and recapture of two elephants along the highway near Lafayette, Oregon. Exactly a year later, you could do a doubletake with UPI's Friday, August 7th accounts of the escape and recapture of an elephant on a road near La Fayette, Ohio.

The Fayette stories continue, but you get the idea.

Jim Brandon feels the triggering element in Fayette, Lafayette, and Fayetteville is the root word "fay/fey." The literal meaning of "fayette" is "little enchantment" or "little fairy" from the Old French *feer*, "to enchant" plus the feminine diminutive, *ette*. Brandon believes the locations may be enchanted by the use of the "fayette" name, and actually given some name power via their entitling.

In parallel research, I have found the use of "fay" intermingled in a significant way with a location important in the Joan of Arc stories. Another meaning, from the French, for "fay" is "beech." Near the home of Joan of Arc was a large old beech tree (French: *fay;* Latin: *fagus*). It was under this tree that the "voices" spoke to Joan. By the 1400s, the tree was considered holy to Our Lady of Domremy, but many people felt it had once been a sacred place during the times of the old pagan religion. Near the beech was a spring where locals came to be cured of disease. At night, fairies were said to dance around the tree.

As T. Douglas Murray noted in *Jeanne d'Arc,* during her trials, Joan of Arc mentioned her involvement with this tree: "Not far from Domremy there is a tree that they call 'The Ladies Tree'— others call it 'The Fairies Tree'. . .. It is a beautiful tree, a beech, from which comes the 'beau mai' (maypole). . .. I have sometimes been to play with young girls, to make garlands for Our Lady of Domremy. Often I have heard the old folk . . . say that the fairies haunt this tree."

The Joan of Arc incident quite clearly points to the "fay," the beech tree being an enchanted spot involved and influenced by mysterious forces quite beyond mortal understanding. What we appear to be seeing in America at all of the present "fayette" sites is merely the threading of this magical web into the modern world.

Has the labeling of certain locations given them some form of occult power or energy magnetism on a level not yet fathomed? The evidence with the "fayette" places, and others, seems to indicate this.

For there are other special places. Speaking of maypoles, let's look at Rowan County, North Carolina, for a second. During the last week in April, and the first in May, 1982, Rowan County was hit with a wave of "wampus cat" (i.e. phantom panther) sightings. Now, interestingly enough, the rowan tree is an extremely important and magical tree in Old England, used in Wicker Man sacrifices and as a maypole. What is to be deduced from the "coincidence" of something mysterious happening in Rowan County, on May the 1st, May Day, the day of the maypole?

Logan is another one of those words. Rocking logan stones are a part of ancient megalithic research. My brother and I interviewed the Lowe family (see Chapter 2) about the big birds' attempted abduction of Marlon from their front yard, in Logan County, Illinois. Another Logan County, this one in Colorado, has had an unusually high number of cattle mutilations, and one 1975 mystery helicopter report. Logan County, Colorado, also has had an 1897 airship account, as has Logan, Ohio. Loganville, Wisconsin, sits but a stone's throw from the woods around Baraboo, said to be haunted by ghost elephants. Logansport, Indiana, is the place a lake monster supposedly made an 1835 appearance. Logan Peak, near Huntsville, Alabama, the location of UFO, Bigfeet and mystery explosion reports, is a short distance north of Hobbs Island. Logan, Kansas, saw some unexplained bird deaths in 1978. Logan, Utah, was a city frequented by UFOs during the late 1940s and early 1950s. A May 1, 1954, flash of light was followed by an explosion and huge crater in Logan, Utah. In the 1980's, women were disappearing from Boston's Logan Airport thus ending this list unended.

Decatur is another "hot" name. During the spring of 1982, my brother Jerry Coleman, investigated black panther sightings between two well-named locales, Decaturville and Devil's Knee, Missouri. Growing up in Decatur, Illinois, I noted all types of phenomena – erratic 'gators, UFOs, panthers, (by the way, Decatur means "dweller at the sign of the cat"!) hairy apes, falls, mutilations, skyquakes, airships – centered on the town. Years later, when attempting to make some sense of the name game, my attention was drawn to the fall of frogs in Decatur, Indiana, in 1937. Charles Fort once wrote that we might gain some insight, we might know an existence by its frogs. In a humorous sort of way, I figured the ole boy was trying to tell me something. But the game

Stephen Decatur – a focus of weird phenomena in person and by way of locations named in his honor. The name game continues.

has sinister tones too. In February, 1981, the town of Decatur, Tennessee, was hit with a month of mutilations. As with the classic pattern of cattle mutilations which peaked in middle America in the 1970s, the Tennessee incident included the surgically skilled removal of one calf's sexual organs, in that Decatur.

The point is made. Cities with certain names appear to have more than their share of strange events taking place in their boundaries. But wait, some cities' "power names" may come from something connected to the individual for whom they were named. Take, for example, Decatur, Illinois. This city and the others were named after Stephen Decatur, naval hero. Not too amazingly, the man seems to be linked to matters occult.

The Stephen Decatur House in Washington, D.C., is haunted. The Decatur House is located on Lafayette Square! Perhaps more amazingly, the Jersey Devil legend involves Stephen Decatur. In about 1804, at the Hanover Iron Works, Brown's Mills, New Jersey, Decatur is said to have observed a bizarre creature flapping its wings as it flew across the cannon firing range. Decatur, the story goes, took aim, shot at "it," but the creature continued on its way. This account adds yet another piece to the puzzle of the name game, and it raises more questions.

Are particular names attached to specific people then the focus of mysterious activity, weird wonders, and strange sightings, akin to the name magic of special places? Surely something is occuring.

Late in 1973, John Keel, anomaly expert extraordinare, was pondering reports I had sent him. These were the Enfield, Illinois critter stories (see Chapter 15) of Henry McDaniel. Keel noted the name McDaniel had crossed his path before. He pointed to the family of that name who were the center of the West Virginia Mothman series he had investigated. Mabel McDaniel had seen Mothman on January 11, 1967, near Tony's Restaurant in Point Pleasant; then later during March, had a run-in with one of those Mad Gasser/Springheel Jack-type fellows, the Men-In-Black. Parke McDaniel had likewise been frightened by the Men-In-Black on December 23, 1967. Keel felt the name McDaniel had a far greater recurrence than should randomly be happening. He had also uncovered an 1870's story of an individual named McDaniel who had met up with the Devil in New York State's Catskill Mountains.

About a decade ago, John Keel raised the question of name selectivity when he wrote: "Hundreds of thousands of phenomenal events have been described in newspapers, magazines and books, and hundreds of thousands of witnesses have been named in print. When dealing with such a large body of evidence – or population – certain laws of probability should surface. We might expect that more Smiths would see UFOs than anyone else, simply because there are more Smiths around. But, in actuality, the name Smith rarely appears in a UFO report."

What Keel found was unusual names were the point of convergence for the phenomena. He saw McDaniel, Reeves/Reaves, Maddox, Heflin, Allen, Hill, and others, as being selected for UFO and related experiences. The Smiths, Browns, Williams and Johnsons – the four top surnames in America – are not the most frequent precipitant name to crop up. I would add that the most unusually named witnesses seem to have the more bizarre encounters.

A good example of such a situation took place in 1958, in the strange case of the two Charlie Wetzels.

On August 27, 1958, Jerry Crew and his men, literally his crew, reported some strange incidents as they were building a new lumber access road near Bluff Creek, California. Soon photographs of giant 17-inch-long plaster casts of human-like tracks were being carried nationwide by the media, and the hunt for Bigfoot was in full swing.

Three months later and 600 miles away, an eerie encounter was to occur in southern California which soon took an aberrant but classic place in the Bigfoot literature. This was the Charlie Wetzel sighting. The details of the story are familiar through the writings of Barker, the Bords, Green, Sanderson, and others, but during 1982 I was able to interview Wetzel and his family personally, coming up with some interesting new information.

Charles Wetzel, born July 8, 1934, was driving his two-door green 1952 Buick Super near Riverside, California, when he saw "it." Saturday, November 8, 1958, is a night Charlie told me he would not soon forget. He even remembers which radio station – KFI in Los Angeles – he had tuned in. Wetzel neared that part of

North Main Street where the Santa Ana River infrequently overflows its banks, and sure enough, at a spot where the road dips, water was rushing across the pavement. So Charles slowed down.

Within moments he was struck by two sensory events which caught him off guard. First, his car radio started to transmit lots of static. He changed stations, he told me, but to no avail. Next, he saw what he thought was a temporary danger sign near the flooded site. Before he could think twice about any of this, Charles Wetzel saw a six-foot-tall creature bound across his field of vision and stop in front of his Buick. It had a "round, scarecrowish head like something out of Halloween," Wetzel told reporters at the time. He described it then and now as having no ears; no nose; a beak-like, protuberant mouth; and fluorescent, shining eyes. The skin was "scaly, like leaves, but definitely not feathers," Wetzel recalled during our 1982 talk.

The creature was waving "sort of funny" with its incredibly long arms, and seemed to be walking from the hips, almost as if it had no knees. Wetzel remembers another detail not noted at the time: the legs stuck out from the sides of the torso, not from the bottom. The gurgling sounds it made were mixed with high-pitched screams. When it saw Wetzel it reached across the hood and began clawing at the windshield. Terrified, Wetzel grabbed the .22 High Standard pistol he kept in the car because he was often on the road at night. Clutching the gun but not wanting to break the one barrier he saw between himself and the beast, the frightened Californian stomped on the gas. "Screeching like a fucker," as Wetzel graphically put it, the creature tumbled forward off the hood and was run over by the car. Wetzel could hear it scrape the pan under the engine, and later police lab tests revealed that something had indeed scrubbed the grease from the Buick's underside.

The police used bloodhounds to search the area, but the dogs found nothing and the officers were left with only the sweeping claw marks on Wetzel's windshield to ponder. Then, the very next night, a black something jumped out of the underbrush near the same site and frightened another motorist.

In recent years, strange three-toed "Bigfeet" have been reported from surrounding areas of southern California, notably the Buena Park smelly eight-footer seen emerging from a drainage ditch in May, 1982. But the Wetzel sighting near Riverside has won classic status among Southern California cases, having been widely discussed and debated by Bigfooters since 1958. Not until 1982 when researcher Ray Boeche passed along an aging newsclip did I learn that *another* Charles Wetzel had seen something strange. For years I had encouraged Boeche, as I had many others, to search their local newspaper libraries beyond the realm of lake-monster and Bigfoot accounts, into the wide weird world of creatures that fill the zoo surrounding us all. I was thus happily amazed to discover that *this* Charles Wetzel was involved with one of my favorites – mysterey kangaroos! The names were the same and the year was the same, 1958; but the scene shifted from California to Nebraska.

I got on the telephone to interview the new Charles Wetzel. The elements of his story were straightforward, as befits a true son of the plains. Charles Wetzel, born March 29, 1888, was at his Platte River cabin, near Grand Island, Nebraska, on the 28th of July, 1958, a Monday. Wetzel reported the thing he first took to be a deer was chasing some dogs, which in itself seemed a bit strange. Then he got within ten yards of it and saw what looked like a kangaroo bound away with ten-foot leaps. To Wetzel, the animal, or whatever it was, appeared to be about six feet tall, brown, with large hind legs and small forelegs that barely touched the ground as it jumped. According to Wetzel, the kangaroo stayed around the cabin for several minutes but finally departed as Wetzel was trying to get closer, first on foot, then in his car. The kangaroo disappeared into an alfalfa field.

Wetzel's report was no isolated event in Nebraska in 1958. Other sightings of kangaroos were reported from towns as distant as 100 miles from each other – Endicott, Stanton and Fairbury among them. Charles Wetzel was operating a brewery in Grand Island at the time of his sighting; he named one of his brands "Wetzel Kangaroo Beer."

In talking with California Charles Wetzel and Nebraska Charles Wetzel, I discovered that both had sons named Charles, but neither family knew of the other. What are we to make of this bit of synchronization of Wetzels, both named Charles, both having encountered creatures way beyond the norm, in the year 1958? After much head-scratching, I thought it might be useful to find some kind of underlying pattern via the name "Wetzel." Now, monsters do not seem to be seen by people with the most common names, but why would a couple of Charlie Wetzels be picked? "Wetzel" is a German name, a corrupted form of "little Varin," from "Warin," meaning "protector." Should we therefore assume some elemental insight from a name that literally means "little protector or guardian"?

Next, I went on a search to determine whether the name "Wetzel" is used geographically. On a map of the United States I discovered but one use of "Wetzel" – it was the name of a very rural county in northern West Virginia. I was not too surprised to find that the folklore of Wetzel County is a repository of historic ghost stories. No surprise, either, to find some curious Fortean items in surrounding areas. Nearby Sisterville, West Virginia, is well known as one of the few eastern American cities to have been visited by the phantom airships of the 1890s. Moundsville, just north of Wetzel is the site of a significant earthen mound built by ancient unknown people. Other mounds are still being discovered in the area; one was recently exposed when a hill was cut away to provide a building site for a glass factory. Bordering counties in Pennsylvania – Greene and Fayette – are the site of many strange accounts of hominoid and UFO visitations in the last few years. All in all, Wetzel County probably feels very at home in the state of the Flatwoods Monster, and Mothman.

Wetzel County, West Virginia, was named after Lewis Wetzel, whom Teddy Roosevelt called a "one-man army, the greatest scout, woodsman and Indian fighter in America's history." Wetzel was credited with killing hundreds of Indians. He was so feared by the Shawnee, they called him the "Dark Destroyer"; the Delawares referred to him as "Deathwind" because of the eerie, hollow cry he let out when he killed. His massacre of Indians continued after the signing of the peace treaties. This led to his capture and escape to Spanish Louisiana, where he was arrested as an American spy.

Wetzel died soon after his release some four years after his imprisonment. In 1808, at the age of 45, Lewis Wetzel was a broken man upon his death.

What kind of influence did his name carry with it to the county in West Virginia? The strange events there appear to have started soon after he died. In 1845, a mysterious "Frenchmen" showed up in the area, and remained awhile without any means of support. He was soon arrested under the vagrancy law, and quickly produced papers stating he was an agent of France, searching for $87,000 buried below a Wetzel County creek. The money was never found. Shortly thereafter, stories circulated that a Mr. Watkins had buried 960 silver dollars, weighing over sixty pounds, sixty steps from the river, under a pawpaw bush.

What I found of interest in the two buried treasure incidents is their connectedness to patterns running through dozens of mysterious sites in America. Buried treasure stories are common fixtures of spook light and Devil's Den sites. Strangers appearing in towns, giving out "disinformation," and leaving a wake of questions in their path occur all too frequently. It happened in the midst of the 1890s airship wave, during the 1960s Mothman episodes, and then again with the Men-In-Black encounters. Wetzel's 1845 "Frenchmen" falls right into this category.

And what of a Mr. Watkins showing up in the tales of Wetzel County? The name is a familiar one in the name game. Alfred Watkins, the English intellectual who formulated the notion of ley lines, comes to mind when thoughts of hidden power points are mentioned. And Watkins Glen, New York, is the site of reoccuring disappearances.

Cryptologic or coincidence?

Jim Brandon is to be credited with calling attention to the name Watts/Watkins/Watson, and its entanglement with inexplicable things. Some other names involved in mysterious events pinpointed by Brandon are Bell, Mason, Parsons, Pike, Vernon and Warren. The influence of such names as Mason, Pike, Warren and Lafayette, for example, issues, in some cryptopolitical and occult way, from their ties to the Masonic tradition. Jim Brandon's *The Rebirth of Pan* discusses this thesis in detail. Clearly, however, a massive name game is being played out across Mysterious America, and the proof of such a hypothesis goes beyond mere chance.

In *Wild Talents,* Charles Fort thought about some of these same things when he wrote: "My liveliest interest is not so much in things, as in relations of things. I have spent much time thinking about the alleged pseudorelations that are called coincidences. What if some of them should not be coincidences?"

Noting that the vanishing act of Ambrose Bierce was followed by the vanishing of Ambrose Small some six years later, Fort continued: "But what could the disappearance of one Ambrose, in Texas, have to do with the disappearance of another Ambrose, in Canada? There was in these questions an appearance of childishness that attracted my respectful attention."

Charles Fort, thus, engaged in the name game, and in an attempt to understand the quick explanation given for it, coincidence.

"In the explanation of *coincidence,*" Fort emphasized in *Wild Talents,* "there is much of laziness, and helplessness, and response to an instinctive fear that a scientific dogma will be endangered. It is a tag, or a label: but of course every tag, or label, fits well enough at times."

So, in the midst of all the Fayettevilles, Wetzels, Decaturs and Devils, someone must feel comfortable in knowing they believe they are merely coincidences.

But ponder Fort: "There is a view by which it can be shown, or more or less demonstrated, that there never has been a coincidence. That is, in anything like a final sense. By a coincidence is meant a false appearance, or suggestion, of relations among circumstances. But anybody who accepts that there is an underlying oneness of all things, accepts that there are no utter absences of relations among circumstances."

And what of any one of our own name games. To look personally, closer at your name or the place you live, is instructive.

For me, one who has examined deeply the pattern in names and things, I was struck by some insights only recently pointed out by Jim Brandon concerning "Coleman." Alfred Watkins, mentioned above, wrote in his *The Old Straight Track,* the "Coleman, who gave his name to all kinds of points and places on the tracks, was a head-man in making them, and probably worked from the Cole-hills, using beacon fires for making out the ley."

In a similar vein, I. Shah's *The Sufis* demonstrates the origin of my name via Coalman, the charcoal burners, the Perceivers, the Carbonari and their links with the occult.

Perhaps, then, the name game has played a special trick on me. I seem predisposed to try to scrutinize names of people and places for the purpose of perceiving the possible hidden meanings and patterns behind them. The lay of the land, and the sighters of the strange, then truly, hold many secrets as we hobnob about America.

22
Some Concluding Thoughts After Some Years On the Trail

Ten years ago, shortly before his death, Ivan Sanderson and I exchanged some interesting letters on the various creature and phantom reports sweeping Mysterious America. Sanderson, a well known investigator of the unexplained and successful Fortean author, had been corresponding with me for over a decade. Trained as a zoologist, as indeed I was, we shared a great deal of similar insights and droll intuitions with regard to the state of mysterious phenomena research of the time.

For example, in 1962, I suggested to Sanderson that an organization be created to deal with an examination of the worldwide abominable snowmen reports, be they termed yeti, bigfeet, or north American ape. He thought that was a good idea, but jokingly said, "The only trouble is that it would probably be full of Russians." Five years later, the Ivan T. Sanderson Foundation was a reality, soon to be followed by his Society for the Investigation of the Unexplained. Sanderson seemed to have had to build a formal organization in response to the incredible numbers of creature reports flooding the countryside of America.

Ivan Sanderson, then of Columbia, New Jersey, and John Green of British Columbia, had been fed reams of case investigations of Eastern U.S.A. creatures accounts by me since the early 1960s, and they were beginning to wonder what was going on. In 1967, Sanderson finally wrote, "Yes . . . Please . . . any reports you have . . . Little Red Men of the . . . or Giant Hairys in the suburbs. The whole bit is getting hotter and hairier by the month; and now we have the damned UFOs mixed up in it."

The lines between cryptozoology, parapsychology and ufology were merging again, after the writers in the 1940s and 1950s had forced artifical boundaries between the creatures, UFOs and phantoms. As Charles Fort had noted after the turn of the century, there is a oneness to it all. During the 1970s this admixture seems to have been rediscovered by authors examining the mysterious. I am a product of this era. I wrote my first article of note in the March 1971 issue of *Fate*.

Living in Illinois at the time, I discussed in the *Fate* article my field investigations into local bipedal hairy creature and black mystery feline reports. I invented the concept of phantom panthers, and began noting these beasts left some very unzoological clues behind.

After reading my article, Ivan Sanderson wrote a long letter to me detailing the dilemma such reports raised for him.

"Dammit. I don't like this sort of 'paraphysical' stuff, and I have kept strictly off it for 20 years now, despite ever increasing volumes of evidence (so called). But, in view of Jacque Vallee's ponderings on UFOs, and holograms, and solid (matter) projections; meaning, one can only assume, teleportation, I begin to wonder if the time has not come to take the proverbial ox by its frontal excrescences, and tackle the issue frontally also. However, it might do more harm than good, because it might put all of us serious minded and sane Forteans right back into the kook-klass in the eyes of both the genuine scientists and the newsmen. Quandary!"

"I have never been able to understand why all things serious
should have to be taken seriously; and, especially, *all* the
time."

—Ivan T. Sanderson

Within two years, Ivan Sanderson was dead. It was left for Vallee, John Keel, Jerome Clark, D. Scott Rogo, myself and others to take the bull by its horns and attempt to answer some of the questions posed by the events breaking out all over Mysterious America. Not coincidentially, when Ivan Sanderson died in 1973, part of the void he left was quickly filled by *Fortean Times* (first called *The News* way back then). Since then, the pages of *Fortean Times,* including a regular column by me, have served as the window on the theoretical mind of weird wonders investigators.

Now in 1983, looking back over the last ten years demonstrates an intriguing evolution in the thinking of those examining the accounts of strange creatures, foggy phantoms, and mysterious locations.

When Jerry Clark and I wrote our first two books in the mid-1970s, we suggested that UFOs and monsters were psychic projections of a collective unconscious, very literally thought forms which took on a solid state existence, be they clawed footprints where a phantom panther stepped, or knocking out of witnesses by a mad gasser.

As we observed, "Extraterrestrial spaceships simply could not be touring the earth in the massive numbers UFO sightings suggest. Neither could massive numbers of large unknown animals be roaming countryside and city streets without long ago having been officially recognized and catalogued (and probably driven into extinction as well).

"Moreover, they could not have done all this in such numbers without providing us with more conclusive physical evidence than they have given us so far. The 'physical evidence' is always just enough to suggest that the reported manifestation was not purely hallucinatory; it is never enough to prove that it was objectively real."

Through the 1970s, the idea that UFOs, monsters and poltergeist activity may be part of the same phenomenon, or as Janet and Colin Bord noted, at least triggered by the same stimulus, gained favor. For example, tales of creatures and phantoms with tattered, checkered shirts were compared to early occult literature by John Keel, Clark and myself. Such stories continue to pour in; the most recent being an account for November 1982 from Thomasville, North Carolina, where employees of the San-Mor furniture factory have seen a 6 foot tall ghost wearing khaki pants and a checkered shirt. And such stories do have an impact. Twelve workers on the night shift quit after seeing the ghost.

The flesh and blood answers of cryptozoologists such as Bernard Heuvelmans and Ray Mackal, or the nuts and bolts solutions of ufologists like Stan Friedman were eclipsed by the paranormal thoughts abounding in the 1970s. *Fortean Times'* Robert J. M. Rickard, and his colleague John Michell's interesting and intelligent notion that monsters might be time-travelers, that is animals teleporting on a temporal plane, added a new twist to the para-whatever school in a novel attempt to account for the tangible intangibility of the creatures. In 1982, Rickard and Michell presented their "theory of revivals" in *Living Wonders,* proposing that animals return from extinction. In 1983, Jim Brandon in *The Rebirth of Pan* detailed his belief that the pagan, earthy energy termed "Pan" in folklore manifests itself from spook lights to sea serpents.

There is lots of enjoyment in hopping from one theory to another to explain phenomena as elusive as this. D. Scott Rogo and Jerome Clark's almost wholesale retreat from their earlier planetary poltergeist positions to embrace their "intermediate reality" or parallel universe is another recent example.

After *Creatures of the Outer Edge* was published, I was aghast at the thought I was being labeled an occultist, a paranormalist, or somesuch. The paraphysical answer was articulated in an exercise in providing yet another possible explanation to the mysterious wonders surrounding us, but what became clearly apparent to me was that theorists are quickly pigeonholed.

This is unfortunate, as I and many other pursuers of the unknown, Forteans all, believe in nonbelief. An open-minded attitude to the many unexplained situations is the stock and trade of the Fortean. Concrete answers, actual flesh and blood critters as the foundation to monster accounts can be accepted by me and the other membership of the International Society of Cryptozoology. But then again, a paranormal illusion may be at work here too with some of these beasts, and the rational conventional undiscovered animal answer may not be viable for all reports.

Lest we not lose our sense of humor about this business, I refer you to the words of Rickard and Michell, from their latest, where they note their theories should be taken "with the customary Fortean promise that it will sit lightly on our shoulders, and that we will gladly give it up as soon as someone finds us something better to wear."

Indeed, I feel some monsters in America are chimpanzee-like dryopithecines, that some mystery cats and maned lions are relic populations of *atrox*, and some lake monsters are primative whales. However, I also have room in my cosmic jokebox for teleporting 'gators, phantom clowns, Dover Demons, and phantom panthers which imitate UFOs in all aspects but flight. Some spook lights in America, those ghostly globes of illumination which seem glued to specific locations, may be related to discharges of electric energy produced by geological fault stresses, to some kind of parapsychological disturbances akin to ghosts, or to a form of astronomical phenomenon as yet not understood.

Simply stated then, I "believe" in nothing and the possibility of everything. Ivan Sanderson once telegraphed me this message: "Forteanism is not an organized anything." Orderly chaos, an openness to the incomprehensible and unthinkable, and a jolly good sense of humor best decribe how I have dealt with America's remarkable array of creatures, phantoms and strange events over the last twenty-five years.

Fortean reality has many levels of satisfaction, and these become more and more apparent to me everyday. The procession of the damned, those wonderful things excluded by science, schools and governments, continues daily. In some sense, in some ways, they exist, these things chased, and seen.

We are like viewers of a grand movie in some unknown foreign language. The pictures are forming images in our heads which at once are familiar, and yet uncomfortable and alien. We know it looks serious sometimes, but at other times we feel we are witness to a great comedy with tragic overtones. All too often, however, the movie becomes three dimensional, and then there is no escaping the fact that this experience is personal, and real or very nearly so. Our mind curds up more rational explanations to make it all fit, but again we come away frustrated and unsatisfied. All the pieces – be they glowing red eyes, silverly balls of light, or rays of blue gas – don't fit the answers proposed. We try to sit back and grasp once again what is going on. Sometimes we succeed – partially. More often than not we fail, and want to agree very quickly with those around us saying this movie is an illusion, a false picture, a pseudoscientific fiction, or at worst, a hoax. It is a struggle, but we remain tied to the idea that the movie is something only mildly reflected and understandable in the context of *Homo sapiens* of the 1980s. There is nothing wrong with not having all of the answers at this stage of the game. Quandary, indeed.

23
The Lists

"There is no money back guarantee that anyone going to these places will see a spook, will-o'-the-wisp, flying saucer, or tumbling geode within the first 10 minutes of arrival. But perhaps there is a certain aura or spirit of place — obviously there is *something* special about these sites — on which we should concentrate our long-dormant powers of total perception."

Jim Brandon
Weird America, 1978.

Appendix I:
Thirty-five Reoccurring "Spook Lights" in America by Mark A. Hall

Mysterious, usually mobile globes of illumination seemingly attached to, and appearing periodically at specific locations are referred to as "spook lights." This phenomenon has fascinated the public for decades. Although their exact origin is still shrouded in mystery, their existence is hardly in doubt.

Country	State, Province	Location	Number	Movement
U.S.A.	Alabama, Lamar Co.	10 miles west of Vernon, road	one	?
U.S.A.	Alaska	mountains rimming Lake Iliamna	multi	?
U.S.A.	California, San Diego Co.	above Oriflamme Mts., near Julian	multi	yes
U.S.A.	Colorado, Custer Co.	a cemetery at Silver Cliff	multi	yes
U.S.A.	Florida, Seminole Co.	State Road 13 near Oviedo	multi	yes

Country	State, Province	Location	Number	Movement
U.S.A.	Hawaii, Hawaii Co.	Parker Ranch	multi	yes
U.S.A.	Iowa, Warren Co.	a farm near St. Mary's	one	?
U.S.A.	Louisiana, Ascension Co.	near Gonzales	one	?
U.S.A.	Maryland, Wicomico Co.	one mile west of Hebron	one	yes
U.S.A.	Missouri, Cedar Co.	10 miles east of El Dorado Springs	one	yes
U.S.A.	Missouri, Newton Co.	12 miles south-west of Joplin	multi	yes
U.S.A.	Nevada, Humbolt Co.	Oregon Canyon Ranch near McDermitt	multi	yes
U.S.A.	New Jersey, Passaic Co.	hills west of Lake Wanaque	multi	yes
U.S.A.	New Mexico, Taos Co.	river near Llano	multi	yes
U.S.A.	North Carolina Brunswick Co.	trestle near Maco	1 or 2	yes
U.S.A.	North Carolina Burke Co.	Brown Mtn. and Catawba Valley	multi	yes
U.S.A.	North Carolina Watauga Co.	Big Laurel	2 or 3	yes
U.S.A.	North Dakota, Cass Co.	road between Fargo and Kindred	one	yes
U.S.A.	Ohio, Ashland Co.	open field and woods near Loudonville	one	yes
U.S.A.	Oklahoma, Cimarron Co.	8 miles east of Kenton	one	no
U.S.A.	Oklahoma, Cimarron Co.	15 miles south-west of Kenton	one	yes
U.S.A.	Oklahoma, Tulsa Co.	2 miles west of Sand Springs	one	yes
U.S.A.	Oregon, Union or Umatilla Co.	road from Weston to Elgin	one	yes

Country	State, Province	Location	Number	Movement
U.S.A.	South Carolina Dorchester Co.	Sheep Island Road near Summerville	one	yes
U.S.A.	Texas, Angelina Co.	RR track near Lufkin	one	yes
U.S.A.	Texas, Bell Co.	bank of the Leon River	one	yes
U.S.A.	Texas, Brazoria Co.	5 miles west of Angleton	one	yes
U.S.A.	Texas, Hardin Co.	Bragg Road north or Saratoga	multi	yes
U.S.A.	Texas, La Salle and McMullen Cos.	along Esperanza Creek	one	yes
U.S.A.	Texas, Presidio Co.	Chinati Mountain	one	yes
U.S.A.	Virginia, Nansemond Co.	Jackson Road south of Suffolk	one	yes
U.S.A.	Washington, Franklin Co.	near Pasco	one	yes
Canada	Manitoba	forest area near Woodridge	one	?
Canada	Ontario	shore of Lake Simcoe near Brechin	one	yes
Canada	Saskatchewan	Buffalo Basin district near Beechy	one	yes

Appendix II:
Erratic Crocodilians and Teleporting 'Gators

Many Forteans have been intrigued by the deep involvement of crocodilians in various mysteries. A survey of the mysterious appearances of alligators and crocodiles, therefore, may be helpful to those interested in finding some more pieces to the puzzle.

As the following list shows, crocodilians fall from the sky and materialize inside cotton bins ranging in places from South Carolina to Texas. They slither and slink to the horror of humans from basement drains and sewers anywhere from Kansas to New York City. Unlike some mystery animals, alligators are caught, killed, and placed in museums. Although actual alligators seem to appear and persist in northern winters (e.g., sightings and finds for Oakland County, Michigan, 1953-1957) to the dismay of herpetologists, random out-of-place finds seem to be the rule.

Pet escapee explanations cannot deal adequately with these accounts of alligators in northern waters – when it is caimans that are being sold as pets.

It should be noted that "found" is used in this list when that is the only word given in the account and proper disposition is not apparent. "Found" may refer to an actual seizure or to a mere noticing of the specimen. Often "found" specimens may be dead or alive, and in incidents where one or the other is clear, it has been noted.

Explanation of "remarks" symbols: **s** = sighted only; **c** = caught; **f** = found; **k** = killed

Ref. No.	Date	Location and Source	Length (inches)	Remarks
1.	1843, July 2	Anson St., Charleston, S.C. WAND-TV, Decatur, Ill., Weather Almanac Feature, July 2, 1971; *Charleston Evening Post*, Charleston, S.C., Aug. 11, 1971	– –	fell from thunder-storm
2.	1877, Dec.	turpentine farm, Aiken Co., S.C. *New York Times*, Dec. 26, 1877	all about 12	6 fell
3.	1892, Feb.	bank, Rock River, Janesville, Wis. *The Books of Charles Fort* (henceforth BCF), page 598. *Chicago Citizen*, Chicago, Ill., Feb. 27, 1892, page 3.	66	f-frozen
4.	1901, Nov.	South Canadian River, Norman, Okla. Lane, H.H., *"Alligator mississippiensis* in Oklahoma," *Science*, Dec. 24, 1909, pp. 923-924.	54	k
5.	1922	Dismal Swamp, Ware, Mass. MacDougall, Curtis D., *Hoaxes*, Dover, 1958, pp. 31-32.	72-96, 24	s c
6.	1926	Potomac River, Md. " 'Baby' Alligators Astray in Northern Rivers," *Literary Digest*, Dec. 11, 1926, pp. 68-72.	36	s
7.	1926	creek, Philadelphia, Pa. *ibid.*	– –	c
8.	1927, Sept. 3	stream, Middleton, N.Y. *New York Times*, Sept. 4, 1927.	"good-sized"	c
9.	1927, Nov.	Mumford River, Mass. *New York Times*, Nov. 13, 1927.	– – one was 34	6 s 2 k
10.	1929, Jun. 17	Galt, Ontario *New York Times*, Jun. 19, 1929.	36	c
11.	1929, Jun. 18	Toronto, Ontario, *ibid.*	60 12	s c

Ref. No.	Date	Location and Source	Length (inches)	Remarks
12.	1929, Jul. 2	Matamoras, Port Jervis, N.Y. *New York Times,* Jul. 3, 1929.	24	c
13.	1929, Sept.	Hackensack Meadows, N.J. *BCF,* p. 591; *New York American,* Sept. 19, 1929.	31	k
14.	1929, Sept.	creek, Wolcott, N.Y. *BCF,* p. 591; *New York Sun,* Sept. 23, 1929.	28	c
15.	1929, Oct. 2	Collender's Point, Darien, Conn. *New York Times,* Oct. 3, 1929.	– –	3 f
16.	1930, Summer	Tulare Lake Basin, Corcoran, Cal. *Sacramento Union,* Sacramento, Cal., May 17, 1971.	72	s
17.	1931, Mar. 22	bushes on estate, Pleasantville, N.Y. *New York Times,* May 22, 1931.	24	c
18.	1932, Jun. 28	Bronx River, Westchester Co., N.Y. *New York Times,* Jun. 30, 1932.	– – 36	2-3 s 1 f dead
19.	1932, Jul. 1	Crestwood Lake, Westchester Co., N.Y. *New York Times,* Jul. 2, 1932.	– –	s
20.	1932, Jul. 7	Shrewsbury River, Wharf St., Red Bank, N.J. *New York Sun,* Jul. 7 or 8, 1932.	14	c
21.	1933, Sept. 11	Passaic River, N.J. *New York Times,* Sept. 12, 1933.	36 30	2 s k
22.	1933, Dec. 4	sandbar, Riverdale, Md. *Times-Herald,* Washington, D.C., Dec. 5, 1933.	46	c
23.	1935, Feb.	sewer, East 123rd St., N.Y., N.Y. (See text.)	90	k
24.	1935, Mar. 7	Northern Yonkers, N.Y. *New York Times,* Mar. 8, 1935.	36	c
25.	1935, Mar.	Grass Sprain, Westchester Co., N.Y. *ibid.*	72	f dead
26.	1935, Jul. 6	Huffman Pond, Xenia, Ohio *New York Times,* Jul. 7, 1935.	36	c
27.	1937, Jun. 1	Pier 9, East River, N.Y., N.Y. *New York Times,* Jun. 7, 1937.	49	c

Ref. No.	Date	Location and Source	Length (inches)	Remarks
28.	1937, Jun. 6	Brooklyn Museum subway station, N.Y., N.Y. *New York Times,* Jun. 7, 1937.	24	c
29.	1937, Jul. 18	brook, Franconia Golf Course, Palmer, Mass. *New York Times,* Jul. 18, 1937.	15 / 18	c / c
30.	1937, Aug. 30	bayou, Lake Decatur, Decatur, Ill. *Decatur Herald,* Decatur, Ill., Sept. 1, 1937, p.3.	--	s
31.	1938	Huron River, Mich. *Detroit News,* Detroit, Mich., Jul. 7, 1955.	22	c
32.	1938, Aug. 11	Huguenot Lake, New Rochelle, N.Y. *New York Times,* Aug. 16, 1938, and Aug. 20, 1938.	longest was 19	5 c
33.	1939, Aug. 7	Honeoye Creek, Staunton, Va. *New York Times,* Aug. 7, 1939.	24	c
34.	1941, Jun.	stream, Lakefield, Minn. *Minneapolis Sunday Tribune and Star Journal,* Minneapolis, Minn., Jun. 22, 1941, p.12.	--	shot but untaken
35.	1942, Aug. 16	Lake Mindowaskin, Westfield, N.Y. *New York Times,* Aug. 17, 1942.	48	k
36.	1942, Nov. 18	Herring Creek, lower Potomac River, Md. *Washington Post,* Washington, D.C., Nov. 19, 1942.	-- / 86	2 s / k
37.	1943, Jun.	Colorado River, Lost Lake, Ariz. *Copeia,* No. 3, 1954, pp. 222-223.	120	k
38.	1946, Dec.	Mariah Creek, Vincennes, Ind. *Indianapolis Star,* Indianapolis, Ind., Dec. 31, 1946.	--	k
39.	1949, Jul.	Rock Creek, Eagletown, Okla. *Copeia,* No. 1, Mar. 30, 1950, p.57.	102	k
40.	1949, Aug. 9-16	Lake Bradford, Princess Anne Co., Va. *Herpetologia,* Vol. 9, No. 2, pp. 71-72.	48 / 36	s / c
41.	1949, Fall	irrigation ditch, Ariz. *Copeia,* No. 3, 1954, pp. 222-223.	15	c

Ref. No.	Date	Location and Source	Length (inches)	Remarks
42.	1950, Spring	tourist court, Tucson, Ariz. *ibid.*	60	c
43.	1950?-1953?	La Paz Slough, Parker, Ariz. *ibid.*	large	s
44.	1953	Elizabeth Lake, Oakland, Co., Mich. *Detroit News,* Detroit, Mich., Jul. 10, 1955.	24	c
45.	1955, Jul. 9	Island Lake, Oakland Co., Mich. *Detroit News,* Detroit, Mich., Jul. 7, 1955.	60-72	c
46.	1955, Jun-Jul.	Lower Long Lake, Oakland Co., Mich. *Detroit News,* Detroit, Mich., Jul 7, 1955.	36-72	s (also tracks found)
47.	1956, Jun.	Harris Lake, Oakland, Co., Mich. *Detroit News,* Detroit, Mich., Jun. 25, 1956.	17	c
48.	1956, Jun.	Susan Lake, Oakland Co. Mich. *ibid.*	– –	rumors
49.	1957, Jul. 10	Lower Long Lake, Oakland Co., Mich. *Detroit News,* Detroit, Mich., Jul. 10, 1957.	57	c
50.	1957, Aug. 4	Susan Lake, Oakland Co., Mich. *Detroit News,* Detroit, Mich., Aug. 5, 1957.	42	k
51.	1957, Sept. -1958, Jun.	Folsom Lake, Calif. Personal communication from Patricia Masterson of the *Folsom Telegraph,* and from Jim McClarin. *Sacramento Union,* Sacramento, Calif., May 17, 1971.	– –	s (of several)
52.	1958, Oct.	Mount Clemens, Mich. *Detroit News,* Detroit, Mich., Oct. 18, 1958.	14	c
53.	1959, Sept.	Fall Creek, Indianapolis, Ind. *Indianapolis Star,* Sept. 10, 1959, p.51.	18	f
54.	1960, Nov. 18	Hines Park, Detroit, Mich. *Detroit News,* Detroit, Mich., Nov. 20, 1960.	36	c
55.	1962, Dec.	Pennsylvania Avenue, Washington, D.C. *Washington Post,* Dec. 23, 1962.	12	c

Ref. No.	Date	Location and Source	Length (inches)	Remarks
56.	1966, Oct. 24	hot water ditch, Lake Decatur, Decatur, Ill. *Decatur Review,* Oct. 26, 1966.	48-72 all were 12	s 13 c
57.	1967, May 31	horticulture pond, MSU, Lansing, Mich. *State Journal,* Lansing, Mich., Jun. 1, 1967.	16	c
58.	1967, Jun. 26	895 West Eldorado, Decatur, Ill. *Decatur Review,* Jun. 27, 1967, p.22.	10	c
59.	1968, Jun. 6	Capitol Building, Lansing, Mich. *State Journal,* Lansing, Mich., Jun. 7, 1968.	18	c
60.	1970, Jul.	basement drain, Newton, Kans. *Newton Kansan,* Newton, Kans., Jul. 16, 1970.	10	k
61.	1970, Jul. 30	shore of man-made lake, Lombard, Ill. *Chicago Tribune,* Jul. 31, 1970, p. 3.	18	c
62.	1970, Aug. 4	pond, Red Hook, N.Y. *Denver Post,* Denver, Colo., Aug. 5, 1970. *Daily Freeman,* Kingston, N.Y., Aug. 5&6, 1970. *Gazette-Advertiser,* Rhinebeck, N.Y., Aug. 6, 1970.	48	k
63.	1970, Sept. 20	Wyandotte St. West, Windsor, Ont. *Windsor Star,* Windsor, Ont., Sept. 21, 1970.	36	c
64.	1970, Sept. 21	cotton bin, Brownsville, Tex. *Brownsville Herald,* Brownsville, Tex., Sept. 21, 1970	18	c
65.	1970, Sept.	neatly clipped lawn, Metaire, La. *New York Times,* Sept. 25, 1970.	48	c
66.	1971, Jul. 9	Pewaukee Lake, Pewaukee, Wis. *Milwaukee Journal,* Milwaukee, Wis., Jul. 10, 1971, p. 1.	30	c
67.	1971, Aug.	Sangamon River, Oakley, Ill. *Decatur Herald,* Decatur, Ill., Aug. 9, 1971.	– –	c
68.	1972, Sept. 22	US 66, Chenoa, Ill. *Courier,* Champaign-Urbana, Ill., Sept. 22, 1972, p. 6.	36	c

Ref. No.	Date	Location and Source	Length (inches)	Remarks
69.	1973, Jul. 28	vacant lot, Montreal, Que. *Toronto Star,* Toronto, Ont., Jul. 30, 1973.	10½	c
70.	1973, late Summer	upper Morris and lower Sussex Counties, N.J. *The Monster Times,* N.Y., N.Y., Nov. 1973, p. 25.	"giant"	s
71.	1975, Oct. 23	Lafayette Lake, Lafayette, California *Lebanon* (PA) *Daily News* 24 Oct., 1975	96	s
72.	1978, Summer	Interstate 70, Olathe, Kansas *Daily News,* Olathe, Kansas 10 Mar. 1979	?	f alive
73.	1978, Jun. 30-Jul. 7	Little Arkansas River, Wichita, Kansas *Wichita Eagle Beacon,* 8 July 1978	120	s
74.	1978, July 2	13th Street Creek, Wichita, Kansas *Wichita Eagle Beacon,* 8 July 1978	18	s
75.	1978, Nov.	Linden, New Jersey *The Patriot,* Harrisburg, Pennsylvania 25 November 1978	36	c
76.	1979, Mar.	small creek, Stilwell, Kansas *Daily News,* Olathe, Kansas 9 Mar 1979	36	f dead
77.	1980, Aug. 24	Edison Board Basin, Edison, New Jersey *News Tribune,* Woodbridge, NJ 27 Aug. 1980	60	s
78.	1980, Sept. 20	backyard, Windsor, Ontario *Windsor* (Ontario) *Star* 33 Sept 1980	24	c
79.	1981, Jun. 23	Kings River, Fresno, California *San Francisco Chronicle* 24 June 1981	48	s
80.	1981, Aug. 5	Feather River, Yuba City, California *San Francisco Examiner,* 13 Aug 1981	82	s & claw prints
81.	1982, Apr. 1	Dover, Delaware *The Sun,* San Bernardino, California 2 Apr. 80	57	c
82.	1982 Aug 7	drainage pipe, Hampton, Virginia *Boston Globe,* 8 Aug 1982	30	c
83.	1982 Aug 9	Kensico Reservior, Valhalla, New York *New York Post,* 12 Aug 1982	26	c
84.	1983 Jun 18	Lake shore, Berne, New York *Schenectady* (New York) *Gazette,* 22 June 1983	28	c

Appendix III:
Phantom Ships
by Mark A. Hall
and Loren Coleman

Ref. No.	Location	Descriptions	When Seen
1.	Tombigee River, Alabama	spectre vessel	?
2.	near Farallon Islands, Calif.	phantom ship	autumn
3.	San Diego Bay, Calif.	phantom ship	spring
4.	off San Francisco Bay, Calif.	clipper ship, *Tennessee*	in fog
5.	New Haven Harbor, Conn.	sailing ship, against wind	June
6.	sea sw of Cortez, Florida	spectre ship	summer
7.	Casco Bay, Maine	the *Dash* with crew and full sails	always in fog; August
8.	near Foggs Point, Smith Island, Maryland	British man-of-war; sounds, voices, music	moonlit nights
9.	off Cape Cod, Mass.	spectre ship with a phantom light	after a storm
10.	Lake Michigan, Michigan	phantom ship	?
11.	Lake Saint Clair, Michigan	phantom ship	?
12.	near Raccourci Island, Miss.	phantom ship	?

Ref. No. Location	Descriptions	When Seen
13. near Isles of Shoals, N.H.	the schooner *White River*	summer twilight; noonday mists
14. Gravesend Bay, New York Harbour, New York	phantom vessel	spring
15. Hudson River, New York	clipper ship	before, after, or during a storm
16. Tappan Zee, New York	"America's *Flying Dutchman*"	summer twilight; calm sea
17. Albemarle Sound to Cape Hatteras, North Carolina	phantom ship	?
18. Devil's Lake, North Dakota	phantom steamboat; lights; sounds	moonless nights
19. over Lake Erie, near Erie, Pennsylvania	burning object 200 or more feet in length	during or after storm
20. off Block Island, Rhode Island	sometimes small; a burning ship; emits luminous rays	late December; sometimes before storms
21. Galveston Bay, Texas, and coast of Mexico	a schooner and two feluccas	?
22. Lake Morey, Vermont	*Aunt Sally,* phantom steamship	moonlit, still, foggy nights; August
23. Dismal Swamp and Lake Drummond, Virginia	phantom canoe; spectre ship	?
24. Rappahannock River, Virginia	phantom ship	?
25. Devil's Lake, Wisconsin	phantom canoe	still, cold nights; mists
26. Platte River, Wyoming	phantom ship	autumn
27. near Vancouver Island, British Columbia	phantom vessel	?
28. Askins Point, Ontario	phantom ship	?
29. Etobicoke Creek, Ontario	phantom vessel	summer
30. near Manitoulin Islands, Lake Huron, Quebec	sailing vessel	during storms
31. off Cape D'Espoir in Gaspe Bay, Quebec	?	?

Ref. No.	Location	Descriptions	When Seen
32.	Chaleur Bay, seen between Dalhousie and Perce Rock, Quebec and New Brunswick	a flame, a burning ship, a great bonfire	before a storm
33.	Bay of Fundy, off St. Martins, New Brunswick	burning ship	September or October
34.	Northumberland Strait off Richibucto, New Brunswick	burning ship; burns for one hour	before a storm; seen every seven years
35.	Northumberland Strait off Cape John, Nova Scotia	burning ship	early December
36.	Northumberland Strait off Merigomish, Nova Scotia	burning ship	before or after the autumnal equinox
37.	Mahone Bay, Nova Scotia	called the "Teazer Light"	?
38.	Gulf of St. Lawrence near Prince Edwards Island	called "Packet Light"; a firebird; a ball of fire; a burning ship	before a storm, after a storm

Appendix IV:
A Few Bedeviled Places

Name of Location	State/County	Phenomena
Devil's Hole Cave	Arkansas/Boone	monster lizard
Canon Diablo	Arizona/Coconino	anomalous meteoritic activity
Devil's Knoll	California/Santa Barbara	mystery deaths
Devil's Gate Reservior	California/Los Angeles	children's disappearances
Mt. Diablo/Devil's Hole	California/Contra Costa	see Chapter 3
Seven Devils Canyon	Idaho/Adams	cattle mutilations
Devil's Kitchen	Illinois/Williamson	see Chapter 3
Devil's Bake Oven & Backbone	Illinois/Jackson	see Chapter 3
Devil's Backbone	Indiana/Lawrence	hauntings; woman's scream
Devil Swamp	Louisiana/West Baton Rouge	bubbling unexplained chemicals
Devil's Den	Maine/Kennebec	hauntings
Devil's Den	Massachusetts/Middlesex	buried treasure; ghost
Devil's Pulpit	Massachusetts/Berkshire	lover's leap lore
Devil's Lake	Michigan/Lenawee	mystery plane crash

Name of Location	State/County	Phenomena
Devil's Track Lake	Minnesota/Cook	evil spirits
Devil's Elbow	Missouri/Pulaski	phantom panthers (see Chapter 21)
Devil's Hole	Nevada/Nye	Charles Manson's "hole in the world"; strange deaths and disappearances
Devil's Den	New Hampshire/Grafton	see Chapter 3
Devil's Highway	New Mexico/Dona Ana	evil spirits; Trinity A-bomb site
Devil's Tramping Ground	North Carolina/Chatham	curious cleared circle; Bigfoot hauntings
Devil's Lake	North Dakota/Ramsey	lake monster; phantom steamboat; mystery drownings
Devil's Promenade	Oklahoma/Ottawa	spook lights; UFOs
Devil's Race Course	Pennsylvania/Bucks	ringing rocks; thunderbird lore
Devil's Foot Rock	Rhode Island/Washington	devil lore; opposite Lafayette House
Hill of the Little Devils	South Dakota/Clay	little evil spirits or elves
Devil's Lake	Wisconsin/Columbia	see Chapter 3
Devil's Tower	Wyoming/Crook	giant phantom bear; CE III movie fame
Devil's Outpost	Labrador	enormous phantom black dogs; horned imps; the devil
Devil's Hole Cave	Ontario/Welland	cold air blasts; evil spirits; misfortune; strange deaths
Le Champ du Diable (Devil's Field)	Quebec	misfortune; bad luck; transformations

Appendix V:
Lake and River Monsters of America

Alaska
  Big Lake
  Crosswind Lake
  Lake Illiamna
  Kalooluk Lake
  Lake Minchumina
  Nonvianuk Lake

Arkansas
  Bedias Creek
  Lake Conway
  Illinois River
  Mud Lake
  White River

California
  Elizabeth Lake
  Lake Elsinore
  Lake Folsom
  Homer Lake
  Lafayette Lake
  Lake Tahoe

Colorado
  Lake Como

Connecticut
  Basile Lake
  Connecticut River

Florida
  Lake Clinch
  Lake Monroe
  North Fork St. Lucie River
  St. John's River
  Suwanee River

Georgia
  Chattahoochie River
  No Man's Friend Pond
  Savannah River
  Smith Lake

Idaho
  Lake Coeur d'Alene
  Lake Payette
  Pend Oreille Lake
  Snake River
  Tautphaus Park Lake

Illinois
  Four Lakes Village Lake

Lake Michigan
Stump Pond
Thompson's Lake
Indiana
Bass Lake
Big Chapman's Lake
Eagle Creek
Hollow Block Lake
Huntington's Lake
Lake Manitou (Devil's Lake)
Lake Maxinkuckee
Wabash River
Iowa
Spirit Lake
Kansas
Kingman County Lake
Kentucky
Herrington Lake
Ohio River
Reynolds Lake
Louisiana
Calcasieu River
Maine
Boyden Lake
Chain Lakes
Machias Lake
Moosehead Lake
Rangeley Lake
Sysladobsis Lake
Massachusetts
Twin Lakes
Silver Lake
Michigan
Au Train Lake
Basswood Lake
Lake Huron
Lake Michigan
Narrow Lake
Paint River
Lake Superior
Swan Lake

Minnesota
Big (or Great) Sandy Lake
Mississippi
Mississippi River
Pascagoula River
Missouri
Lake Creve Coeur
Kansas River
Mississippi River
Missouri River
Lake of the Ozarks
Montana
Flathead Lake
Missouri River
Waterton Lake
Nebraska
Alkali Lake
(renamed Walgren Lake)
Missouri River
Nevada
Lake Mead
Pegrand Lake
Pyramid Lake
Lake Walker
New Jersey
North Shrewsbury River
Passaic Falls
New York
Baldwinsville Mill Pond
Black River
Canandaigua Lake
Lake Champlain
Lake George
Hudson River
McGuire's Pond
Lake Onondago
Lake Ontario
Silver Lake
Spirit Lake
Wading River
Lake of the Woods

North Carolina
Little Tennessee River
Valley River
North Dakota
Devil's Lake
Ohio
Lake Erie
Olentangy River
Slaven's Pond
Oregon
Crater Lake
Crescent Lake
Forked Mountain Lake
Hollow Block Lake
Upper Klamath Lake
Wallowa Lake
Pennsylvania
Wolf Pond
South Carolina
Goose Creek Lagoon
South Dakota
Campbell Lake
Texas
Brazos River
Klamath Lake
Utah
Bear Lake
Great Salt Lake
Mud Lake
Sevier Lake
Utah Lake
Vermont
Lake Champlain
Connecticut River
Dead Creek
Lake Memphremagog
Winooski River
Washington
Chelan Lake
Omak Lake
Quinault Lake
Rock Lake

Lake Washington
Wisconsin
Brown's Lake
Chippewa Lake
Devil's Lake
Elkhart Lake
Fowler Lake
Lake Geneva
Madison Four Lakes
Mendota Lake
Mississippi River
Lake Monova
Pewaukee Lake
Red Cedar Lake and River
Rock Lake
Lake Superior
Lake Waubeau
Lake Winnebago
Yellow River
Wyoming
Lake DeSmet
Hutton Lake
Lake Katherine
Lake La Metrie
Alberta
Battle River
North Saskatchewan River
British Columbia
Campbell River
Lake Cowichan
Harrison Lake
Lake Okanagan
Seton Lake
Sushwap Lake
Lake Tagai
Thetis Lake
Manitoba
Cedar Lake
Lake Dauphin
Dirty Water Lake
Lake Manitoba
Lake Winnipeg
Lake Winnipegosis

New Brunswick
Skiff Lake
Lake Utopia
Ontario
Lake of Bays
Berens Lake
Deschenes Lake
Mazinaw Lake
Muskrat Lake
Lake Ontario
Ottawa River
Lake Simcoe
Quebec
Lac Aylmer
Lac Baskatong
Blue Sea Lake

Lake Champlain
Reservior Gouin
Lac Massawippi
Lac Mekinac
Lac Memphremagog
Mocking Lake
Moffat Lake
Lac-des-Piles
Lac Pohengamok
Lac Remi
Lac St. Clair
Lac St. Francois
Lac St. Jean
Lac-a-la-Tortue
Les-Trois-Lac
Lake Williams

Mysterious America:
A Regional Bibliography

Two publications well worth obtaining for news of the latest mysterious outbreaks in America are:

UFO and Fortean News Service
Route One, Box 220
Plumerville, Arkansas 72127 USA

and

BM – *The Fortean Times* – LC
London WC1N 3XX
United Kingdom.

The charting of a journey, be it on the road or through the library, can begin in many ways. Investigators of Mysterious America may be in pursuit of a specific unknown creature or phenomenon, or in quest of all inexplicable events for a specific area. For the use of those readers who wish to explore the unexplained happenings of a particular location, I have assembled this bibliography of books which I find the most helpful for regional inquiries.

North America

Bord, Janet and Colin.
The Bigfoot Casebook.
Harrisburg: Stackpole, 1982.

Corliss, William R.
Lightning, Auroras, Nocturnal Lights and Related Luminous Phenomena.
Glen Arm, MD: Sourcebook Project, 1983.

Costello, Peter.
In Search of Lake Monsters.
New York: Coward, McCann & Georghegan, 1974.

Eberhart, George M.
A Geo-Biblography of Anomalies.
Westport, Conn.: Greenwood, 1980.

Eberhart, George M.
Monsters: A Guide to Information on Unaccounted-for Creatures, Including Bigfoot, Many Water Monster, and Other Irregular Animals.
New York: Garland, 1983.

Fort, Charles.
The Books of Charles Fort.
New York: Dover Publications, 1974.

Green, John.
Sasquatch: The Apes Among Us.
Seattle: Hancock House, 1976.

Heuvelmans, Bernard.
In the Wake of the Sea-Serpents.
New York: Hill & Wang, 1968.

Hitching, Francis.
The Mysterious World: An Atlas of the Unexplained.
New York: Holt, Rinehart & Winston, 1979.

Michell, John and Robert J. M. Rickard.
Living Wonders.
London: Thames & Hudson, 1982.

Phillips, Ted.
Physical Traces Associated with UFO Sightings.
Evanston: Center for UFO Studies, 1975.

Sanderson, Ivan T.
The Continent We Live On.
New York: Random House, 1961.

United States of America

Bolte, Mary.
Haunted New England.
Riverside, Conn.: Chatham, 1972.

Botkin, B. A.
A Treasury of New England Folklore.
New York: Crown, 1965.

Botkin, B. A.
A Treasury of Western Folklore.
New York: Crown, 1975.

Brandon, Jim.
Rebirth of Pan: Hidden Faces of the American Earth Spirit.
Dunlap, IL: Firebird, 1983.

Brandon, Jim.
Weird America.
New York: Dutton, 1978.

Carey, George.
A Faraway Time and Place: Lore of the Eastern Shore.
New York: R. B. Luce, 1971.

Clark, Jerome and Loren Coleman.
Creatures of the Outer Edge.
New York: Warner, 1978.

Davidson, James Dale.
An Eccentric Guide to the United States.
New York: Berkley, 1977.

Fawcett, George D.
Quarter Century of Studies of UFOs in Florida, North Carolina and Tennessee.
Mount Airy: Pioneer, 1975.

Federal Writers' Program.
Each state's edition.
Produced during the 1930s – 1950s.

Fell, Barry.
America B.C.
New York: Quadrangle, 1976.

Folsom, Franklin.
America's Ancient Treasures.
New York: Rand McNally, 1974.

Goodwin, John.
Occult America.
Garden City: Doubleday, 1972.

Holzer, Hans.
Haunted Houses.
New York: Crown, 1971.

Holzer, Hans.
Yankee Ghosts.
New York: Ace, 1966.

Life Editors.
The Life Treasury of American Folklore.
New York: Time, 1961.

Miller, Tom.
On the Border.
New York: Harper and Row, 1981.

Reynolds, James.
Ghosts in American Houses.
New York: Paperback Library, 1967.

Skinner, Charles.
American Myths and Legends. (2 volumes)
Detroit: Gale Research (reprint), 1974.

Skinner, Charles.
Myths and Legends of Our Own Land. (2 volumes)
Philadelphia: Lippincott, 1896.

Squier, E. G. and E. H. Davis.
Ancient Monuments of the Mississippi Valley.
Washington, D.C.: Smithsonian, 1848.

Stern, Jane and Micheal.
Amazing America.
New York: Random House/Obst Books, 1978.

Trento, Salvatore Michael.
The Search for Lost America.
Chicago: Contemporary, 1978.

Webb, Richard.
Great Ghosts of the West.
Los Angeles: Nash, 1971.

Williams, Brad and Choral Pepper.
Lost Treasures of the West.
New York: Holt, Rinehart & Winston, 1975.

Williams, Brad and Choral Pepper.
The Mysterious West.
New York. World, 1967.

Yankee Editors.
Mysterious New England.
Dublin, NH: Yankee, 1971.

Alabama

Windham, Kathryn Tucker and Margaret Gillis Figh.
13 Alabama Ghosts and Jeffrey.
Huntsville: Strode, 1969.

Alaska

Badlam, Alexander.
The Wonders of Alaska.
San Francisco: The Author, 1891.
Carrighar, Sally.
Wild Voice of the North.
New York: Garden City, 1959.
Colp, Harry D.
The Strangest Story Ever Told.
New York: Exposition, 1953.
Higginson, Ella.
Alaska: The Great Country.
New York: Macmillan, 1917.
Marshall, Robert.
Arctic Village.
New York: Literary Guild, 1933.

Arizona

Barry, Bill.
The Ultimate Encounter.
New York: Pocket Books, 1978.
Gentry, Curt.
The Killer Mountains.
New York: New American Library, 1968.
Jennings, Gary.
Treasure of the Superstition Mountains.
New York: Norton, 1973.
Kluckholn, Clyde.
Navaho Witchcraft.
Boston: Beacon, 1962.
Walton, Travis.
The Walton Encounter.
New York: Berkley, 1978.
Waters, Frank.
Book of the Hopi.
New York: Viking, 1963.

Arkansas

Allsop, Fred.
Folklore of Romantic Arkansas.
New York: Grolier, 1931.
Crabtree, Smokey.
Smokey and the Fouke Monster.
Fouke: Days Creek Production, 1974.

Randolph, Vance.
Ozark Superstitions.
New York: Columbia University Press, 1947.

Randolph, Vance.
We Always Lie to Strangers.
New York: Columbia University Press, 1951.

California

Andrews, Richard.
The Truth Behind the Legends of Mt. Shasta.
New York: Carleton, 1976.

Bailey, Philip A.
Golden Mirages.
New York: Macmillian, 1940.

Bell, Horace.
On the Old West Coast.
New York: William Morrow, 1930.

Druffel, Ann and D. Scott Rogo.
The Tujunga Canyon Contacts.
Englewood Cliffs: Prentice-Hall, 1980.

Eichorn, A. F.
The Mt. Shasta Story.
Mt. Shasta: The Herald, 1957.

Gross, Loren E.
The UFO Wave of 1896.
Fremont: The Author, 1974.

Holzer, Hans.
Ghosts of the Golden West.
New York: Ace, 1968.

Reinstadt, Randall A.
Ghosts, Bandits and Legends of Old Monterey.
Carmel: Ghost Town Publications, 1972.

St. Clair, David.
The Psychic World of California.
New York: Bantam, 1973.

Colorado

Davidson, Lavette J. and Forrester Blake.
Rocky Mountain Tales.
Norman: University of Oklahoma, 1947.

Eberhart, Perry.
Treasure Tales of the Rockies.
Chicago: Swallow, 1968.

Orr, Cathy M. and Michael J. Preston.
Urban Folklore from Colorado.
Ann Arbor, MI: Xerox, 1976.
Smith, Frederick W.
Cattle Mutilation: The Unthinkable Truth.
Cedaredge: Freedland, 1976.

Connecticut
Taylor, John M.
The Witchcraft Delusion in Colonial Connecticut.
New York: Grafton, 1908.

District of Columbia
Alexander, John.
Ghosts: Washington's Most Famous Ghost Stories.
Washington, D.C.: Washingtonian Books, 1975.
INFO Editors.
Weird Washington Guidebook.
Arlington, VA: International Fortean Organization, 1976.

Delaware
Baker, Denise.
Delaware Folklore.
Sussex County: Delaware Arts Council, 1978.

Florida
Fuller, Elizabeth.
My Search for the Ghost of Flight 401.
New York: Berkley, 1978.
Fuller, John.
The Ghost of Flight 401.
New York: Berkley, 1976.
Tinsley, Jim Bob.
The Florida Panther.
St. Petersburg: Great Outdoors, 1970.

Georgia
Fancher, Betsy.
The Lost Legacy of Georgia's Golden Isles.
Garden City: Doubleday, 1971.
McQueen, A. S. and H. Mizell.
History of the Okefenokee Swamp.
Folkston: The Authors, 1949.

Hawaii
Armitage, George T. and Henry Judd.
Ghost Dog and Other Hawaiian Legends.
Honolulu: Advertiser, 1944.

Beckwith, Martha.
Hawaiian Mythology.
New Haven: Yale University, 1940.

Cox, Halley.
Hawaiian Petroglyphs.
Honolulu: Bishop Museum, 1970.

Kalakaua, David.
The Legends and Myths of Hawaii.
Rutland, VT: Tuttle, 1972.

Rice, William H.
Hawaiian Legends.
Honolulu: Bishop Museum, 1977.

Thrum, Thomas.
Hawaiian Folk Tales.
Chicago: McClurg, 1917.

Westervelt, W. D.
Hawaiian Legends of Volcanoes.
Boston: George Ellis, 1916.

Westervelt, W. D.
Legends of Old Honolulu.
Boston: George Ellis, 1915.

Idaho

Bird, Annie L.
Boise: The Peace Valley.
Boise: Canyon County Historical Society, 1975.

Erwin, Richard.
Indian Rock Writing in Idaho.
Boise: Idaho Historical Society, 1930.

Fisher, Vardis.
Idaho Lore.
Caldwell: Caxton, 1939.

Illinois

Allen, John W.
Legends and Lore of Southern Illinois.
Carbondale: Southern Illinois University, 1963.

Angle, Paul M., ed.
The Great Chicago Fire.
Chicago: Chicago Historical Society, 1946.

Hyatt, Harry Middleton.
Folklore from Adams County, Illinois.
Hannibal, MO: Hyatt Foundation, 1965.

Means, Ruth.
The Piasa.
Alton: Alton-Godfrey Rotary Club, n.d.
St. Clair, David.
Watseka.
Chicago: Playboy, 1977.
Steiger, Brad.
Psychic City: Chicago.
Garden City: Doubleday, 1976.

Indiana
Black, Glenn.
Angel Site.
Indianapolis: Indiana Historical Society, 1967.
Hartle, Orvil R.
A Carbon Experiment?
LaPorte: The Author, 1963.
Kellar, James.
An Introduction to the Prehistory of Indiana.
Indianapolis: Indiana Historical Society, 1973.

Iowa
McKusick, Marshall.
The Davenport Conspiracy.
Iowa City: University of Iowa, 1970.
McKusick, Marshall.
Men of Ancient Iowa.
Ames: Iowa State University, 1964.
Steiger, Brad.
Irene Hughes on Psychic Safari.
New York: Warner, 1972.
Steiger, Brad.
Mysteries of Time and Space.
New York: Dell, 1972.

Kansas
Koch, William E., ed.
Folklore from Kansas: Customs, Beliefs and Superstitions.
Lawrence: Regent Press of Kansas, 1980.
Sackett, Samuel and William E. Koch.
Kansas Folklore.
Lincoln: University of Nebraska, 1961.

Kentucky
Atkinson, Paul Lewis.
Kentucky: Land of Legend and Lore.
Fort Thomas: Northern Kentucky Historical Society, 1962.

Davis, Isabel and Ted Bloecher.
Close Encounter at Kelly and Others of 1955.
Evanston: Center for UFO Studies, 1978.

Meloy, Harold.
Mummies of Mammoth Cave.
Shelbyville, IN: Micron, 1973.

Montell, William Lynwood.
Ghosts Along the Cumberland: Deathlore in the Kentucky Foothills.
Knoxville: University of Tennessee, 1975.

Louisiana

de Lavigne, Jeanne.
Ghost Stores of Old New Orleans.
New York: Rinehart, 1946.

Kane, Harnett T.
The Bayous of Louisiana.
New York: William Morrow, 1943.

Saxon, Lyle.
Gumbo Ya-Ya.
New York: Houghton-Miffllin, 1945.

Saxon, Lyle.
Fabulous New Orleans.
New York: Appleton-Century, 1935.

Tallant, Robert.
Voodoo in New Orleans.
New York: Macmillan, 1946.

Maine

Beck, Horace.
The Folklore of Maine.
Philadelphia: Lippincott, 1957.

Reich, Wilhelm.
Contact with Space.
Rangeley: Core Pilot, 1957.

Snow, Edward Rowe.
Romance of Casco Bay.
New York: Dodd, Mead, 1975.

Verrill, A. Hyatt.
Romantic and Historic Maine.
New York: Dodd, Mead, 1938.

Maryland

Carey, George C.
Maryland Folk Legends and Folk Songs.
Cambridge, MO: Tidewater, 1971.

Parke, Francis Neal.
Witchcraft in Maryland.
Baltimore: Maryland Historical Society, 1937.

Massachusetts

Allen, Joseph.
Tales and Trails of Martha's Vineyard.
Boston: Little Brown, 1938.

Delabarre, Edmund Burke.
Dighton Rock.
New York: Walter Neale, 1928.

Fowler, Raymond E.
The Andreasson Affair.
Englewood Cliffs: Prentice-Hall, 1979.

Fowler, Raymond E.
UFOs: Interplanetary Visitors.
Jericho, NY: Exposition, 1974.

Hansen, Chadwick.
Witchcraft at Salem.
New York: George Braziller, 1969.

Snow, Edward Rowe.
Boston Bay Mysteries and Other Tales.
New York: Dodd, Mead, 1977.

Snow, Edward Rowe
The Islands of Boston Harbor.
New York: Dodd, Mead, 1971.

Snow, Edward Rowe.
Mysterious Tales of the New England Coast.
New York: Dodd, Mead, 1961.

Summers, Montague.
The Geography of Witchcraft.
Secaucus, NJ: Citadel, 1965.

Michigan

Boyer, Dwight.
Ghost Ships of the Great Lakes.
New York: Dodd, Mead, 1968.

Boyer, Dwight.
Ghost Stories of the Great Lakes.
New York: Dodd, Mead, 1966.

Boyer, Dwight.
Strange Adventures of the Great Lakes.
New York: Dodd, Mead, 1974.

Boyer, Dwight.
True Tales of the Great Lakes.
New York: Dodd, Mead, 1971.

Dorson, Richard M.
Bloodstoppers and Bearwalkers: Folk Traditions of the Upper Peninsula.
Cambridge: Harvard University, 1952.

Dorson, Richard M.
Negro Folktales in Michigan.
Cambridge: Harvard University, 1956.

Gourley, Jay.
The Great Lakes Triangle.
Greenwich, CT: Fawcett, 1977.

Minnesota

Blegen, Theodore C.
The Kensington Rune Stone: New Light on an Old Riddle.
St. Paul: Minnesota Historical Society, 1968.

Festinger, Leon and Henry W. Riecken, Stanley Schachter.
When Prophecy Fails.
Minneapolis: University of Minnesota, 1956.

Holland, Hjalmar.
The Kensington Stone.
Ephraim, WI: The Author, 1932.

Mississippi

Claiborne, J. F. H.
Mississippi: As a Province, Territory and State.
Baton Rouge: Louisiana State University, 1964.

Missouri

Collins, Earl.
Folktales of Missouri.
Boston: Christopher, 1935.

Collins, Earl.
Legends and Lore of Missouri.
San Antonio: Naylor, 1951.

Loftin, Bob.
Spookville's Ghost Lights.
Tulsa: The Author, 1967.

Moore, Tom.
Mysterious Tales and Legends of the Ozarks.
Philadelphia: Dorrance, 1938.

Randolph, Vance.
Ozark Ghost Stories.
Girard, KS: Haldeman-Julius, 1944.

Randolph, Vance.
Tall Tales from the Ozarks.
Girard, KS: Haldeman-Julius, 1944.

Randolph, Vance.
Wild Stories from the Ozarks.
Girard, KS: Haldeman-Julius, 1943.

Rayburn, Otto.
Ozark Country.
New York: Duell, Sloan & Pearce, 1941.

Montana

Donovan, Roberta and Keith Wolverton.
Mystery Stalks the Prairie.
Raynesford: THAR, 1976.

Nebraska

Pound, Louise.
Nebraska Folklore.
Lincoln: University of Nebraska, 1959.

Welsch, Roger L.
A Treasury of Nebraska Pioneer Folklore.
Lincoln: University of Nebraska, 1966.

Nevada

Chalfant, Willy.
Gold Guns and Ghost Towns.
Palo Alto: Stanford University, 1947.

Greenway, John.
Folklore of the Great West.
Palo Alto: Western Folkways, 1969.

Heizer R. F. and M. A. Baumhoff.
Prehistoric Rock Paintings of Nevada and Eastern California.
Berkeley: University of California, 1962.

New Hampshire

Glynn, Frank.
Report of Excavations at North Salem.
Harrisburg, PA: Eastern States Archaeological Federation, 1959.

Goodwin, William B.
The Ruins of Great Ireland in New England.
Boston: Meador, 1946.

Gore, M. P. and Eva Speare.
New Hampshire Folktales.
Plymouth: NH Federation of Women's Clubs, 1932.

Feldman, Mark.
The Mystery Hill Story.
Derry: Mystery Hill Press, 1977.

Fuller, John.
The Incident at Exeter.
New York: Putnam, 1966.

Fuller, John.
The Interrupted Journey.
New York: Dial Press, 1966.

Speare, Eva.
New Hampshire Folk Tales.
Plymouth: The Author, 1964.

New Jersey

McCloy, James F. and Ray Miller, Jr.
The Jersey Devil.
Wallingford, PA: Middle Atlantic Press, 1976.

McMahon, William H.
Pine Barren Legends, Lore and Lies.
Wallingford, PA: Middle Atlantic Press, 1980.

United States Naval Research Laboratory.
NRL Investigations of East Coast Acoustics Events.
Washington, DC: Government Printing Office, 1978.

New Mexico

Berlitz, Charles and William L. Moore.
The Roswell Incident.
New York: Grosset & Dunlap, 1980.

Bullock, Alice.
Living Legends of Santa Fe Country.
Santa Fe: Sunstone, 1972.

Cushing, Frank.
My Adventures in Zuni Country.
Palo Alto: American West, 1970.

Fry, Daniel.
The White Sands Incident.
Los Angeles: New Age, 1954.

James, George Wharton.
New Mexico: The Land of Delight Makers.
Boston: Page, 1920.

Simmons, Marc.
Witchcraft in the Southwest.
Flagstaff: Northland, 1974.

New York

Merrill, Auch.
The White Woman and Her Valley.
Rochester: Creek Books, n.d.

Jones, Louis C.
Spooks of the Valley.
Boston: Houghton-Mifflin, 1948.

Jones, Louis C.
Things That Go Bump in the Night.
New York: Hill & Wang, 1959.

Thomas, Howard.
Folklore from the Adirondack Foothills.
Prospect: Prospect Books, 1958.

Thompson, Harold W.
Body, Boots and Britches.
Philadelphia: Lippincott, 1940.

North Carolina

Harden, John.
The Devil's Tramping Ground.
Chapel Hill: University of North Carolina, 1949.

Harden, John.
Tar Heel Ghosts.
Chapel Hill: University of North Carolina, 1954.

Howe, C. K.
Solving the Riddle of the Lost Colony.
Beaufort: Skarren, 1947.

Lael, Ralph I.
The Brown Mountain Lights.
Morgantown: The Author, 1965.

Mansfield, George Rogers.
Origin of the "Brown Mountain Light" in North Carolina.
Washington, DC: US Geological Survey, 1971.

Morgan, Fred T.
Ghost Tales of the Uwharries.
Winston-Salem: John T. Blair, 1968.

Roberts, Nancy.
An Illustrated Guide to Ghosts and Mysterious Occurrences in the Old North State.
Charlotte: Heritage House, 1959.

Robinson, Melvin.
Riddle of the Lost Colony.
New Bern: Owen G. Dunn, 1946.
Whedbee, Charles.
The Flaming Ship of Ocracoke.
Winston-Salem: John T. Blair, 1971.
Whedbee, Charles.
Legends of the Outer Banks.
Winston-Salem: John T. Blair, 1966.

North Dakota
Bicentennial Committee.
Devil's Lake Bicentennial History.
Devil's Lake: Bicentennial Committee, 1976.
Devil's Lake Diamond Jubilee Committee.
Devil's Lake: 75 Years.
Devil's Lake: Ness Press, 1957.
Pioneers' Society.
Devil's Lake Region.
Devil's Lake: Daily Journal, circa 1923.

Ohio
Greenman, Emerson F.
Serpent Mound.
Columbus: Ohio Historic Society, 1970.
Page Research Editors.
Bigfoot: Tales of Unexplained Creatures.
Rome, OH: Page Research, 1978.
Pilichis, Dennis.
Night Siege: The Northern Ohio UFO-Creature Invasion.
Rome, OH: Page Research, 1982.
Stringfield, Leonard H.
Situation Red: The UFO Siege.
New York: Fawcett Crest, 1977.

Oklahoma
Farley, Gloria.
The Vikings Were Here.
Poteau: The Independent, 1970.
Landsverk, O. G.
Ancient Messages on American Stones.
Glendale, CA: Norseman, 1969.

Oregon

Hult, Ruby.
Lost Mines and Treasures of the Pacific Northwest.
Portland: Binford & Mort, 1957.

Jones, Suzi
Oregon Folklore.
Eugene: University of Oregon, 1977.

Pennsylvania

Barach, Sally M.
Haunts of Adams and Other Counties.
Indiana PA: Halldin, 1972.

Jeffrey, Adi-Kent Thomas.
Ghosts in the Valley.
New Hope: New Hope Art, 1970.

Jeffrey, Adi-Kent Thomas.
More Ghosts in the Valley.
New Hope: New Hope Art, 1973.

Korson, George.
Black Rock: Mining Folklore of the Pennsylvania Dutch.
Baltimore: John Hopkins, 1960.

Korson, George.
Pennsylvania Songs and Legends.
Philadelphia: University of Pennsylvania, 1949.

Lewis, Arthur.
Hex.
New York: Trident, 1969.

Lyman, Robert R.
Amazing Indeed!
Coudersport: Potter Enterprise, 1973.

Lyman, Robert R.
Forbidden Land.
Coudersport: Potter Enterprise, 1971.

Rhode Island

Bacon, Edgar.
Narragansett Bay: Its Historic and Romantic Associations.
New York: Putnam, 1904.

Means, Philip.
The Newport Tower.
New York: Holt, 1942.

Weber, Ken.
Twenty-five Walks in Rhode Island.
Somersworth, NH: New Hampshire Publishing Co., 1978.

South Carolina

Kershaw, C. D.
The Gray Lady: A Legend of Old Camden.
Charleston: Walker, Evans & Coggswell, n.d.

Martin, Margaret Rhett.
Charleston Ghosts.
Columbia: University of South Carolina, 1963.

Roberts, Nancy and Bruce.
Ghosts of the Carolinas.
Charlotte: McNally & Loftin, 1962.

South Dakota

Bennett, Estalline.
Old Deadwood Days.
New York: Charles Scribner's Sons, 1935.

Tennessee

Bell, Charles B.
The Bell Witch: A Mysterious Spirit.
Nashville: Lark, 1934.

Faulkner, Charles H.
The Old Stone Fort.
Knoxville: University of Tennessee, 1968.

Windham, Kathryn Tucker.
Thirteen Tennessee Ghosts and Jeffrey.
Huntsville: Strode, 1977.

Texas

Abernathy, Francis.
Tales from the Big Thicket.
Austin: University of Texas, 1966.

Clarke, Sally Ann.
The Lake Worth Monster.
Fort Worth: The Author, 1969.

Dobie, J. Frank.
Tales of Old-Time Texas.
Boston: Little, Brown, 1955.

Miles, Elton.
Tales of the Big Bend.
College State: Texas A & M, 1976.

Wheeler, David R.
The Lubbock Lights.
New York: Award, 1977.

Utah

Lee, Hector.
The Three Nephites: The Substance and Significance of the Legend in Folklore.
Albuquerque: University of New Mexico, 1949.

Salisbury, Frank B.
The Utah UFO Display.
Old Greenwich, CT: Devin-Adair, 1974.

Vermont

Cook, Warren L.
Ancient Vermont.
Rutland: Academy, 1978.

Olcott, Henry S.
People from the Other World.
Rutland: Tuttle, 1972 (reprint).

Virginia

Tucker, George H.
Virginia Supernatural Tales.
Norfolk: Donning, 1977.

Washington

Arnold, Kenneth and Ray Palmer.
The Coming of the Saucers.
Boise: The Authors, 1952.

Beck, Fred and R.A.
I Fought the Apeman of Mt. St. Helens.
Washington State: The Authors, 1967.

Finke, Mary J.
Legends of Four High Mountains.
Portland: Portland Historical Journal, 1944.

West Virginia

Barker, Gray.
The Silver Bridge.
Clarksburg: Saucerian, 1970.

Keel, John A.
The Mothman Prophecies.
New York: Saturday Review Press/Dutton, 1975.

Musick, Ruth Ann.
Coffin Hollow.
Lexington: University of Kentucky, 1977.

Musick, Ruth Ann.
The Telltale Lilac Bush.
Lexington: University of Kentucky, 1965.

Wisconsin

Brown, Charles E.
Sea Serpents: Wisconsin Occurrences of These Weird Water Monsters.
Madison: Wisconsin Folklore Society, 1942.

Salisbury, Rollin D. and Wallace W. Atwood.
The Geography of the Region About Devil's Lake.
Madison: Wisconsin Geological and Natural History Survey, 1900.

Wells, Robert W.
Fire at Peshtigo.
Englewood Cliffs: Prentice-Hall, 1968.

Wyman, Walker D.
Wisconsin Folklore.
River Falls: University of Wisconsin, 1979.

Wyoming

Gebhard, David.
The Rock Art of Dinwoody, Wyoming.
Santa Barbara: Unversity of California, 1969.

Canada

Berton, Pierre.
The Mysterious North.
New York: Knopf, 1956.

Colombo, John Robert.
Colombo's Book of Marvels.
Toronto: NC Press, 1979.

Fowke, Edith.
Folklore of Canada.
Toronto: McClelland & Stewart, 1976.

Garner, Betty Sanders.
Canada's Monsters.
Hamilton, Ont.: Potlatch, 1976.

Hervey, Sheila.
Some Canadian Ghosts.
Richmond Hill, Ont.: Pocket, 1973.

Lambert, R. S.
Exploring the Supernatural: The Weird in Canadian Folklore.
Toronto: McClelland & Stewart, 1955.

Owen, A. R. G.
Psychic Mysteries of the North.
New York: Harper & Row, 1975.

Skinner, Charles M.
Myths and Legends Beyond Our Borders.
Philadelphia: Lippincott, 1899.

Sonin, Eileen.
More Canadian Ghosts.
Richmond Hill, Ont.: Pocket, 1974.

British Columbia

Buckland, Frank M.
Story of Ogopogo.
Kelowna: Okanagan Historical Society, 1943.

Corner, John.
Pictograms in the Interior of British Columbia.
Vernon: Wayside, 1968.

LeBlond, Paul J. and John Sibert.
Observations of Large Unidentified Marine Animals in British Columbia and Adjacent Waters.
Vancouver: University of British Columbia, 1973.

Moon, Mary.
Ogopogo.
Vancouver: J. J. Douglas, 1977.

New Brunswick

Trueman, Stuart.
Ghosts, Pirates and Treasure Trove: The Phantoms that Haunt New Brunswick.
Toronto: McClelland & Stewart, 1975.

Truman, Stuart.
An Intimate History of New Brunswick.
Toronto: McClelland & Stewart, 1970.

Wright, Bruce S.
The Eastern Panther.
Toronto: Clark, Irwin, 1972.

Wright, Bruce S.
The Ghost of North America.
New York: Vantage, 1959.

Newfoundland

Mowat, Farley.
Westviking.
Totowa, NJ: Minerva, 1965.

Smallwood, Joseph.
The Book of Newfoundland.
St. John's: Newfoundland, 1937.

Nova Scotia

Creighton, Helen.
Bluenose Ghosts.
Toronto: Ryerson, 1957.

Fraser, Mary L.
Folklore of Nova Scotia.
Toronto: Catholic Truth, 1931.

Furneaux, Rupert.
The Money Pit Mystery.
New York: Dodd, Mead, 1972.

Sherwood, Roland H.
The Phantom Ship of Northumberland Strait.
Windsor, NS: Lancelot, 1975.

Ontario

Cochrane, Hugh.
Gateway to Oblivion: The Great Lakes' Bermuda Triangle.
New York: Avon, 1980.

Haisell, David.
The Missing Seven Hours.
Markham: Paperjacks, 1978.

Tushingham, A. D.
The Beardmore Relics: Hoax or History?
Toronto: Royal Ontario Museum, 1966.

Prince Edward Island

Ramsey, Sterling.
Folklore: Prince Edward Island.
Charlottetown: Square Deal, 1973.

Quebec

Davies, Blodwen.
Romantic Quebec.
New York: Dodd, Mead, 1932.

Gagnon, Claude and Michael Meurger.
Monsters In Quebec Lakes: Myths and Troublesome Realities.
Montreal: Alain Stanke, 1983. Published in French, (*Monstres des Lacs du Québec*), in 1982.

Deep appreciation to George Eberhart and Monique Denoeu Cone for their assistance and the exchange of information in the compilation of this bibliography.

Loren Coleman
P.O. Box 109
Rangeley, Maine, 04970